NOBODY IS
PROTECTED

ALSO BY REECE JONES

Border Walls

Violent Borders

White Borders

NOBODY IS PROTECTED

How the Border Patrol Became
the Most Dangerous Police Force
in the United States

REECE JONES

Counterpoint
Berkeley, California

Library of Congress Cataloging-in-Publication Data

Names: Jones, Reece, author.
Title: Nobody is protected : how the Border Patrol became the most dangerous police force in the United States / Reece Jones.
Description: First Hardcover Edition. | Berkeley, California : Counterpoint Press, [2022] | Includes bibliographical references.
Identifiers: LCCN 2021044902 | ISBN 9781640095205 (Hardcover) | ISBN 9781640095212 (eBook)
Subjects: LCSH: U.S. Border Patrol. | Border security—United States. | National security—Law and legislation—United States. | Border patrols—United States—Evaluation. | Racial profiling in law enforcement—United States. | Searches and seizures—United States. | Civil rights—United States—Cases. | Security sector—United States. | Military-industrial complex—United States.
Classification: LCC JV6483 .J65 2022 | DDC 363.28/50973—dc23/eng/20220206
LC record available at https://lccn.loc.gov/2021044902

Jacket design by Dana Li
Book design by Laura Berry

COUNTERPOINT
2560 Ninth Street, Suite 318
Berkeley, CA 94710
www.counterpointpress.com

Printed in the United States of America

10 9 8 7 6 5 4 3 2 1

Contents

Part III
The One-Hundred-Mile Zone

NOBODY IS
PROTECTED

Introduction

Out of Control

THE WINDSHIELD WIPERS SWIPED BACK AND FORTH AS Border Patrol Agents Brady and Harkins waited by the side of Interstate 5 near San Clemente, California. It was early in the evening of Sunday, March 11, 1973.[1] On the news, there were reports about the standoff between the American Indian Movement and federal officers at Wounded Knee, the brewing Watergate scandal, and the impending departure of the last American troops from Vietnam. The agents' vehicle was parked perpendicular to traffic and their headlights lit up the raindrops splashing onto the pavement, growing into pools on the side of the highway. The clouds obscured the glow of the moon that normally reflected off the Pacific Ocean, only a few hundred feet to the west. Every few moments, a northbound vehicle passed through the headlight beams, briefly illuminating the profiles of the passengers inside.

The rainy weather and a shortage of agents on duty that night forced Brady and Hawkins to close the permanent Border Patrol checkpoint on the interstate, which was about halfway between San Diego and the rapidly expanding southern suburbs of Los Angeles. They were sixty-six miles north of the busiest border crossing in the world, where the San Ysidro Port of Entry leads to Tijuana on the other side. The agents knew from experience that smugglers monitored the interior check-point on I-5 and waited until it was closed to send their human cargo north. The Border Patrol regularly closed the checkpoint on Sunday afternoons so as not to inconvenience Americans traveling back home to Los Angeles from a weekend outing in San Diego, but it also occasionally closed due to inclement weather or lack of staffing, as was the case this evening.

Although the agents were not eager to get out in the driving rain and the 50°F temperatures, they carefully observed the passing cars to see if the brief glimpse of the silhouettes suggested the vehicle contained undocumented immigrants. After a few minutes, a 1969 Chevrolet sedan caught their attention. There were three people in the vehicle, two men and a woman. After quickly discussing it, the Border Patrol agents agreed that all three looked Mexican. They switched on their siren, put the car in gear, and began the pursuit.

Felix Brignoni-Ponce looked nervously in his rearview mirror as the flashing lights danced around in the driving rain.[2] He hoped they had safely slipped past the shuttered Border Patrol checkpoint, but as the patrol car picked up speed and settled in behind them, he knew they were in trouble. Felix had no other option but to pull over to the side of the interstate and wait for the Border Patrol agents to approach.

The patrol car doors opened, and the agents' flashlights signaled that one agent was coming to the driver's side door while the other was positioned behind the passenger side of the Chevy. Felix rolled down his window and raindrops landed on his arm. The agent asked about the citizenship of the people in the car. Felix did not speak much English, but it became clear that the agents' hunch that he was from Mexico was wrong. He grew up in Puerto Rico and was a U.S. citizen. He produced his ID card and showed it to the agent. Agent Harkins asked him to step out of the vehicle and they walked back to the trunk, which Felix opened and Agent Harkins inspected.

Agent Brady rapped his knuckles on the passenger-side window and identified himself. As the window rolled down, he asked the two passengers about their citizenship in English. They indicated that they only spoke Spanish, so he asked them again in Spanish. Elsa Marina Hernández Serabia did not have an ID card but informed the agent that she was not Mexican, but Guatemalan. She did not have documents that gave her the right to be in the United States. The only person from Mexico in the vehicle was José Nuñez Ayala, but he also did not have the proper documents to be in the United States. Elsa and José were handcuffed and taken to the San Clemente Border Patrol station for processing.

Although Felix Brignoni-Ponce was an American citizen, he was also arrested and charged with a felony: knowingly transporting illegal aliens.[3] Using a card from his pocket, Agent Brady read Felix his Miranda rights in Spanish, and he was also taken to the San Clemente station. On March 14, his bond was set at $7,500 ($43,500 in 2022, adjusted for inflation) and he was assigned a federal public defender. On April 12, his jury trial began in the court of Judge Howard Turrentine. Turrentine was appointed to the bench in 1970 by Richard Nixon, and his rugged tough-guy appearance belied his kindness and reasonable approach to the job.[4] Felix's two passengers were called as witnesses in the trial; the following day, the charges against them were dropped and they were deported. On May 14, 1973, the jury found Felix guilty on both counts. Judge Turrentine sentenced him to four years in federal prison followed by five years of probation.

In their report about the stop and in their sworn testimony at the trial, Agents Brady and Harkins stated that the only reason they stopped the vehicle was the Mexican appearance of the people inside. Felix, with the help of his tireless lawyers from the Federal Defenders of San Diego, appealed to the Ninth Circuit Court of Appeals in San Francisco, arguing that race alone did not meet the standard of reasonable suspicion to justify a traffic stop by the Border Patrol. Indeed, Felix was a U.S. citizen and was of Puerto Rican, not Mexican, origin. The fundamental question of the case was whether the Border Patrol could use racial profiling to make a warrantless stop on an American interstate highway over sixty miles north of the border.

The Fourth Amendment of the Constitution protects everyone inside the territory of the United States, both citizens and noncitizens, from unreasonable searches and seizures. It requires police officers to obtain a warrant from a judge based on probable cause that a crime has been committed in order to carry out a search. Can the Border Patrol really stop a car on a highway over sixty miles north of the border based only on the fact that the driver and passengers looked Mexican? The case would go all the way to the highest court in the land, but at the time Agents Brady and Harkins made the stop, they were operating well within the loosely defined regulations that guided the actions for the Border Patrol in its first fifty years of existence.

When the United States Supreme Court heard Felix Brignoni-Ponce's case in 1975, it faced a difficult decision about what took precedence on American roads: the authority of the Border Patrol to search for undocumented immigrants, or the Fourth Amendment's constitutional protections against unreasonable searches and seizures. The verdict that the justices reached about the legality of the Border Patrol's stop continues to shape the lives of hundreds of millions of Americans and immigrants through the present day.

=

In the summer of 2020, there were civil demonstrations across the United States after the killing of George Floyd, an unarmed Black man, by Minneapolis police. Among the many videos of excessive police violence that circulated that summer, a series of videos stood out that documented mysterious late-night detentions by heavily armed agents in Portland, Oregon, in July 2020.

One video begins at a typical urban intersection with two men approaching on a crosswalk. Across the street, the headlights of an idling minivan illuminate the road while green leaves sway in the streetlights. A WE'RE OPEN sign is strung across a Starbucks behind them, but it is in fact closed because it is the middle of the night. After a couple of frames, it is clear that the two men are not regular pedestrians but are incongruously dressed in desert-toned camouflage and body armor. The only marking to identify them is a yellow patch that says POLICE on the front of their bulletproof vests. They wear helmets and sunglasses, even though it is the dead of night. The woman holding the camera, apparently a mom, instructs them to "use your words" and then asks, "What are you doing?" They do not respond, but one of the men pulls a camo mask up over his face as he passes her.[5]

The camerawoman turns to follow them, and their prey comes into view. Dressed in black with hands up, a person stands beside the graffiti-covered plywood of a boarded-up building. The camerawoman again encourages the armed men to "use your words" but as they close in, panic creeps into her voice. "What are you doing?" she yells.

Their target is wearing a black mask, a black helmet with a headlamp, and a black sweatshirt. The person in black says, "I didn't do anything wrong."

The camouflaged men reply, "Let's go."

The individual puts their hands behind their back to be cuffed, but the armed men don't use handcuffs. Instead, they grab the individual's arms on each side and walk them to the waiting minivan across the street.

The camerawoman asks again, "What is going on? Who are you?" No one answers. A few other people on the street try to get the person in black to give them their name, but they wisely remain quiet. As the armed men force the person in black into the van, the camerawoman says, "We got you, friend. Someone will get you out."

Another man makes sounds of disgust as if he has just tasted something unexpected and terrible. He says, "They're just kidnapping people." Then the minivan speeds away.

At first, there was confusion about the identities of the armed men. As the Black Lives Matter protests of 2020 spread across the United States, heavily armed white civilians began appearing at the protests, many associated with the far-right Three Percenters, Oathkeepers, Proud Boys, and Boogaloo movements. There was concern that the video documented a kidnapping by one of these militia groups. However, others quickly realized the men in camo were likely members of the U.S. Border Patrol. There were already reports that a Border Patrol Tactical Unit (BORTAC) was in Portland to protect the Mark O. Hatfield United States Courthouse and other federal buildings during the ongoing protests. Within a day, it was confirmed that the Border Patrol carried out the mysterious late-night detentions.

Customs and Border Protection, the parent agency of the Border Patrol, is the largest law enforcement force in the United States, yet the extent of the Border Patrol's authority is not well known or understood. For many Americans, the fact that the Border Patrol was operating so far from what they considered to be the border was a baffling revelation. Black Lives Matter and social justice activist Bree Newsome Bass tweeted, "WTF is Border Patrol doing in a place that's not the border???"[6] Others asked why the Border Patrol was detaining American citizens in the middle of the night at a protest against police violence. What could that possibly have to do with the Border Patrol's mission to conduct immigration enforcement?

==

In my own research at the border, I experienced the seemingly unchecked authority of the Border Patrol in 2011 when I was driving on a public road with a rancher named Bill Addington.[7] It was a sunny and warm March afternoon, and we were headed to see a section of the border wall near his land in Sierra Blanca, about an hour southeast of El Paso, Texas. To the east, we could see the Quitman Mountains; across the green valley of the Rio Grande, the dry desert landscape of Chihuahua, Mexico, sprawled out in the distance.

Despite the beauty, Bill was irritated because the U.S. Border Patrol would not leave us alone. "Well, it gets old," he said with exasperation. Dressed in a plaid shirt, timeworn jeans, and a dusty baseball cap, Bill's weathered face and gap-toothed smile looked the part of hardscrabble rancher. Bill's family has lived on this land since before the Border Patrol even existed. His grandfather founded the Guerra Farm in 1919 to use the water of the Rio Grande to grow cotton and raise cattle. Bill's mother continued the tradition and now it has passed onto Bill, who knows every inch of the land like it is a part of his being. The Border Patrol agents, though, do not know Bill or his deep roots. They all commute back and forth from El Paso.

The first two agents began following us as soon as the dust kicked up behind my rental car after we turned onto the gravel of Route 192, headed toward the border. Knowing what was coming, Bill tried to be proactive. We pulled over and told them what we were doing. The second, third, and fourth Border Patrol trucks pulled us over during the thirty minutes we spent driving down the public road to see the border wall and the wetlands beyond it.

"Don't they have a radio?" Bill asked, hoping in vain that they would use it to let the other agents in the area know what we were up to. By the time the fifth Border Patrol truck sped up behind us with its lights flashing, Bill was fed up. "Getting stopped by the Border Patrol is a regular thing for me, but I get tired of it. It's like living in Russia where they check you at checkpoints. I guess Germany was worse. It's similar to that."

My drive along the border with Bill made me wonder how the border zone had become the focus of such intense policing inside the United States. Was it really possible that the Border Patrol can legally stop the same vehicle five times in less than an hour while driving along a public road in the United States?

A few days later, I was in El Paso recounting my drive with Bill to a Mexican American community organizer, who smiled and laughed. "Just think if you really fit the profile. They would have had three cars there, put you in the back, and then asked questions . . . Sometimes I feel like the Constitution does not exist here at the border."

The drive with Bill and particularly the comment of the community organizer stuck in my mind and led me to write this book. I assumed the U.S. Constitution applied equally everywhere in the territory of the United States, but being stopped and interrogated five times in less than an hour on a public road left me with many unanswered questions. The late-night Border Patrol kidnappings of protesters in Portland left others with similar questions. Why can the Border Patrol operate so far from the actual borders of the United States? How does the ability of the Border Patrol to make seemingly unlimited stops square with the Fourth Amendment of the Constitution, which protects against unreasonable searches and seizures and requires a warrant in most instances? Should the Border Patrol be able to use race in their decision to make a stop?

I traveled the border zone and worked my way through the archives, looking for answers. Along the way, I uncovered the untold story of how the courts have granted the Border Patrol exceptions to the Fourth Amendment to an extent that would shock most Americans. Furthermore, the Border Patrol is authorized to use these special rules in an area much larger than most Americans would ever guess. Perhaps most surprisingly, the expansive border zone and the use of racial profiling by the Border Patrol was reviewed, and largely approved, by the United States Supreme Court in a series of decisions in the 1970s that remain in force to the present day.

As I dug deeper, I discovered the outrageous behavior of early Border Patrol agents who operated with impunity, bringing a "shoot first, ask questions later" ethos to the enforcement of immigration laws. Almost a century later, those excesses have never been curtailed. Today, Border Patrol agents are arrested for off-duty criminal activity at a rate five times higher than regular police officers. However, Border Patrol agents are rarely disciplined for on-duty infractions. A 2021 report from Human Rights Watch based on internal DHS records described 160 sexual assaults and violent incidents by Border Patrol agents, including an agent offering to release a woman in exchange for oral sex, an agent undressing and touching a child in custody, and agents withholding food from a detainee until he signed a document he did not understand. A 2013 survey found that 11 percent of migrants said they were assaulted by agents during or after their apprehension, including being intentionally hit by vehicles, beaten while in custody, and sexually assaulted. Most never reported the abuse. However, another study found that 95 percent of abuse complaints that were filed resulted in no action taken by the agency.[8]

Since 2010, 119 people have been killed by the Border Patrol, including at least six who were standing in Mexico at the time. James Tomsheck, the Border Patrol's inspector general during the Obama administration, has said that one-quarter of the killings by Border Patrol agents during his tenure were under suspicious circumstances, but he was prevented from properly investigating. Only once in the history of the Border Patrol has an agent been charged for an on-duty killing, and even then, that agent was not convicted of the crime.[9]

During the Trump presidency, the border became the focus of intense media coverage as a symbol of the worst atrocities of the administration. The "no tolerance policy" resulted in children separated from their families, and some were held for days in prisons cells meant for violent criminals. This came to be known as "kids in cages."[10] Other stories like the unwanted medical procedures performed on women in the custody of Immigration and Customs Enforcement, a separate agency tasked with interior deportations, reinforced the idea that the Trump administration represented a radical break with previous American policies.[11]

In reality, the violence of the Trump era was a continuation of decades-long patterns of violence toward immigrants at the border. The expansion and transformation of the Border Patrol described in this book is more insidious because it occurred under both Republican and Democratic administrations, as the agency has slowly but methodically accrued legislative and judicial precedents that legalize its extreme actions.

As Bree Newsome Bass's tweet asking why the Border Patrol was even in Portland suggested, most Americans assume that the border zone is defined as an area relatively close to the actual border. They think of the border as a distant place that does not affect them, but that turns out not to be the case. In a 1947 administrative decision, made without public input, the Department of Justice defined the border zone as within one hundred miles of borders *and coastlines*, a vast area that includes nine of the ten largest cities in the United States and two-thirds of the American population.[12]

Portland, where the late-night detentions occurred in the summer of 2020, is within that zone, as are Boston, Chicago, Detroit, Houston, Los Angeles, Miami, New York, San Francisco, Seattle, and Washington, D.C. The entire states of Connecticut, Delaware, Florida, Hawai'i, Maine, Massachusetts, Michigan, New Hampshire, New Jersey, and Rhode Island are in the border zone. If you are reading this book in the United States, the odds are that you are, at this moment, in the border zone.

Even though Portland falls within the hundred-mile border zone, it turns out that the agents at the summer 2020 demonstrations were operating under a completely different and novel interpretation of the U.S. code. Under this other section of the law, agents are no longer required to have an immigration purpose for their work and are allowed to operate across the entire United States.[13] The result is that the Border Patrol is moving ever closer to becoming something the United States has never had: a national police force.

=====

Nobody Is Protected tells the story of how the Border Patrol grew from a small and underfunded frontier agency, established in 1924, into a modern, sophisticated paramilitary force of 19,000 agents that claims the legal right to sweep people off the streets of an American city without a warrant or even probable cause that a crime was committed. The first section of the book begins with the Wild West origins of the Border Patrol and the failed efforts of a few government officials to rein in its most violent practices and prevent it from operating deep inside the United States. While all other police are bound by the Fourth Amendment, which protects citizens and noncitizens alike from unreasonable searches and seizures, the Border Patrol's 1925 congressional authorization allowed agents to stop vehicles without a warrant for immigration inspections within the border zone.

For the first fifty years of the Border Patrol's existence, the courts did not resolve this contradiction between the constitutional protections of the Fourth Amendment and the Border Patrol's regulations, so agents stopped and searched anyone they wanted. The earliest Border Patrol agents were drawn from the rough-and-tumble world of the Texas Rangers and frontier law enforcement. They brought an "anything goes" ethos to the enforcement of the country's immigration laws in the remote and desolate stretches of the border.

It was not until the 1970s that the questionable practices of the Border Patrol received any oversight from the Supreme Court of the United States. Its scrutiny then is largely due to the work of a few scrappy lawyers from a fledgling public defender's office in San Diego. The four most significant Border Patrol cases, which are detailed in the second section of the book, were all argued by the same two lawyers, John Cleary and Chuck Sevilla. Cleary and Sevilla were young and idealistic but also unwavering in their pursuit of justice for their poor, immigrant clients. Their aggressive tactics in court garnered them the nickname "terrorists in suits" but also won them the grudging respect of prosecutors and judges in the courtrooms of Southern California. As they pressed the constitutional arguments against the Border Patrol's invasive and racialized practices, the Supreme Court was forced to consider the expansive authority of the Border Patrol to make stops in the border zone without a warrant as well as whether race could be used as the only factor to make a stop.

Cleary and Sevilla faced an uphill battle at the Supreme Court, which had taken a much more conservative and pro–law enforcement turn in the early 1970s. Richard Nixon was elected president in 1968, promising a law-and-order crackdown across the country, and he was given the unique opportunity to appoint four new Supreme Court justices in his first term in office. However, one of those law-and-order

Nixon appointees was a wild card whose careful, deliberative style often resulted in surprising decisions. Justice Lewis Powell had been a conservative corporate lawyer for decades, representing the likes of tobacco giant Philip Morris, but when he arrived at the court, he often found himself in the middle looking for compromise. Lewis Powell did not have any experience with the border or immigration, but he played a critical role in all the Supreme Court's Border Patrol cases in the early 1970s, changing his mind at the last minute in the first case and writing the opinion in the next three.

In the four most significant Border Patrol cases, the Supreme Court decided whether Border Patrol agents could search a vehicle without any justification in *Almeida-Sanchez* (1973) and *Ortiz* (1975); could stop vehicles in the United States based only on the race of the driver and passengers in *Brignoni-Ponce* (1975); and could set up permanent checkpoints on interior roads inside the United States to briefly detain all vehicles in order to ask drivers about their immigration status in *Martinez-Fuerte* (1976).

In the first of those cases, *Almeida-Sanchez v. United States* in 1973, Justice Thurgood Marshall, an icon of the civil rights movement and the first Black man to serve on the Supreme Court, asked a series of questions that pressed the government's lawyers about the true extent of the Border Patrol's authority on American highways deep inside the United States. Unsatisfied with the responses, Marshall finally asked if the Border Patrol could legally stop and search the vehicle of the president of the United States without any evidence or suspicion whatsoever. When the lawyer said "Yes," Marshall concluded, "Nobody is protected."

===

The decisions in the 1970s Border Patrol cases set the parameters that are still in force today, giving the Border Patrol wide discretion to police for immigration violations inside the United States. The Border

Patrol can stop virtually any vehicle or pedestrian in a zone within one hundred miles of the border and coastlines. In that interior zone, the Border Patrol can set up permanent checkpoints where they stop and detain every single vehicle, whether on a lonely back road or a major interstate highway. In all these interactions, the Supreme Court ruled that Border Patrol can legally use the race of the individual as a factor when selecting which vehicles to stop.

There were only 1,500 Border Patrol agents in the 1970s, but over 600,000 apprehensions per year at the border. In the decades since, even as the Border Patrol has become a completely different organization, the Supreme Court has not revisited the legality of racial profiling, warrantless stops, and the construction of interior checkpoints up to one hundred miles from the border.[14] Today, there are over 19,000 agents. After the terrorist attacks of September 11, 2001, the Border Patrol rebranded itself as the front line against terrorist infiltration into the United States. The flood of national security appropriations that followed allowed not only the huge increase in agents but also the acquisition of a wide range of sophisticated military hardware ranging from high-tech surveillance equipment to the largest fleet of drones in the United States.

Despite this massive expansion, the average number of apprehensions per year has declined by 33 percent. From 2010 to 2020, the average Border Patrol agent made 22 apprehensions in the entire year, or less than 2 per month.[15] In 2021, the number of apprehensions increased substantially to 1.7 million. However, that figure is misleading because it occurred when the United States used Title 42, a health directive, during the COVID-19 pandemic to immediately remove large numbers of people apprehended at the border. Consequently, the Border Patrol's data shows that one-third of apprehensions were of people already apprehended and removed earlier in the year. There were only 1.1 million unique encounters in 2021.[16] Even using the full 1.7 million figure, it equates to only 7 apprehensions per month per agent.

The result is a large and powerful border force with relatively little immigration-related work to do. Consequently, the agents have time to get involved in many other things that have nothing to do with the immigration enforcement mission of the agency. The implications of a heavily militarized border force that can operate in large swaths of the United States is considered in the final section of this book.

The Supreme Court's decisions in these Border Patrol cases, which legalized racial profiling and carved out exceptions to constitutional protections against unreasonable searches and seizures, deserve further scrutiny. Although they occurred over forty years ago, they continue to affect the lives of hundreds of millions of Americans and count-less more migrants to the United States. Despite their significant and far-reaching implications, the Border Patrol decisions of the 1970s are almost unknown outside law enforcement, legal, and academic circles.

This book brings these cases to light and argues that two of those decisions, *United States v. Brignoni-Ponce* in 1975 and *United States v. Martinez-Fuerte* in 1976, which legalized racial profiling for the Bor-der Patrol, should be seen in the same light as some of the most noto-rious racist decisions in the history of the Supreme Court, such as *Dred Scott v. Sandford*, *Plessy v. Ferguson*, and *Korematsu v. United States*. As Justice William Brennan wrote in his dissent in *Martinez-Fuerte*, the Supreme Court's Border Patrol decisions amounted to an "evisceration" of the reasonableness requirement in the Fourth Amendment, allow-ing agents "to stop any or all motorists without explanation or excuse" and "target motorists of Mexican appearance." However, among those symbols of America's racist past, *Brignoni-Ponce* and *Martinez-Fuerte* stand alone because they are still put into practice by the Border Patrol every day. The "anything goes" origins of the Border Patrol, combined with the Supreme Court's approval of racial profiling and warrantless stops, have made the Border Patrol the most dangerous police force in the United States. This is the story of how it happened.

Part I

The Wild West Origins of the Border Patrol

1.

Send Two Coffins

THE FIRST FEDERAL AGENT HIRED TO PATROL THE BORDERS of the United States was named after the president of the Confederacy. Jefferson Davis Milton was born during the first year of the Civil War on November 7, 1861, and his father, John Milton, chose to honor his close friend, Jefferson Davis, by naming his son after him. John Milton, named after the famous poet who was also their ancestor, led the effort for secession in Florida. The Florida legislature voted to secede from the United States on January 10, 1861, becoming the third state to join the separatist movement to protect the institution of slavery after South Carolina and Mississippi.[1] John Milton became the Confederate governor of Florida a month before his son was born and remained in that role throughout the Civil War. He served until his death on April 1, 1865, the day before Richmond, the capital of the Confederacy, fell to Union forces. Milton's family and local media called it a hunting accident, but *The New York Times* reported that he committed suicide.[2]

After the war, the Milton family struggled to reestablish their prominence. As a young man of fifteen, Jefferson Davis Milton moved out west in search of a fresh start. He found work as a ranch hand, but soon realized his calling lay in the rough-and-tumble world of frontier law enforcement. In 1878, he joined the newly revived Texas Rangers by pretending to be eighteen.

The Rangers were first established when Texas was an independent republic and remained in periodic use as a frontier patrol during its early years as a state. The Rangers were disbanded after the Civil War as the federal government occupied the former Confederate states and implemented Reconstruction. Texas was readmitted to the Union in 1870 and it reestablished the Rangers in 1874. Ostensibly, their purpose was to protect citizens from attack by Mexican or Native American raids, but in practice they often harassed and displaced Native Americans and Mexicans who lived in the region.[3] The Rangers operated in open lands with little oversight, which led to frequent excesses, including intimidation, torture, and executions. A history of the Rangers explains, "The earliest rangers were frontiersmen—and frontiersmen were never noted for obedience to anybody."[4]

With a handlebar mustache and piercing eyes below his cowboy hat, Milton was restless and rarely remained in a job for long. He left the Texas Rangers after a couple of years and roamed the wild lands of the desert Southwest. He found a job as a U.S. Marshal in New Mexico before arriving in Tombstone, Arizona, in 1886, only a few years after the infamous shootout at the O.K. Corral. Milton would tell people in saloons, "I never killed a man who didn't need killing, and I never shot an animal except for meat."[5] Once a rattlesnake got in his bedding while he was camped in the desert. Instead of killing it, he simply shook out the bedding and shooed the snake away in appreciation for it not biting him.

In Tombstone, Milton had landed in a town where his moral judgments about who should be killed fit in just fine. Cochise County, in the southeastern corner of the Arizona Territory, was the archetype of the Wild West, with snowcapped mountains in the distance and tumbleweed flats as far as the eye could see. The boomtown of Tombstone grew up overnight after the discovery of silver in 1879 by a prospector named Ed Schieffelin. By the early 1880s, the town swelled to over 10,000 people as adventurers, fortune seekers, entrepreneurs, and thieves descended on the area. Within a few years, Tombstone's dusty streets boasted a bowling alley, an opera house, and three newspapers as well as several Chinese restaurants, a French restaurant, and even an ice cream parlor.[6] It also had over one hundred saloons along with numerous gambling halls and brothels. The town was close to Mexico and became a conduit for cattle rustlers who stole from across the unmarked border.

From the start, there was tension between the industrialists from the northern states who ran the silver mines and the cattle rustlers and bandits, collectively called the cowboys, who were mostly Confederate veterans from the Civil War. The famous gunfight in 1881 grew out of this conflict, as simmering personal disputes boiled over between the cowboys and U.S. Marshal Virgil Earp and several of his deputies, Wyatt Earp, Morgan Earp, and Doc Holliday.

In frontier territories, the idea of the rule of law was fragile, and many wealthy individuals employed hired guns to protect their interests. In this case, the hired guns of the industrialists had the authority of the law behind them, while the hired guns of the cowboys did not. Nevertheless, both sides engaged in violent and lawless behavior as the conflict escalated. Doc Holliday, thin and sickly from tuberculosis, was accused of robbing one of the cowboys a few months before the shootout. The cowboys were blamed for a rash of stagecoach holdups around the town.

Despite the famous name, the gunfight on October 26, 1881, did not occur at the O.K. Corral, but a few doors down at an empty lot beside a photography studio. The U.S. Marshals unexpectedly stumbled across a group of the cowboys, and guns were quickly drawn. As the dust settled, thirty shots had been fired in thirty seconds and three of the cowboys were dead. The Earps and Doc Holliday were accused of murder but were found by a judge to have acted within the law. The cowboys nevertheless carried out their vigilante revenge, severely injuring U.S. Marshal Virgil Earp and killing his brother Morgan in 1882. Wyatt Earp and Holliday formed a posse that killed several more of the cowboys before fleeing the Territory of Arizona after warrants were put out for their arrests.

When Jeff Milton arrived in Cochise County four years later, the Earps and Doc Holiday were gone but the chaotic conflict between law enforcement and the cowboys remained. There had been dozens of stagecoach robberies in the county, and several gangs roamed the wild lands near the Mexican border. In 1886, John Slaughter, a slim and upright man, was elected the new sheriff of the county, and Milton became one of his deputies. Together they worked to eliminate the gangs that operated in the wilds around Tombstone. Slaughter and Milton doggedly pursued the Jack Taylor Gang through the winter of 1886 and 1887, even tracking the gang into Mexico, where they raided another bandit's hideout. They killed several bandits that day but missed Taylor. He was captured a few weeks later in Sonora.

After several years as a sheriff's deputy in Tombstone, Milton moved to El Paso, Texas, where he became the police chief. In the 1890s, he continued to move every few years to new law enforcement jobs in New Mexico and Texas, including time as a customs agent. In 1895, Milton arrested a well-known cattle rustler named Martin McRose, who died mysteriously in Milton's custody before he got him back to the county jail. Another bandit bragged for years in the saloons across Texas that he paid Milton to do the killing.

On February 15, 1900, Milton filled in for a sick friend on a shift as a railroad guard for a payroll train headed west. When the train stopped to unload cargo in Fairbank, Arizona, just a few miles outside Milton's old stomping grounds in Tombstone, it was ambushed by "Three Fingered" Jack Dunlop and his gang of train robbers. Milton shot Dunlop, who died a few days later from his wounds, and killed another robber. However, he was outnumbered, and Milton was gravely injured when he took a bullet to his left arm. With blood gushing out of his wound, Milton tossed the keys to the train's safe into a pile of boxes at the far end of the car and played dead just as the remaining bandits dismounted their horses and climbed onto the train. Without the keys, the thieves could not crack the safe and left with only a few dollars instead of the $10,000 ($310,000 in 2022, adjusted for inflation) payroll on board. Before they rode off, one of the bandits was going to finish Milton off, but the train conductor told him to save his bullets because Milton was already as good as dead.[7]

After the bandits left, Milton tied a tourniquet around his bleeding arm and the railroad employees sent a special engine to transport him to Tucson for treatment. Tucson was a small outpost at the time, and they did not have the proper equipment, so they sent him on to San Francisco. After the long journey to the Pacific Coast, the doctors there thought the only option was to amputate the arm, but Milton refused and found another doctor who patched it up as best he could. Milton never regained use of it, but never had it amputated either. Within a few months, he was back to work in law enforcement.

With a quick draw and a reputation for fearlessness, Jefferson Davis Milton was an obvious choice to be hired in 1904 to patrol the borders of the United States as a "mounted Chinese inspector," a precursor to the U.S. Border Patrol.

Racial Immigration Laws

Although Milton was the first federal officer hired to patrol the border, he was not the first to enforce racial boundaries in the United States.

From the arrival of the first slave ship in 1619, the English colonies in
North America were a laboratory for organized policing. As the colonies became dependent on slave labor, the slave population grew to
outnumber the free white population in parts of the South, creating the
potential for rebellion. The slave owners relied on violence and menace
to prevent rebellions through organized militias of local men and, later,
more formal slave patrols.

The first official slave patrol was created in South Carolina in 1704;
Virginia followed in 1726. They became common across the South in
the decades that followed.[8] Slave patrols tracked down runaway slaves,
sowed fear to prevent revolts, and enforced plantation rules, which
were not formal laws.[9] By the time the United States won its independence from England, these local militias were crucial to maintaining
control over the slave populations across the South. Militias also contributed to the Revolutionary War effort. Consequently, the need to
maintain citizen militias was formalized in the founding documents
of the country. The Second Amendment of the Constitution says, "A
well-regulated Militia, being necessary to the security of a free State,
the right of the people to keep and bear Arms, shall not be infringed."
The Second Amendment has become controversial in the modern era,
but part of the original purpose of the right to bear arms was to allow
civilians to participate in slave patrol militias in the South.[10]

Slave patrols often worked at night, walking the borders of plantations as well as the streams and paths that led away from them in
search of curfew violators and runaways. Free Blacks had to carry
passes at all times that proved they had the right to move around. The
slave patrols became expert trackers who looked for signs in the landscape of human beings fleeing to the free northern states or Mexico
for freedom and opportunity. Slave patrols were also union busters,
tasked with breaking up unauthorized slave meetings at night and
preventing insurrections. The slave patrols could enter slave quarters

without a warrant and search for contraband, such as weapons and means of communication like paper and writing instruments. They also did headcounts to determine if anyone was out breaking curfew. After the end of slavery, many of the same tactics became common with the emergent Ku Klux Klan. Like the slave patrols, the KKK was a local militia that rode at night and terrorized the Black population of the South, preventing them from organizing in a way that could challenge white supremacy.[11]

Through the early 1870s, the United States did not have any federal limits on immigration, although there were some state-level restrictions. Massachusetts and New York had rules barring the poor, the infirm, and the insane, but many other states had no immigration regulations at all.[12] The U.S. Supreme Court decided in 1849 in the *Passenger Cases* that immigration rules were a federal concern, which invalidated these local restrictions and left the task of regulating immigration with Congress. The Supreme Court again invalidated state-level restrictions in 1875 in *Chy Lung v. Freeman* and *Henderson v. Mayor of City of New York*. Even after it was established that only the federal government could limit immigration, Congress did not pass any limits on immigration until non-white immigrants started to arrive on America's shores.

In the first decades after the American Revolution, the slave trade remained legal through 1808 and free immigration to the United States was not substantial. Those who came were mostly from England and Northern Europe. The first large wave of new immigrants was from Ireland in the 1840s as the potato famine forced people onto ships across the Atlantic. The Treaty of Guadalupe Hidalgo at the end of the Mexican–American War also gave the United States control of large swaths of the west, populated primarily by Native Americans and former Mexican citizens. After the discovery of gold in California in 1848, the United States began to see the first free non-white immigrants arriving from China. The explosive political issue of Chinese immigration was initially confined to the new states on the Pacific Coast, but by the 1870s, non-white immigration became a political issue in the entire United States.

As whites grappled with the reality of free Black citizens in the aftermath of slavery, there was a concerted effort to prevent the admittance of any more free non-white peoples. Senator La Fayette Grover of Oregon explained the problem of non-white immigration on the Senate floor in 1882. "Our ancestors," he said, "proceeded forthwith to drive out the aborigines from the land with fire and sword, and to occupy it for themselves and for us their posterity."[13] For him, this is the evidence that the founders did not intend the United States to be anything other than a white country.

Grover acknowledged that they had to deal with the freed slaves and remaining Native Americans, but they should not take any more non-white people. "While we are to treat the poor remnant of the Indian race among us and the African who was forcibly brought here with that justice and humanity becoming to a great people," he argued, "it is of the gravest importance to the future peace and well-being of this country that we do not voluntarily create other relations with colored foreign peoples which will force upon us complications in our civil and political relations."

Senator Grover expressed the mainstream opinion of the country at the time, and Congress passed a series of laws to prevent Chinese immigration. In 1875, the Page Act, which sought to reduce the number of Chinese laborers, was the first national immigration limits of any kind in the United States. In 1882, Congress completely banned Chinese immigration to the country in the Chinese Exclusion Act. It was initially enforced only at ports, where the vast majority of people arrived in the United States. Throughout this era, the United States had customs officials who checked shipments at ports, but for decades there were no federal officers tasked with enforcing the new ban on Chinese immigration at other sections of the border or in the interior.

Mounted Chinese Inspectors

The mounted Chinese Inspectors were established to search for Chinese people who bypassed the enforcement at the ports by crossing from Mexico or Canada. The mounted Chinese Inspectors' mission was based on racial profiling. They would roam border towns looking for Chinese people, then inspect their documents to see if they had the right to be in the United States. If not, they detained them and sent them back across the border. Akin to the previous generation's slave patrols, the mounted Chinese Inspectors were tasked with patrolling the borders to look for people violating the racial social order of the United States.[14]

In his job as a mounted Chinese Inspector, Jeff Milton followed the same approach he used as a Texas Ranger and a sheriff's deputy in Tombstone, bringing a "shoot first, ask questions later" attitude to the role of federal border agent. Soon after he was hired, he got a report of three bank robbers who had just crossed into the United States from Mexico. The one-armed Milton grabbed some provisions and ammunition, then jumped onto his horse and rode off alone in search of the three hardened criminals who were desperate to escape the law. His friends were not surprised, but they did begin to worry when he did not return after a few days. They eyed the horizon in hopes of seeing him riding back through the sagebrush and eventually grew concerned enough to mount a search party. As they were organizing men and discussing where to look for his body, a telegram arrived that would join the lore of the Border Patrol. All it said was "Send two coffins and a doctor. Jeff Milton." Neither the coffins nor the doctor were for Milton.[15] An early book about the Border Patrol spoke fondly of the

exploits of Milton and the other mounted inspectors, saying, "the tra-
ditions they set are revered and followed by the men of the modern
Border Patrol."[16]

The mounted Chinese Inspectors never had more than seventy-
five men working along the remote and rugged 1,954-mile border with
Mexico as well as the border with Canada. In the early years, Milton
and the other federal inspectors relied heavily on local and state law
enforcement to help monitor the border. These state militias carried out
what would today be called an ethnic cleansing of the newly conquered
frontier lands of the United States as they drove out Native Americans
and Mexican citizens. Milton's former colleagues in the Texas Rangers
were among the most extreme practitioners of frontier justice.

As the Mexican Revolution unfolded in the 1910s, cross-border
incursions became increasingly common and deadly, often leading to
brutal acts of violence. Among the most gruesome were the raid on the
Brite Ranch on Christmas Day 1917 and the revenge carried out by the
Texas Rangers in the town of Porvenir a few weeks later.

2.

The Texas Rangers

As THE FIRST RAYS OF SUNLIGHT PEEKED OVER THE HORIzon on Christmas morning 1917, Sam Neill was sipping a cup of coffee when he heard the rumble of forty-five horses galloping into the Brite Ranch.[1] The Mexican Revolution had been spilling into Texas for several months as refugees fled north in search of safety and groups of armed men from Mexico raided border communities for supplies. The riders from Mexico forded the Rio Grande before sunrise and made their way fifteen miles over rocky hills and dry, grassy plains toward Marfa, Texas, intending to raid the Brite Ranch.

The ranch, normally teeming with farmhands readying for the morning's work, was deserted because everyone had gone home for Christmas. Sleeping inside the home was Sam's son, ranch supervisor T.T., and T.T.'s wife. There were only a handful of farmhands still in their quarters. Two were quickly detained by the bandits but a few others slipped away. Inside the house, Sam and T.T. were able to gather their rifles and kill one of the bandits. Sam, a former Texas Ranger, was also hit twice, on the nose and the leg.

A standoff ensued. The bandits sent one of the farmhands, José Sánchez, into the house to negotiate a surrender. Instead, the Neills gave the bandits the keys to the general store and told them to take what they needed and leave. They were in the process of looting the store and stealing all the horses from the corrals when an unsuspecting mail carrier, Mickey Welch, pulled his cart into the ranch with two other men. The Mexican bandits, mistaking the mail carrier for reinforcements for the besieged family, shot and killed the two passengers and lynched Welch, leaving his body hanging in the store.

About twenty-five miles away in Valentine, Texas, Bob Keil and the rest of his company of Troop G of the United States Cavalry were just tucking into their Christmas Day meal when they got word of the raid.[2] The company was often dispatched to the border to guard against such raids, so they abandoned their uneaten food and set off for the ranch. They had their horses in the corral at Valentine, but it would have taken over two hours of hard riding to reach the ranch. Instead, they turned to local residents who had new automobiles. Within a few minutes, they had twelve Oldsmobiles and Hupmobiles ready to make the trip. The poor condition of the roads slowed the drive, and one car had to be abandoned after it got a second flat tire.

By the time they reached the ranch, the bandits were gone, but the soldiers were horrified to see Welch's body hanging in the store. Sam Neill told them that the bandits had left only an hour before and he pointed the way. The soldiers pulled out their field glasses and spotted dust kicked up by the horses on the horizon. The cavalry chased the bandits toward the border using both the automobiles and horses from the ranch. They killed several en route before the bandits crossed the Rio Grande at a spot called Los Fresnos, near the new refugee town of Porvenir that had sprung up on the U.S. side of the border.

The brazen cross-border raid and the killing of three people en-
raged the white community of the sparsely populated region. Bob Keil
of the cavalry remembered, "A deathly quiet settled over the Big Bend.
It was certainly noticeable on the river. No one had a name for it, but it
was like the stillness that precedes a cyclone."[3]

The Texas Rangers also had a company of fifteen men at
Marfa, mostly green new recruits, who were tasked with patrolling
the 38,000-square-mile Big Bend region for border incursions. The
Rangers set out to find a scapegoat for the deadly raid and they settled
on the village of Porvenir, on the flimsy logic that since the bandits
chose to cross the Rio Grande nearby, the Mexican refugee population
must have been involved.[4] On January 26, 1918, the Texas Rangers rode
into the village of 140 people and searched all the homes for weapons or
other evidence that would demonstrate loyalty to the rebels across the
border. They found only a pistol in the home of a white man and a rifle
in the home of an American citizen of Mexican descent. The Rangers
left the village but would return the next day to exact their revenge.

"There Will Be No Way of Subduing Them, but Extermination"

The image of the Texas Rangers as a fabled frontier force that brought
justice to the wilds of the Southwest is primarily the creation of pop-
ular culture in the twentieth century. From *The Lone Ranger* of 1950s
television to *Walker, Texas Ranger* of the 1990s, the Rangers evoke the
idea of honorable men serving as the last line of defense against lawless
frontier violence. As with many historical fables, the rosy picture of the
Texas Rangers does not match the gritty reality of their early years.

When Stephen F. Austin led the first band of American settlers
into Texas in 1825, the region was claimed on the map by Mexico
but inhabited by Native Americans who had lived there for centuries.
Mexico won its independence from Spain in 1821 and the fledgling

country was struggling to organize its government and stabilize its economy. It had little presence in the remote northern reaches of the state of Coahuila y Tejas.

The Mexican government did not pay too much attention to the request from Austin to settle the wild coast of the Gulf of Mexico near the Colorado and Brazos Rivers, what is today the region between Corpus Christi and Galveston. Austin recruited settlers, and by 1825, there were three hundred families working to establish homesteads in the region. Many of the settlers were from New Orleans and brought slaves with them to farm cotton.

On his first expedition, Austin encountered a band of Karankawa, Native Americans who lived in the area in the winter to eat mussels and fish from the Gulf of Mexico. The band were friendly and they parted on good terms. Nevertheless, Austin had a more sinister view of their presence, writing at the time, "There will be no way of subduing them, but extermination."[5] Austin spread false rumors that the Karankawa were dangerous and possibly cannibals, and he set up a group of rangers to battle the Native Americans. These settlers were ruthless, killing entire villages and stealing their supplies. The remaining Karankawa fled to Padre Island in the 1840s, but another extermination effort by the Texas settlers in the following decade eliminated the remaining members of the tribe.

By the 1830s, the Mexican government became wary of the growing American colony inside its territory and was particularly uncomfortable with its reliance on slavery, which was banned in Mexico in 1829. During an uprising in Mexico in 1832, the Texian settlers, as they called themselves, forced Mexican troops out of their colony and demanded revisions to their agreement with Mexico. Stephen F. Austin was detained in January 1834 and taken to Mexico City. He was never charged with anything and was released in August 1835.

That fall, Mexico dispatched troops to pacify the restive territory.

Skirmishes continued through the new year when the Mexican president, Antonio López de Santa Anna, led a regiment into Texas to put down the rebellion. In March 1836, Santa Anna laid seige to a small band of Texians at Béxar, in what is now San Antonio. The Texians, including the famed frontiersmen Davy Crockett and Jim Bowie, holed up in the Catholic mission called the Alamo. After a thirteen-day siege, the Mexican troops attacked, killing all of the approximately two hundred men inside. The Mexican army lost at least double that number in the attack. The Alamo was not militarily significant, but the bravery of the men inside and the killing of all of them by the Mexican forces became a rallying cry for the Texian rebels.

The conflict concluded a month later at San Jacinto, north of the present-day city of Houston. The rebels routed Santa Anna's troops on April 21 and even captured the Mexican president as he hid in some brush, attempting to flee. Rather than execute Santa Anna, the Texian general, Sam Houston, forced him to order the removal of all Mexican troops from Texas. Texas declared its independence but also sent a request to Washington, D.C., that the United States annex the territory.

Although Mexico withdrew its troops, it did not recognize the independence of Texas. Skirmishes continued in contested territory between the Rio Grande and the Nueces River, known as the Nueces Strip. In 1836, the Texas government formally established the Texas Rangers as "Mounted Gunmen to act as Rangers on the Western and Southwestern frontier."[6] They patrolled the loosely defined borders of the new republic, fending off attacks from Mexico from the south as well as Native Americans to the west and north in what is today Oklahoma. The Rangers had little training but carried out this mission with ruthless violence, destroying Native American settlements, killing men, women, and children indiscriminately, and often scalping their victims. They also served as slave patrols to stop the southern Underground Railroad that ferried people to Mexico.

John Coffee "Jack" Hays epitomized the early Texas Rangers. Hays was born in Little Cedar Lick, Tennessee, in 1817 and was only nineteen when he arrived in the Texas Republic and joined the Rangers. With boyish good looks and stylish hair, Hays did not look the part of frontier law enforcement, but he quickly rose through the ranks to become captain of a Rangers unit in 1840. After a series of Mexican raids, Sam Houston, the president of the Republic of Texas at the time, declared martial law in the Nueces Strip in 1843, giving Hays and his Rangers broad authority to prevent Mexican incursions in the area. A local newspaper reported that Hays used that authority to summarily execute three men he thought to be Mexican spies.[7]

Hays's unit of Rangers was later redeployed to track and fight the Comanche, a fierce band of Native Americans that controlled an area known as Comancheria that ranged from what is today southern Colorado through western Kansas, Oklahoma, and eastern New Mexico, as well as most of western Texas. The Comanche were a formidable foe for the Texians because they had honed the use of horses to attack quickly and then escape the more plodding advances of the Texian forces. For many years, the Comanche proved stronger and seemed impossible to defeat.

Hays and his unit of Rangers led the battle that changed the course of the conflict with the Comanche and sped the ethnic cleansing of West Texas. The problem the Rangers faced was that although they had rifles, in the 1840s they still only afforded a single shot and took almost a minute to reload. The Comanche learned to send a few warriors out to draw the first volley of shots, and then as the Texians were reloading, they would quickly charge their lines on horseback.

Back east in New Jersey, inventor Samuel Colt had designed a new pistol with a revolving chamber, hypothetically allowing multiple shots before reloading. At first, the new gun did not sell well. The early designs were fragile and liable to explode as it was fired. It was also expensive. As his new company struggled to sell the weapon, they did deliver an order of 180 functioning revolvers to the navy of the Republic of Texas. Texas disbanded the navy in 1843 and the revolvers were transferred to other units, including Hays's band of Rangers.

They put the new guns to use in an encounter with Comanche at Walker's Creek. The Rangers were outnumbered but killed twenty Comanche while suffering only one casualty before the Comanche fled. After the battle, Hays wrote, "I cannot recommend these arms too highly. Had it not been for them, I doubt what the consequences would have been."[8] As word of the new weapon spread, Colt continued to refine the design, and the Colt Revolver came to be known as the "the gun that won the west."

After Texas was annexed by the United States in 1845, disputes with Mexico over the Nueces Strip increased. At the same time, politicians in Washington, D.C., had imperial designs on further westward expansion, leading to the Mexican–American War. During the war, the Rangers were assigned to U.S. Army units and fought on campaigns deep into Mexico. They gained a rough reputation for violence and thuggery. As the U.S. Army occupied Mexico City toward the end of the war, the Rangers under Hays's command killed ten Mexican citizens on the march into town, then eighty more in a slum after a Ranger was killed there while exploring the city. The U.S. general Winfield Scott scolded Hays but did little more.[9] A Catholic priest from France named Emmanuel Domenech was more direct: "The Rangers . . . are the very dregs of society and the most degraded of human creatures. They slew all, neither woman nor child was spared. These blood-thirsty men . . . have neither faith nor moral feeling."[10]

After the war, the Rangers, which were not a permanent force but rather mustered in times of need, were disbanded and the U.S. Army fought Native Americans on the frontier. Jack Hays joined thousands of other prospectors as he traveled to California in the Gold

Rush of 1849.[11] Instead of prospecting, he became the sheriff of San Francisco in 1850. Later he was named the surveyor general of California, and he was instrumental in the early foundations of the city of Oakland.

The Creation of the Border

For most of its first century of existence, the United States was not focused on marking or protecting its borders, but on expanding them.[12] This happened through killing and displacing native populations and through purchasing land from other colonial powers. When the United States was founded, it consisted of thirteen colonies on the Atlantic coast of the continent. Even the western parts of those original states were not yet occupied by settlers. The Louisiana Purchase of 1803 added, on paper, the western plains ranging from Louisiana on the Gulf of Mexico all the way to Montana. In 1821, the United States purchased Florida from Spain. In 1846, the United States and Britain signed the Treaty of Oregon, establishing the 49th parallel as their territorial boundary in the Pacific Northwest.

At the end of the Mexican–American war, the United States took half of Mexico's territory including all of California, Nevada, and Utah along with parts of Arizona, Colorado, Kansas, New Mexico, Oklahoma, and Wyoming. The border was finalized with the Gadsden Purchase of 1853, which added the southern parts of New Mexico and Arizona to allow for a more direct southern railway route to California and to give the United States control of the new mines being discovered in the region, including those that would give rise to Tombstone a few decades later. By 1853, the territorial outline of the lower forty-eight states was complete.

Like many documents at the time, the Treaty of Guadalupe Hidalgo, which established the border between the United States and

Mexico at the end of the war, was an agreement on paper, not a reflection of the reality on the ground. The document makes clear that neither the Mexican nor the American governments knew much about the land they were awarding to each other: "And, in order to preclude all difficulty in tracing upon the ground the limit separating Upper from Lower California, it is agreed that the said limit shall consist of a straight line drawn from the middle of the Rio Gila, where it unites with the Colorado, to a point on the coast of the Pacific Ocean, distant one marine league due south of the southernmost point of the port of San Diego."[13] The area was vast and largely unknown to white settlers, so they simply agreed to draw a line on the map and figure it out on the ground later.

The treaty called for the two countries to nominate surveyors to work together to mark the border on the ground within one year. A few markers were placed in the 1850s at key locations, but it ended up taking almost fifty years for the two countries to get around to the daunting task of locating the line through the entire 1,954 miles of sparsely populated and remote landscapes.[14] In the nineteenth century, marking the border on the ground was a low priority for both countries because the physical line did not really matter. Since there were no immigration regulations between the countries, it was not necessary to locate, much less patrol, the vast stretches of the remote border.

With its economy based heavily on slavery, Texas joined the Confederacy during the Civil War. In the aftermath, during the Reconstruction period, the white population chafed under federal occupation. Texas was readmitted to the union in 1870, and in 1874, the Texas legislature reconstituted the Texas Rangers as a state police force to lessen the reliance on the hated federal officials. Seventeen-year-old Jeff Milton joined the Rangers only three years after it was reconstituted. The new Rangers had two units. One was placed on the frontier and focused on pushing Native Americans out of Texas, and the other worked along the border with Mexico to prevent Mexican incursions and to get cattle rustlers and bandits under control. As an early history of the Rangers explains, "they were irregular as hell, in everything except getting the job done."[15]

In the 1890s, Mexican and American surveyors worked together to place markers along the length of the border and inscribe it into the landscape. The white obelisks they installed are still visible at some locations along the border today. The United States set up customs checkpoints in the towns along the border—including Brownsville-Matamoros, Laredo–Nuevo Laredo, El Paso–Ciudad Juárez, Nogales-Nogales, and Tijuana–San Diego—but it did not have a federal force to patrol in between the checkpoints except for the small contingent of mounted Chinese Inspectors.[16] Consequently, the Texas Rangers were the primary force patrolling the U.S.–Mexico border in the first decades of the twentieth century.

The Porvenir Massacre

There were many instances of extreme and wanton violence by the Texas Rangers, but the Porvenir Massacre is perhaps the most egregious. After three people were killed in the Mexican raid on the Brite Ranch on Christmas Day 1917, the Texas Rangers were dead set on revenge and identified the settlement of Porvenir as their target. The village was full of refugees who had fled the violence of the Mexican Civil War, but it was adjacent to the spot where the Brite Ranch raiders crossed back into Mexico, so the Rangers assumed the villagers were involved. Even though their initial search of Porvenir turned up very little, the Rangers returned to the village with an army cavalry unit late on the night of January 27, 1918, and ordered everyone out of their homes.

Bob Keil and the other cavalrymen had been surprised when the

Rangers had showed up earlier that evening requesting support for the raid. Keil had been in Porvenir that very afternoon to buy some eggs for the camp mess and was amused that the Rangers thought there might be bandits there. He remembered thinking, "If we find a butcher knife down there, it will be a surprise to me."[17]

It was a cold night, and they lit a large fire for warmth after rounding up all the villagers and taking them out of their homes. The Rangers stood back while the cavalry did their work. When they were finished, they reported to the Rangers that they did not see any bandits. Moreover, the soldiers knew most of the residents of Porvenir personally and knew they were just farmers.

The Rangers thanked the cavalry and then told them to stand back, as the Rangers wanted to talk directly to the villagers. As the flames flickered in their faces, the Rangers systematically selected thirteen Mexican men and three teenaged boys, including thirteen-year-old Juan Flores and his father, Longino. At the last minute, one of the Rangers decided that Juan was too young and shoved him over to the huddled group of villagers. They marched the remaining fifteen out of the town.

As the villagers shivered and cowered near the fire, the late-night silence was pierced by a volley of gunshots. The Rangers then galloped out of town, leaving Keil and the cavalry unit confused. They stayed in the town for a while, then rode away.[18] Thirteen-year-old Juan slipped out of Porvenir and made his way toward Marfa, to the home of his schoolteacher, Henry Warren, the only white man he knew and trusted. The other residents remained in their homes until dawn, peeking through windows, praying that the Rangers would not return, and hoping against hope that the fifteen were alive. The wife of one of the missing men went into labor and delivered a baby in the anxious hours before dawn.

As the sun rose, Juan Flores returned to Porvenir with Henry

Warren. They searched the nearby countryside and came upon the grisly scene on a hillside. The bodies of the fifteen men and boys, ranging in age from fifteen to seventy-two, were dead with gunshot wounds. Many had been shot multiple times in the face, making them difficult to identify, but Juan immediately saw that his father was among the dead. The remaining residents of Porvenir gathered their possessions and crossed the river back into Mexico in search of safety. A few days later, the cavalry unit returned to the abandoned site and destroyed the entire village.

The Rangers involved in the murders did not write up an incident report for a few days. When they did, the report said that the villagers were suspected of being involved in the Brite Ranch raid and had fired first. All the deaths were in the crossfire. However, that story unraveled.

Henry Warren sent a letter to the governor of Texas informing him of what happened, "to call to your attention this unprovoked and wholesale murder by Texas Rangers." Warren wrote, "these men were all farmers . . . there was not a single bandit in the 15 slain men."[19] Mexican authorities took testimony from the survivors, and the Mexican ambassador in D.C. filed a complaint. After a review, five of the Rangers were fired and the unit was disbanded. The unit's captain was forced to resign. A broader investigation of the entire Rangers organization in 1919 found that the Rangers had been responsible for up to 5,000 extrajudicial killings in the previous five years.[20]

Despite, or perhaps because of, this violent history, many of the first Border Patrol agents were hired directly from the Texas Rangers.

3.

Closing the Back Gate

IN 1924, THE UNITED STATES CONGRESS PASSED A MASSIVE
overhaul of the immigration system that was designed, in the words
of President Calvin Coolidge, to "Keep America American." The law,
often referred to as the National Origins Quotas, was based on the
prevailing racial pseudoscience of the era that claimed that whites from
Northern Europe were racially superior to people from everywhere else
around the world. Senator David Reed of Pennsylvania, one of the authors of the bill, explained, "Our incoming immigrants should hereafter
be of the same races as those of us who are already here."[1] While the
law's supporters took victory laps in the press, it was less clear how
exactly the rules would be enforced at the thousands of miles of un-
guarded and unmarked borders and coastlines of the United States. At
the time, Jeff Milton and the seventy-five Mounted Inspectors were the
only federal officials tasked with patrolling the borders of the United
States away from ports of entry.

Although the 1924 Immigration Act severely restricted immigration from most places in the world through low entry quotas, it was also notable for the immigrants that it continued to allow. The non-quota immigrant categories included "An immigrant born in the Dominion of Canada, Newfoundland, the Republic of Mexico, the Republic of Cuba, the Republic of Haiti, the Dominican Republic, the Canal Zone, or an independent country of Central or South America."[2] In the context of today's immigration debates, it might seem surprising that immigration from Mexico, the Caribbean, and all of Central and South America was not restricted. This exemption was fought for by agriculture interests in the west, which relied heavily on migrant workers. The land reclamation acts of the early twentieth century turned California into the breadbasket of the country by building dams and irrigating the land. The only limitation was the availability of labor. White workers tended to demand higher wages and were unwilling to do the most grueling jobs. Workers from China were banned in the 1882 Chinese Exclusion Act, and workers from Japan were restricted after the Gentleman's Agreement of 1907. There was local racist resistance to bringing Black workers to the fields, so most agricultural businesses relied on labor from Mexico. By the 1920s, 80 percent of California's farm labor were seasonal migrants from Mexico. In 1900, there were 100,000 Mexican citizens residing in the United States; by 1930 it was 1.5 million.[3]

The implications of open immigration along the Mexican border were already under discussion before the Immigration Act even passed. In April 1924, Representative Cyrenus Cole of Iowa introduced a letter written by Secretary of Labor James Davis into the congressional record. Cole had asked Davis about the impact that restrictions on European migration might have on the land borders of the United States. Davis replied on April 15, 1924: "The greater the restriction against Europe, the greater will be the number of Mexican and Canadian admissions, unless the same restriction is made to apply to the countries of this hemisphere. If a demand exists for common labor and that labor is not permitted to come in from Europe, the employers of labor are going to look toward Mexico and Canada as a source of supply."[4]

Davis explained that Mexicans were crossing the border easily because "From El Paso west there is only an imaginary line through a thousand miles of desert, and many people find it convenient to cross to the states from Mexico at points where there is no human habitation for a hundred miles." The labor secretary concluded his letter: "I know you will agree with me that we should not lock the front door without supplying some means of closing the back gate."[5]

The secretary's wish was granted just two days after President Calvin Coolidge signed the National Origins Quotas into law. Tucked into the Labor Appropriation Act of 1924 was a provision to establish the United States Land Border Patrol. The Land Border Patrol's sole mission was to enforce the new eugenics-derived rules about who could enter the United States.[6] Their job was to patrol the borders of the United States and prevent the entry of non-white people banned by the Immigration Act. Jeff Milton was sixty-two years old when he was appointed as the first Border Patrol agent in 1924, and he remained on the force until he was seventy.[7]

The Border Patrol

The fledgling Land Border Patrol's task was immense. The United States had a 1,954-mile border with Mexico as well as a 5,525-mile border with Canada to the north. In 1925, coastlines were added to the Border Patrol's assignment and "Land" was removed from their name. The United States had 2,069 miles of Atlantic coastline, 1,631 miles of Gulf of Mexico coastline, and 1,293 miles of Pacific coastline. Alaska and Hawai'i were still territories in 1924, but they add an additional 6,330 miles of coastline, and Alaska also has a 1,538-mile border with Canada. In total, that is 20,340 miles of border to patrol.

Most of these borders were imaginary lines, as Labor Secretary Davis suggested, that existed on maps but were not inscribed into the physical landscape in any meaningful way.

When the Border Patrol was established, it had a tiny budget, no clear mission, and uncertain authority.[8] The initial budget was $1 million ($14 million in 2022, adjusted for inflation). That is the equivalent of less than one-tenth of 1 percent of Customs and Border Protection's 2020 budget of $15 billion. The agency's job was to enforce the new prohibition on "smuggling, harboring, concealing, or assisting an alien not duly admitted by an immigrant inspector or not lawfully entitled to enter or reside in the United States." The appropriation, however, did not actually give the agency law enforcement authority. Nevertheless, it was established quickly, and 104 agents were on duty by July 1, 1924.[9] The agents had to have their own horse and saddle but were provided with a badge, an old-model revolver, and feed for their horses. Their annual salary was $1,680 ($25,000 in 2022, adjusted for inflation).[10] There was no training. Many of the newly hired agents were not sure exactly what they were supposed to do.

Immediately after it was created, the Border Patrol realized that agents like Jeff Milton had not been given authority to do, well, anything. Congress had appropriated funding for the new agency but had not given them police powers to stop vehicles or to use force. The commissioner-general of the Bureau of Immigration wrote to a field office over the summer of 1924 explaining the problem: "If the bureau is right in its understanding of the matter, the border patrols are now without the slightest authority to stop a vehicle crossing the border for the purposes of a search, or otherwise, nor can they legally prevent the entry of an alien in violation of the law. In other words, they possess no more powers than does the ordinary citizen." If they did use force, he concluded, "They would be guilty of assault."[11]

Congress gave the Border Patrol law enforcement authority on

February 27, 1925.[12] Although it took nine months, the authority the agents received was broad and has remained largely unchanged since. The law allows agents to "arrest any alien who in his presence or view is entering or attempting to enter the United States in violation of any law." Additionally, agents can "board and search for aliens any vessel within the territorial waters of the United States, railway car, conveyance, or vehicle, in which he believes aliens are being brought into the United States."

The agents finally had police authority, but many specifics in the legislation were vague. The legislation implied that Border Patrol agents could operate to some extent inside the United States but provided no guidance on how far into the interior they could go. The second clause gave agents the ability to detain and search vehicles based only on a belief that someone is undocumented. While the legislation allowed the agents to detain an individual for interrogation while they "board and search," it did not indicate how long the detention could last. It was also unclear whether they could look for other illegal items during the search of the vehicle for undocumented immigrants. Finally, the legislation gave the Border Patrol a much lower standard of evidence compared to other police. They needed neither probable cause nor a warrant to board and search a vehicle. The legislation does not elaborate on what level of certainty is necessary to have the reasonable suspicion that someone is undocumented. Can the race of the individual justify that belief, as had been the practice of the Chinese Inspectors?

Focus on Mexicans

Even though there was no cap on Mexican immigration, the Border Patrol heavily patrolled Mexicans in the United States from the start. The Border Patrol was underfunded, and it was expensive to detain Chinese or European people while their status was adjudicated in the courts. Although Mexicans were allowed to enter the United States, there was a head tax of $8 per person ($120 in 2022, adjusted for inflation), which was a large sum at the time, particularly for manual laborers. Additionally, there were sanitation checks at the border posts that were demeaning. Crossing at an official point often meant stripping naked and being sprayed with chemicals or doused with kerosene to kill lice. Since the border with Mexico was long and open, many people opted to cross without paying the tax and without undergoing the humiliation.

In 1929, Congress made it illegal to cross the border between crossing points.[13] The Border Patrol also established a voluntary return policy for Mexicans in which they agreed to return to their home country in exchange for not being officially charged. In most cases, the agent would simply drive them to a checkpoint within a few hours of being detained. This practice continued well into the 2000s.

Operating in the remote border zone away from scrutiny of the media or most citizens, and with broad police authority to stop people without a warrant, the early Border Patrol agents continued the pattern of frontier law enforcement officers like Jeff Milton and the Texas Rangers, who filled their early ranks. The result was numerous racist and violent incidents involving Border Patrol agents that were never investigated or prosecuted. Many of the stories are recounted in the autobiographies of the agents themselves—not as embarrassing indiscretions, but rather as funny anecdotes and proud achievements.

In the 1920s, local agents wondered whether they were allowed to search vehicles for alcohol during the Prohibition era, even though their primary duty was to look for people. In response, the acting chief inspector for the U.S. Border Patrol in El Paso assured the agents that as long as they were using racial profiling and only targeting people of Mexican appearance, the seizures were fine. He wrote, "as long as Patrol Inspectors use their heads when stopping Mexicans to inquire into their alienage and later find liquor, the arrests will be upheld. Had the two persons been white Americans, the case would have been thrown out on account of illegal search, as it would have been absurd to say they believed the Americans to be aliens."[14]

Clifford Perkins, a Border Patrol agent from 1924 until 1953, wrote in his memoir about a trip to the Dallas area to conduct immigration checks in 1926.[15] At the time, Perkins was the chief patrol inspector in San Antonio, but he did not know any officials in Dallas or Fort Worth, where he was hoping to raid brothels and round up prostitutes who lacked papers. Without contacts in the city, he asked officials in San Antonio to write letters of introduction for their counterparts in Dallas. He went to only two people for these letters: the bishop of the San Antonio Diocese and the Grand Dragon of the Ku Klux Klan in San Antonio.

On the same trip, when Perkins realized that many of the prostitutes had been tipped off about the raids, he arrested a prostitute of Mexican heritage who he knew was an American citizen. He threatened to deport her if she did not give up the other prostitutes' location. When she protested that Perkins knew she was a citizen, he said he did not see any documents right now and told another officer to take her away. Perkins gleefully explains in his memoir that the threat to deport the American citizen worked and she gave up the location of the other women.

In the ethos of the early Border Patrol, only whites were of value. Everyone else was something lesser that could be killed without consequences. When Border Patrol Agent Jack Cottingham's brother Jim was shot by a Mexican liquor smuggler, Jack went to the edge of the Rio Grande and "killed every person that came in sight on the Mexican side of the river."[16] Agent Charles Askins wrote in his book *Unrepentant Sinner* that in his lifetime he had killed twenty-seven people, but that only included whites. He bragged that he did not even bother to count Black and Brown people.[17]

Jeff Milton and the other early Border Patrol agents brought a

frontier policing mindset to the new job of immigration law enforcement, drawing on their previous experience as Texas Rangers and
sheriffs in the Wild West. The Border Patrol's 1925 congressional authorization said that agents had special authority to board and search
vehicles when they observed someone crossing the border or en route
to the interior. While the legislators meant for the Border Patrol to remain close to the border itself, the agents understood it broadly and began to patrol deeper inside the United States. That approach appalled
legislators in Washington, D.C., who became concerned that the aggressive and violent actions of the agents were spilling into the interior
of the county and affecting American citizens.

4.

They Have No Right to Go into the Interior

OGDEN MILLS SHOOK HANDS AND GREETED HIS FORMER colleagues as he took his seat before the House Committee on Interstate and Foreign Commerce on April 24, 1930, where he would propose a plan to rein in the Border Patrol. Born into wealth and social status, Mills attended Harvard for his undergraduate and law degrees before pursuing a political career, serving first in the New York State Senate and then three terms in the U.S. House of Representatives from 1921 to 1927.[1] He had the square jaw and gravitas of a politician and seemed destined for higher office. He ran for governor of New York in 1926 but lost to Democrat Alfred E. Smith, who would be the Democratic nominee for the presidency two years later. After the loss, Mills used his connections to be nominated as treasury undersecretary, the number two position, in the administration of Calvin Coolidge, and then stayed on with Herbert Hoover. He served under Treasury Secretary Andrew W. Mellon, the famed banker. Mellon, aging and aloof, was not interested in the public duties of the job. Mills assumed this role and became the face of the Treasury, testifying before Congress and speaking with the media at the height of the economic boom in the Roaring Twenties.

After the 1929 market crash, Mellon's reputation was tarnished and Mills played an even bigger role. In 1932, Hoover was fed up with Mellon and sent him abroad as the ambassador to the United Kingdom. Mills was confirmed as treasury secretary for the final year of Hoover's term. Mills's legacy would be his insistence that in the face of the Great Depression, the country needed austerity measures to maintain a balanced budget, a policy that is today widely viewed as having deepened the crisis. Although he was a childhood friend and neighbor of Franklin Delano Roosevelt, Mills campaigned vigorously against him in the 1932 election and remained an outspoken critic of the New Deal. He wrote two books about the ideological shift that had occurred as Republicans became the party of individualism while Democrats backed the big government programs of the New Deal, which he referred to as "well-fed" collectivism. His second book, *The Seventeen Million*, sought to provide a voice for the 17 million people who had voted against Roosevelt in 1936, an idea that presaged today's Republican messaging around the 74 million who voted for Donald Trump in 2020.[2] Mills was discussed as a possible Republican presidential candidate until his early death in 1937 from a heart attack at age fifty-three.

In April 1930, Mills was appearing before the House Committee to discuss a proposed bill to reshape and rein in the Border Patrol at the behest of border communities.[3] There was already concern in Congress about the broad search authority and the still-undefined extent of the border zone. Local residents strongly disliked the new police presence in their communities. Some, of course, engaged in smuggling and were threatened by the new policing. Others were ranchers or farmers who relied on Mexican labor. Still others were American citizens of Latino/a descent who were constantly being hassled by the Border Patrol.

The Border Patrol recognized from the beginning that they could not effectively watch the border line itself because they did not have enough agents. Consequently, many agents opted to patrol within the United States, which meant they could not observe an individual violating immigration laws by crossing the border, so they had to use other means to decide whom to stop. This often meant racial profiling people of presumed Mexican appearance in order to stop a vehicle without a warrant to check an individual's documents.[4] In its first decade of existence, the number of people the Border Patrol apprehended peaked at 35,274 people in 1926. The agents, however, made many more stops to question people: 2,220,952 in that same year. In other words, 98 percent of stops and interrogations did not result in an apprehension.[5] In some sectors, the numbers of stops far exceeded the population of the area, which meant that many individuals were being stopped repeatedly to ask for their documents.

One of the authors of National Origins Quotas, Senator David Reed of Pennsylvania, assured concerned lawmakers that the Border Patrol's mandate "only applies to the arrest of aliens in the act of entering the country. There has been some doubt about the authority of those men to make arrests. We want to make it very clear that they have no right to make arrest except on sign of a violation of the immigration law as to illegal entry. They have no right to go into the interior city and pick up aliens in the street and arrest them, but it is just at the border where they are patrolling that we want them to have this authority . . . [the illegal entry] must be in sight of the officer himself; otherwise, he has to get a warrant. We are all on alert against granting too much power to these officials to act without warrant."[6]

Senator Reed's interpretation of the law was overly optimistic and was not how it was used in practice. Border Patrol agents asked superiors about how they should interpret the phrases "entering or attempting to enter" and "in his presence or view." The Border Patrol relied on an earlier federal court ruling that "the expression 'entering the United States' has been construed by the courts to mean that an alien is engaged in the act of entering until he reaches his final destination."[7] This reading of the law meant that if the agents came across someone traveling, they could be described as on the way to their final destination. Some agents would simply wait for people they suspected of being undocumented to leave their place of work to stop them on the road and say they were traveling to their final destination.[8]

"You Will Have a Border Patrol Where It Belongs, and That Is on the Border"

Ogden Mills proposed several fixes to end warrantless internal stops and searches. Although the Border Patrol was in the Department of Commerce and Labor, the Customs Agency was in the Treasury Department. Mills wanted to merge them.

Mills began his presentation by expressing his shock at the current practices of the Border Patrol, which he found completely inappropriate. He had trouble understanding why the Border Patrol would be operating twenty miles inside the United States, where no one would expect them to be. He said, "I do not know what you gentlemen would do, but if I were traveling 20 miles inside the borders of the United States and I had not been out of the country and someone stepped out from the side of the road and told me to stop, I would not stop because I would think I was being held up."[9]

The Treasury Department's solution combined the Border Patrol, the Customs Bureau, and the Coast Guard into a single agency focused on patrolling only the border itself at coastlines, crossing points, and along the border lines. Part of the problem in 1930 was that American citizens were still free to cross the border at any location they wanted, and they were required to visit a checkpoint only if they had goods to declare. Mills proposed expanding the number of border checkpoints and then requiring everyone cross at those locations. That would funnel traffic there and allow the Border Patrol to watch the line in between. He said, "The concentration of attention on the border will also have the result of eliminating the evils which have arisen out of the attempts to detect smuggling on interior roads. . . . It is not surprising that errors and misjudgments of those officers have occasionally had unfortunate consequences, and there have been many protests."

Mills also suggested that maybe the Border Patrol should be an arm of the military, because it would be "likely to get probably better men, a higher standard of morale," rather than the rough and violent men that were currently causing havoc along the border. He assured the committee that if Congress passed the bill, "you will not have a Border Patrol operating 20 miles inside the United States. You will have a Border Patrol where it belongs, and that is on the border."[10]

Mills said that the key was to find a balance between government expenditure and control over the border. He speculated that if Congress invested enough money, "you can put 25,000 men along the borders and you can probably make it absolutely so tight that no one can come in." Milton Garber, a Republican from Oklahoma, scoffed at that idea: "There is no intention on the part of anyone to go to the extreme."

In the end, Mills's proposed bill failed not because congressional leaders were opposed to reining in the Border Patrol, but rather due to the costs associated with it. The stock market had crashed only a few months earlier and Congress was not open to new spending bills during a period of financial uncertainty and declining tax revenues. The bill would have doubled the budget for the new border agency. As the country turned its attention to the approaching Depression, jobs were scarce and immigration across the border was declining, seemingly reducing the need for enforcement.

In June 1933, rather than combining the Border Patrol with the Customs Bureau as Mills suggested (which would not occur until 2003), Congress instead merged the Border Patrol with the Naturalization Bureau in the Labor Department. Daniel MacCormack took over as the first commissioner general of the Immigration and Naturalization Service (INS). MacCormack conducted a review of the Border Patrol and immediately shared Mills's concerns about the agents' practices. In his first month on the job, he reined in the agents by requiring warrants for all stops. He issued "confidential orders to all district directors prohibiting the apprehension of immigrants without an arrest warrant."[11] Agents and supervisors on the ground were incensed and argued that the order did not recognize the impracticality of agents in remote locations having to contact their supervisors and then judges before making a stop.

In the months that followed the new rules, there was a dramatic reduction in Border Patrol apprehensions. In the El Paso sector, apprehensions were cut in half from June to July 1933.[12] In 1934, apprehensions dropped to 11,016, the lowest level on record and only one-third of the rate of previous years. MacCormack also began trainings with field agents to familiarize them with regulations and to weed out violent and unprofessional behavior.[13] The first class of thirty-four entered the INS Border Patrol Training School in December 1934.

MacCormack's efforts to reform and professionalize the Border Patrol were cut short when he died while still in office on January 1, 1937, at the age of fifty-seven. His successors bowed to the will of field agents and rescinded the warrant process because it was impractical. The efforts by Senator Reed and Treasury Undersecretary Mills to end

interior enforcement and keep the Border Patrol at the border itself
also failed.

On the ground, agents resumed operating as they had originally.
Throughout the era, the Border Patrol remained a small force, never
more than 1,000 agents, operating in a vast and still sparsely populated
border zone. Their small numbers and their remote workplaces meant
that their violence toward immigrants and their loose interpretations
of the law received little scrutiny. The unanswered questions of whom
the agents could legally stop, what amount of cause they needed, and
whether they could search a vehicle in the interior of the United States
lingered for decades.

One story of a Border Patrol agent who raided a campsite of men
he suspected to be smugglers illustrates the "anything goes" ethos
in the early years. The agent spotted tracks that indicated a group of
men, likely carrying a load of smuggled goods. He followed the trail
until he located the men camped for the night around a fire. As the
men relaxed, he took them by surprise and was able to subdue them
even though he was outnumbered. As the agent searched the camp,
he confiscated their guns. One of the men asked under what law he
was allowed to seize their weapons. The agent responded, "The law of
self-preservation." An early history of the Border Patrol commended
his approach: "No one, then or later, questions his wise interpretation
of the rules."[14]

However, despite the 1925 legislation that gave expansive authority to conduct stops and searches in the border zone, and the Border Patrol's culture of writing their own rules, the smuggler was right
to question the legality of the agent's actions. The United States has
core constitutional protections for individuals, including the Fourth
Amendment, which protects everyone in the United States from unreasonable searches and seizures. The Border Patrol's regulation that

authorized agents to stop and search people without a warrant was at odds with the Constitution.

The Border Patrol's stop and search authority was destined to be reviewed by the Supreme Court, but that would not happen for almost fifty years. In the meantime, the Supreme Court weighed in on several other cases that established the extent of Fourth Amendment protections in the United States. These cases became the precedent against which the Border Patrol would eventually be judged.

5.

Unreasonable Searches and Seizures

GEORGE CARROLL AND HIS FRIEND JOHN KIRO WERE TRY-
ing to keep warm as they drove from Detroit back to Grand Rapids,
Michigan, on December 15, 1921. Even a top-of-the-line automobile
like Carroll's Oldsmobile Roadster did not, at that time, have a heating
system. The soft-top roof provided barely any barrier against the Michigan winter. The two men, bundled up in coats, sweaters, and gloves,
had been on the road for hours and were only sixteen miles from Grand
Rapids when another car passed them, headed in the opposite direction. The Roadster did not have any mirrors, but if Carroll had glanced
behind him, he would have seen the other vehicle slam on the brakes
and quickly do a U-turn. Inside the other vehicle were three federal
Prohibition officers, Agents Cronenwett, Scully, and Thayer, as well as
a state police officer named Peterson.[1] The officers' vehicle picked up
speed as it began to pursue Carroll's Oldsmobile.

It is easy to forget that the United States banned the sale of alcohol only two weeks into the decade that came to be known as the Roaring Twenties. The decade evokes images of the postwar and post-flu-pandemic boom with people dancing in clubs and luxuriating in the new consumer items that flooded the American marketplace. Yet during the entire decade, alcohol was banned across the United States. Alcohol consumption, and particularly the raucous male culture of saloons, was a political flashpoint in the country for decades as the temperance movement pushed for more restrictions on what they considered to be a dangerous and deadly drink. Temperance found support in conservative religious communities as well as in the burgeoning women's suffrage movement. Alcohol was blamed for many social ills, from lazy workers to violence against women. Saloons were painted as dens of corruption where secret deals were made and inappropriate behaviors tolerated.

The Eighteenth Amendment, which prohibited the production, transport, and sale of alcohol, passed in 1917 but required ratification by two-thirds of the states to go into force. Nebraska became the thirty-sixth state to ratify it on January 16, 1919, and Prohibition went into effect one year later on January 17, 1920. In October 1919, Congress passed the Volstead Act, which filled in the details on the alcohol ban and authorized 1,520 federal Prohibition agents to enforce it. Immediately after Prohibition, clandestine stills were set up across the country and smuggling networks appeared on the Mexican and Canadian borders. The Prohibition agents were fighting a losing cause, but they dutifully set to work smashing barrels in the streets and destroying moonshine operations across the country.

The Prohibition agents in Grand Rapids had suspected Carroll and Kiro were smugglers for months but were not able to catch them in the act. Earlier that fall, on September 29, 1921, agents Cronenwett and Scully were working undercover, posing as buyers on the black market. They set up a meeting at an apartment in Grand Rapids, with Cronenwett playing the role of a Mr. Stafford, a fictional employee of the Michigan Chair Company interested in buying three cases of whiskey. Carroll and Kiro agreed to a price of $13 ($190 in 2022, adjusted for inflation) per case and promised to return with the contraband in about an hour. The agents waited, but Carroll and Kiro never showed up. The agents presumed their ruse had been discovered. At their initial meeting, the agents had noted Carroll's vehicle, an Oldsmobile Roadster, and the license plate. They kept an eye out for it around Grand Rapids.

The following week, on October 6, the agents were monitoring the highway on the outskirts of Grand Rapids for suspicious vehicles headed into the city. They knew most of the liquor in the region was smuggled in from Canada at the border between Windsor, Ontario, and Detroit. The agents would position themselves on the highway from Detroit and look for cars they thought might be smuggling. Agent Scully was outside the car eating his lunch when Cronenwett spotted Carroll's Oldsmobile leaving Grand Rapids and driving toward Detroit. Cronenwett called out to Scully, who jumped into the passenger seat as they sped off to follow them. The Prohibition agents decided not to stop Carroll because they assumed he was headed to pick up a shipment. A stop before he got to Detroit would not produce any evidence. The agents were able to keep an eye on the car until it reached East Lansing, but they lost track of it in the city. The agents returned to Grand Rapids empty-handed but even more convinced that Carroll was smuggling alcohol in from Detroit.

The agents finally spotted Carroll's Oldsmobile again on that cold December evening. The agents spun their car around and began the pursuit. After the agents sped up behind him and signaled him to stop, Carroll eased his Oldsmobile to the side of the road. He taunted the agents when they arrived at his car window, addressing them by their real names, not the fake identities given to him under cover. Carroll was jovial and confident while he waited as the agents searched the car. They initially found nothing. There was nothing visible in the open areas of the car and Carroll was happy to open up the trunk, which was also empty. However, as one of the agents bent down to look under the seats, he thought the leather seemed harder than normal. The other agents pressed the seat and agreed.

Carroll protested as the agents cut into the leather, but their hunch was right. They found sixty-eight quarts of alcohol, labeled as Scotch Whiskey and Gordon's Gin. Carroll knew he was caught and resorted to a strategy that had gotten him out of tight spots previously. He pulled out his money clip, which held wads of $10 bills, and said to Agent Cronenwett, "Take the liquor and give us one more chance and I will make it right with you." Perhaps if there were fewer officers present, the bribes might have worked, but with four men from different agencies, they refused.

At his initial trial, Carroll was convicted of illegally transporting alcohol. He appealed, and the case reached the Supreme Court. The case was argued on March 14, 1924, two months before Congress created the Border Patrol. The court was presented with two very different views of the search. The government suggested that Congress gave the Prohibition agents the right to search any vehicle for alcohol. If that was not what Congress intended, they should change the law. Additionally, the lawyers noted that requiring a warrant was not practical because a vehicle could flee the scene, easily crossing jurisdictional boundaries before a warrant was received. Indeed, the Prohibition agents had pursued Carroll and Kiro previously but lost track of them. It was a fundamentally different case than a search of a fixed location like a house.

Carroll's lawyers argued that the law was a gross violation of the Fourth Amendment of the Constitution, which prohibited unreasonable searches and seizures. As a constitutional right, they argued, it was inviolable. If the Supreme Court allowed the Prohibition agents to stop and search anyone, it would turn the country into a police state. Consequently, the evidence from the illegal search of Carroll's vehicle should be suppressed and the Volstead Act's sweeping authority for Prohibition agents invalidated.

The Supreme Court took almost a year to weigh the different arguments and the decision was not announced until March 2, 1925. The fundamental question was how to balance the legitimate need of the police to enforce laws with the constitutional protections of citizens to be free of unreasonable searches and seizures. The decision they made in the *Carroll* case would prove to be a key precedent for the coming Border Patrol disputes, as well as for the constitutional rights of everyone inside the United States.

The Fourth Amendment

The Fourth Amendment to the U.S. Constitution was written in response to the experiences of people living in the English colonies prior to the revolution. The English wanted to crack down on smuggling that was undermining the taxes meant to be collected in the colonies. In order to find the contraband and properly tax it, they used general writs of assistance that worked like a blanket warrant and allowed the inspectors to enter any house they wanted.

In 1760, James Otis, a lawyer and political activist in Massachusetts who coined the phrase "taxation without representation is tyranny," led an effort against the writs of assistance, which he ultimately lost. However, his stand against the writs informed the rights that the founders of the United States wanted to protect in the Bill of Rights.

The Fourth Amendment of the United States Constitution reads: "The right of the people to be secure in their persons, houses, papers, and effects, against unreasonable searches and seizures, shall not be violated, and no Warrants shall issue, but upon probable cause, supported by Oath or affirmation, and particularly describing the place to be searched, and the persons or things to be seized." The Amendment was sent to the states by Congress on September 28, 1789, and was ratified by December 15, 1791.

Although the language of the Fourth Amendment seems straightforward, the devil is in the details. Police generally need to go to a judge, show probable cause that a crime has been committed, and get a warrant if they want to conduct a search, unless an individual consents to a search. However, when there are exigent circumstances—other, time-sensitive factors—courts have ruled that warrantless searches do not violate the Fourth Amendment. These are often decided on a case-by-case basis, but some examples of exigent circumstances would be if screams or gunshots are heard inside a house or if the police receive a credible tip that a crime is occurring. Once the location is secure, they need a warrant from a judge to conduct a proper search. A house cannot flee, and the delay while requesting a warrant does not impede the search.

The Fourth Amendment was written in the era before rapid transportation. There was no way for the framers of the Bill of Rights to account for new technologies like trains, planes, and vehicles that would allow an individual to flee and quickly cross into a different jurisdiction, which makes the requirement of waiting for a warrant from a judge onerous. Consequently, it was up to the Supreme Court to decide how to interpret the Fourth Amendment protections against unreasonable searches and seizures in the context of new technologies like George Carroll's Oldsmobile Roadster.

The Supreme Court's March 2, 1925, decision in the Carroll case was written by Chief Justice William Howard Taft. Taft, stout with a handlebar mustache, is the only person to serve as both the president of the United States and the chief justice of the Supreme Court. The 6–2 verdict found a middle ground, which came to be known as the *Carroll* doctrine.

The court decided that the stop of George Carroll was legal because it fulfilled two tests. The first was whether the agents had probable cause. Probable cause exists if they have enough evidence to believe that if they were to take it to a judge and request a warrant, it would be approved. The second test was whether there were exigent circumstances that meant that they did not have time to go to a judge. If both conditions are met, then the officers can stop and search a car without a warrant. In George Carroll's case, the court agreed that both conditions were met, so his conviction was upheld.

The *Carroll* ruling seemed to have settled the rules for when a federal agent could stop and search a vehicle in the United States. However, only three days before the ruling, on February 27, 1925, Congress gave the Border Patrol its broad authority to stop vehicles without a warrant for immigration inspections. Consequently, while other federal agents were required to have probable cause and exigent circumstances to make a vehicle stop, the Border Patrol followed their own regulations throughout the still-undefined border zone.

Stop and Frisk

Until the 1960s, it was thought that the Fourth Amendment of the Constitution applied only to federal police, not state officials. The 1961 Supreme Court decision in *Mapp v. Ohio* dramatically altered that understanding by ruling that the Fourth Amendment applied to both state and federal police.[2] The ruling established the exclusionary rule, also known as the suppression doctrine, which prevents the inclusion of evidence in a trial that was collected or analyzed in violation of the defendant's constitutional rights. The ruling required police, both federal and state, to follow proper procedures for gathering evidence in order for that evidence to be admissible at trial. For many critics of the liberal Supreme Court decisions in the 1960s, the exclusionary rule from *Mapp* was particularly despised because it did not just protect innocent people from unreasonable searches, but also constrained the police and freed people who committed crimes.

The 1960s saw a number of other Fourth Amendment cases before the Supreme Court. The most significant was *Terry v. Ohio,* which was decided in 1968. On October 31, 1963, John Terry, a Black man, and two friends were observed walking around in front of a jewelry store in Cleveland by a veteran detective named Martin McFadden. McFadden, suspecting the men were casing the store for a possible robbery, decided to stop and interrogate them. After the men did not respond clearly to his questions, McFadden said he feared for his safety and decided to frisk them to search for weapons.

The search located a pistol in Terry's coat pocket and a revolver in the pocket of his friend, Richard Chilton. The third man had no weapons. McFadden arrested Terry and Chilton and charged them with carrying concealed weapons. The men were found guilty by the Cuyahoga County court after the judge ruled that the stop was lawful and that the evidence found in the search should not be suppressed. Terry appealed and the case reached the Supreme Court in the fall of 1967.

The Supreme Court in the 1960s was liberal and handed down a string of rulings that created more rights for defendants, including the exclusionary rule from *Mapp* and the well-known *Miranda* ruling of 1966, which held that the police had to inform people in custody of their rights to remain silent and to have access to a lawyer. The Supreme Court ruling in *Terry,* written by Chief Justice Earl Warren, attempted to find a balance between the need to prevent crimes and the real prospect of harassment by the police if they could stop and frisk anyone. The court worried it could result in "The wholesale harassment by certain elements of the police community, of which minority groups, particularly Negroes, frequently complain."[3]

The court ended up with a middle ground that allowed stops but only those based on some set of facts. The standard they produced was "reasonable suspicion" based on articulable facts from the officer for why they made the stop. Crucially, they decided these facts did not have to amount to probable cause, but the stops had to be very brief and were not akin to detention. The reasonable suspicion needed to be about the safety of the officer and the public in that location. If these conditions are met, the evidence found in this sort of a stop is admissible in court. They ruled that the conditions were met in Terry's case and his conviction was upheld.

Although the Warren court expressed concern about the potential for racial profiling in the practice of stop and frisk, the end result certainly allows for it and it has played out on street corners for decades. The police must have more than a hunch that the individuals are engaged in illegal activity, but they do not need formal probable cause to briefly stop and search individuals in public spaces.

In practice, stop and frisk is often used in predominantly Black neighborhoods that are identified as areas of drug sales and gang activity. It is a form of racial profiling masked by geography. If an officer sees a group of young men hanging around on a street corner known for drug sales, they can use those articulable facts of reasonable suspicion to briefly talk to the men and search them for weapons or drugs. Justice William Douglas, who was known for his solitary liberal opinions, cast the lone dissenting opinion. He criticized the ruling because he saw it as a step toward a police state: "To give the police greater power than a magistrate is to take a long step down the totalitarian path."[4]

When combined, *Carroll*, *Mapp*, and *Terry* established the basic parameters for how Fourth Amendment protections were applicable to police stops in public spaces without a warrant. If the officer had probable cause and worried that a vehicle was going to flee, they could stop and search the vehicle. If the officer had reasonable suspicion with articulable facts that an individual was a potential danger to the officer or the public, they could briefly stop them in order to ask a few questions and frisk them. However, in all other circumstances, police officers needed a warrant or consent in order to conduct a search if they wanted the evidence to be admissible in court.

The Border Patrol's Unexamined Authority

The Border Patrol's authority to stop anyone in the border zone for any reason was in conflict with the Supreme Court's decisions that law enforcement officials needed probable cause for searches and reasonable suspicion for brief interrogations in the United States. Just as the Volstead Act of 1919 gave Prohibition agents seemingly unchecked authority to stop vehicles to search for alcohol, the Border Patrol's authorization in 1925 gave agents seemingly unchecked authority to stop vehicles to search for undocumented immigrants. However, the Supreme Court curtailed the Prohibition agents' authority within a few years of its implementation through the *Carroll* doctrine. By contrast, the Border Patrol continued to operate in the remote border zone for decades before the Supreme Court considered the implications of its ability to conduct warrantless stops inside the United States.

In those intervening decades, the agency interpreted the law as they wished. They also continuously sought to expand the definition of the border zone, where their unchecked authority could be put into practice every day. It would not be until 1947 that the exact boundaries of the Border Patrol's special zone of operations would finally be established. That zone turned out to be vast.

6.

A Reasonable Distance

HERBERT BROWNELL JR. KNEW NOTHING ABOUT THE BOR-
der when he became the attorney general of the United States in 1953,
but decisions he would make continue to affect the lives of people in the
border zone to this day. Brownell was born in the tiny town of Peru, Nebraska, in 1904 and attended the University of Nebraska and Yale Law
School. He then settled in New York and became active in Republican
politics. Brownell served in the New York State Assembly in the 1930s
and then became the campaign manager for Thomas Dewey's success-
ful campaign for governor of New York in 1942. In 1944, Brownell was
elected chair of the Republican National Committee, and he managed
Dewey's presidential campaigns in 1944 and 1948. In 1948, Dewey was
the heavy favorite over the unpopular incumbent Harry Truman, and
several newspapers, including the *Chicago Daily Tribune,* went to press
early on election night with the headline DEWEY DEFEATS TRUMAN.
The shock loss for Dewey led to the famous photos of a beam-
ing Truman holding the erroneous headlines. For the 1952 election,

Brownell turned his attention to Dwight D. Eisenhower and encouraged him to run. Brownell was instrumental in helping Eisenhower win a contested convention over Robert A. Taft, a senator from Ohio and the eldest son of William Howard Taft, the twenty-seventh president of the United States and the chief justice of the Supreme Court who wrote the opinion that became the *Carroll* doctrine. After Eisenhower won the presidency, he nominated Brownell as his first attorney general.

Herbert Brownell was among the most prominent members of Eisenhower's cabinet and appeared on the cover of *Time Magazine* a few weeks into his new job, under the title "A Legal Mind and a Political Brain." However, he had an unassuming manner and a rather plain appearance. On one occasion, he wore mismatched shoes to testify before Congress. When it was pointed out, he joked, "Just wanted to let the folks know I owned two pairs of shoes."[1] The *Time* cover story began with an anecdote about a secretary at Eisenhower's New York campaign headquarters stealing a glance at the famous campaign strategist when she heard he was in the waiting room. As she peeked around the door, she realized that she had seen him walk by her desk dozens of times before. She exclaimed, "Oh, is that him? He looked so unimportant I didn't think he could possibly be Mr. Brownell."[2]

Brownell guided the Department of Justice through the early years of the civil rights movement and supported desegregation efforts, which resulted in many enemies in the South. He proved instrumental in convincing Eisenhower to send federal troops to Little Rock, Arkansas, in 1957 to ensure the desegregation of Central High School. Brownell also established the system of having the American Bar Association vet judicial nominees. Eisenhower considered him for several Supreme Court seats that opened up late in his term, but decided that southern senators would derail his nomination. These seats instead went to William Brennan, Charles Whittaker, and Potter Stewart. Brownell was again considered for the court in 1969 by Richard Nixon, but he withdrew his name from consideration for the seat that went to Warren Burger.

Despite his lack of familiarity with the border, as the attorney general of the United States from 1953 to 1957, Brownell found himself in charge of the Immigration and Naturalization Service, which had been moved from the Department of Labor to the Department of Justice in 1940. The week before Eisenhower's inauguration, *The New York Times* ran a front-page story under the headline, TIDE OF 'WETBACKS' REACHES CREST; 1,500,000 IN SOUTHWEST IN 1952.[3] *Wetback*, a racist term used to describe undocumented people from Mexico, was derived from the idea that immigrants had to swim across the Rio Grande to reach the United States. The use of the term by the U.S. government and by a newspaper like *The New York Times* illustrates the casually pejorative view of immigrants at the time. The article calls the Mexicans "invaders" while stating that although the Mexicans are "guileless laborers, there is nothing to prevent their hordes from being infiltrated by subversive foreign agents." Without providing evidence, the article states that they undercut American wages and are a "major factor in the chronic economic and social distress" of many American citizens.

As his term began, Eisenhower tasked Brownell with getting the situation under control. In his four years as attorney general, Brownell would make a series of significant decisions about the border, including authorizing one of the largest roundups of immigrants in the history of the United States.

The Bracero Program

World War II changed the relationship between farmers in the Southwest, Mexican laborers, and the Border Patrol. From Texas to California, large agricultural interests became dependent on cheap labor from

Mexico to work the fields. This labor was less important to small mom-and-pop farms but became crucial to the massive ranches and corporate agribusinesses that dominated the region. In the prewar years, the open border and unlimited Mexican immigration, combined with the Border Patrol's selective internal enforcement, resulted in a large, accessible labor force, but one that was precarious and did not have the same rights as citizen workers. The constant threat of the Border Patrol meant that Mexican workers were forced into compliance: they were less likely to demand higher wages or complain about dangerous conditions.

Border Patrol officials routinely gave congressional testimony describing the dual role of patrolling the border and ensuring workers for agricultural businesses. The Border Patrol did not attempt to prevent immigration completely. Instead, it controlled and managed immigration so that business interests ended up with the type of workers they desired, a role not that distinct from the slave patrols that had ensured compliant labor for plantations a century before.

Willard Kelly, the Border Patrol chief at the time, told a Presidential Commission in 1950 that "Service officers were instructed to defer apprehensions of Mexicans employed on Texas farms where to remove them would likely result in the loss of crops."[4] Instead, they would focus on the period after the harvest in order to send the workers back to Mexico. Similarly, during economic downturns, the Border Patrol would step up enforcement to ensure the state did not have to provide for the unemployed laborers. These roundups would often happen just before payday, so agribusinesses got the labor and the agents got their apprehension quotas, but the Mexican workers were not paid.[5]

At other times, when the agribusinesses were desperately in need of labor, the Immigration and Naturalization Service (INS), the parent agency of the Border Patrol, recruited more labor through schemes like the Bracero program. In 1942, as the United States ramped up its war effort in the Pacific, many American men were enlisted, and labor sources for farms dried up. American and Mexican officials drew up a guest worker program to bring Mexican workers to the United States to fill this gap. In the negotiations, the Mexican government demanded protections and minimum wages for their workers, while the U.S. officials negotiated on behalf of the American agribusinesses. During the war, 219,500 Mexican workers came to twenty-four states through the program.[6]

The Bracero program formalized the relationship between agribusinesses in the Southwest and Mexican laborers, establishing a mutually beneficial system. The Braceros sent money home, so other Mexican laborers learned it was profitable to travel to the United States to work. The jobs were difficult and the living conditions poor, but for many it was still better than their options at home. The only real opposition to the system was from labor unions on both sides of the border.[7] After the war, the Bracero program briefly expired but was then renewed and continued through the 1960s.

Expanding the Border Zone

While there had been legislative and administrative attempts in the 1930s to rein in the Border Patrol by Undersecretary of the Treasury Ogden Mills and INS Commissioner Daniel MacCormack, in the 1940s and 1950s a series of decisions expanded their already significant authority. A 1946 revision to the Border Patrol authorization removed the phrase "in which he believes aliens are being brought into the United States" and replaced it with "within a reasonable distance from any external boundary of the United States." Previously, agents were supposed to have some belief that a person lacked documents, but after 1946, all warrantless stops were allowed within the geographic area of the "reasonable distance" from the border.[8] Congress left the extent of that reasonable distance undefined.

In July 1947, the Justice Department published a routine update on immigration policies in the *Federal Register*. While Congress writes the laws that govern the executive branch of the government, the individual agencies interpret and implement those laws. The *Federal Register* is the record of the definitions they are using of terms in the laws and specifics on how they are applied. Buried on page 5071, among the three columns of tiny print, there was a clarification of what "reasonable distance" meant for how far the Border Patrol's special rules extended into the interior of the United States. Without public comment or consultation, the Department of Justice defined reasonable distance as "a distance not exceeding 100 air miles from any external boundary of the United States."[9] This simple administrative decision on the size of the border zone has remained in place ever since, allowing the Border Patrol to use its special authority to make stops based on lower evidence standards in large sections of the interior of the United States.

In 1952, Congress revised the Border Patrol's regulations again to allow warrantless searches of property within twenty-five miles of the border.[10] Agents had been frustrated that they could not access private property in the border zone except with exigent circumstances such as a continuous pursuit. As the relationships between agribusinesses and Mexican workers expanded, many farmers became more resistant to intrusions from the Border Patrol. They put up fences, No Trespassing signs, and actively dissuaded the Border Patrol from accessing their lands. The new rules meant that agents were allowed onto private land without a warrant, but they could not enter buildings or houses.

Although the revision passed, it was opposed by many border state senators and representatives. Representative Ovie Fisher, a Democrat from Texas, explained his discomfort with it: "The Constitution authorizes search warrants for the limited purpose of seizing persons or things. It does not authorize fishing expeditions. It does not authorize searches for the purpose of interrogating people."[11] Nevertheless, that is precisely the authority that the Border Patrol agents had in the border zone.

By the early 1950s, the postwar economic boom, combined with the established migration networks between southwestern agribusinesses and Mexican towns, led to a substantial growth in laborers outside the formal Bracero program. The Border Patrol continued to operate in a gray area between an enforcement organization and a labor recruiter for agribusinesses. One change was that the Border Patrol began to legalize some workers it found in the United States, rather than relying on Mexico to identify and send them. They often referred to this process as "drying out wetbacks." This benefited the agribusinesses because it circumvented the Mexican government's rules about working conditions and wages. It also benefited laborers because it accelerated the process. They no longer had to wait for a formal invitation; they just crossed the border and began working without proper documents. If the Border Patrol found them, then they received documents on the spot. By the time Herbert Brownell became attorney general, five times as many Bracero workers were legalized after clandestine crossings than came through the official channel.

These local, agribusiness-friendly procedures did not play well at the national political level. The Border Patrol chief, Willard Kelly, called these migrations "the greatest peacetime invasion ever complacently suffered by any country."[12] The 1951 President's Commission on Migratory Labor reached the same conclusion. It noted that there had been cross-border traffic prior to World War II, but it was never "overwhelming in numbers." However, in the years since, "The magnitude of the wetback traffic has reached entirely new levels" and is "virtually an invasion."[13] A *New York Times* radio report in 1951 stated, "There is nothing to stop the whole nation [of Mexico] moving into the United States, if it wants to."[14] While the United States removed about 11,000 Mexicans in 1943, the number was over 835,000 by 1953. That same year, outgoing INS commissioner Argyle Mackey complained of "the human tide of 'wetbacks'" and called it the "most serious enforcement problem of the Service."[15]

Operation Wetback

As he took office in January 1953, President Dwight D. Eisenhower was feeling substantial pressure to bring some order at the border. The media and congressional attention to immigration meant the border situation became one of the first issues Herbert Brownell tackled as the new attorney general. Brownell took a two-day tour of the border in August 1953 and came away "shocked" by the "serious and thoroughly unsatisfactory situation."[16] Although he had no knowledge of the border, or of diplomatic relations with Mexico, Brownell was an expert at campaigning and creating a spectacle to signify action. He began working on several steps to orchestrate a well-publicized crackdown at the border. Mexican Secretary of Foreign Affairs Luis Padilla Nervo, however, presciently noted that the problem was difficult to solve: "as long as the wetbacks could find work, the illegal border traffic would continue."[17]

Brownell's first step was an immediate increase in the number of Border Patrol agents. At the time, there were only 1,080 agents, 750 of whom were on the Mexican border. He proposed adding 200 more agents to the Mexican border. Brownell also began working on a plan called Operation Cloudburst that would send 4,000 U.S. troops to the border in a show of force to impress the American public and demonstrate action on the issue.

Brownell took the finalized plan for Operation Cloudburst to Eisenhower for his consideration, but Eisenhower did not make a decision right away. Instead, he discussed it with an old friend from his military days, retired Lieutenant General Joseph Swing. Swing was concerned by the use of the military within the United States, which was banned in most instances under the Posse Comitatus Act of 1878, which removed federal troops from the South in the aftermath of the Civil War. Swing instead suggested another idea: Eisenhower should nominate him as the next INS commissioner so he could solve the problem of the border himself.

With a hair-trigger temper but a reputation for loyalty to his troops, Joseph Swing was a career military officer who served in France in World War I and was the commander of the 11th Airborne Division in World War II.[18] He graduated from West Point in 1915 in the same class as future president Eisenhower and his first commission was with General John Pershing at Fort Bliss in El Paso, Texas, in 1916, when he was part of a three-week incursion into Mexico in an attempt to arrest Pancho Villa, which became a diplomatic dispute. Swing's experience in Mexico made him particularly sensitive about the impact of American troops on diplomatic relations with Mexico.

When Eisenhower told Swing about Attorney General Brownell's plan to send troops to the border to solve the immigration issue, Swing was alarmed. He knew the presence of troops would be terrible for international relations and he volunteered that he could solve the problem using only Border Patrol agents from the INS. Eisenhower was impressed with his former West Point classmate's plan and nominated Swing to be commissioner of the INS.

During his tenure, Swing treated the INS as his own fiefdom, similar to how his contemporary, J. Edgar Hoover, ran the FBI. Eyebrows were raised when he put his daughter on the payroll. He was also criticized for taking five hunting trips to Mexico on taxpayer funds, ostensibly to maintain good relations with his counterparts in the Mexican government.

Swing was confirmed by the Senate in late May 1954, and by early June he already had a plan in place for a crackdown.[19] However, he was

an adept political operator and he ensured that he had all the important constituencies on board before he acted. Swing framed his plan as
something that would benefit the politically powerful agribusinesses of
the Southwest, and he reassured them that the result would be more
reliable, legal workers through the Bracero program.[20] He argued that
his plan would eliminate the unfair advantage of some competitors
who were using lower-cost undocumented workers.

With agribusinesses on board, Attorney General Brownell announced "Operation Wetback" on June 9, 1954. The Border Patrol
joined with local police to set up roadblocks and blockade immigrant
neighborhoods to round up people without the proper work documents. They started in California, with plans to move east to Texas
later in the summer, and then target interior cities like Saint Louis and
Kansas City in the fall.

The media covered the operation heavily, which was part of
Brownell and Swing's strategy. The goal was the illusion of a powerful
sweep, with the hope that some people might leave and others would
delay coming.[21] It was also designed to allay fears in the public about
the border. *The New York Times* reporter on the immigration beat somewhat credulously called it "a widespread round up of border jumpers"
that was "aimed at permanently sealing the nation's 2,000-mile Southwestern boundary against a decades-long illegal alien influx."[22] Only
two days later, when agents had just begun in California, the same reporter celebrated Operation Wetback as a success: "Federal men think
they have border-jumping in hand by patrol system."[23] The reporter
noted that there were hardly any disputes as the raids were carried
out: "[Mexicans] know that if caught, although technically liable to
imprisonment, they will, because of their overwhelming numbers, be
trundled back across the border. So when rounded up, hoeing in a field,
trudging across country, or riding northbound freight trains, they accept their fate with characteristic Mexican impassivity and grace." Only

two days into the operation, with no steps taken outside of California, the newspaper of record was already reporting that the immigration issue was essentially solved.

For people caught up in the crackdown, it was horrible. Mexican laborers, many of whom already lived in squalid conditions and worked long hours for meager wages, now had to continuously look over their shoulder for the Border Patrol. The roundup captured an unknown number of American citizens of Mexican heritage who happened not to have a proper ID document on them when they were swept up. There were also tragedies, such as the eighty-eight people who died in Mexicali in July 1955, when temperatures reached 112°F after they were deposited across the border without money or a place to go.[24]

Operation Wetback was lauded in the press, and even today it is often reported that the Border Patrol apprehended over 1 million people in 1954. However, the 1954 fiscal year ended on July 1, only three weeks after Swing's operation began. Therefore, only a small fraction of the 1954 apprehensions were from Operation Wetback.[25] After the media attention died down in the fall of 1954, Swing reduced the number of agents at the border. The result of fewer agents was a precipitous decline in apprehensions, which Swing used to claim fewer people were crossing the border after the crackdown. In the 1955 fiscal year, which included the majority of the sweeps from Operation Wetback, there were only 225,186 apprehensions.

The 1965 Immigration Act

For President Eisenhower and Attorney General Brownell, Operation Wetback was a success because it turned attention away from the border while southwestern agribusinesses continued to have access to low-cost labor through the Bracero program. General Swing had promised to replace removed workers with legal Bracero workers and he did. While there were 201,380 Bracero workers in 1953, the number increased to 445,197 by 1956.[26] The Border Patrol returned to its normal practice of rounding up Mexicans in the border zone and returning them to Mexico in a voluntary removal on the same day. General Swing's drawing down of agents at the border meant that removals declined from over 1 million in 1954 to only 60,000 in 1960.[27]

At the end of Brownell's term as attorney general in 1957, there was another update to immigration definitions in the *Federal Register*, and the one-hundred-mile border zone was kept, as it has been in every revision to the Border Patrol's regulations in the decades since.[28]

By the early 1960s, the Bracero program became mired in an interagency dispute between the INS and the Department of Labor.[29] While the INS consistently represented the needs of large agribusinesses in the Southwest, the Department of Labor was influenced by labor unions to crack down on low-cost workers from Mexico. By 1963, the Bracero program was viewed as a relic of the past. The program was criticized for its poor conditions for Mexican workers, its low wages that were said to undercut American wages, and its impact on small farms who did not have the same ability to access the program as massive factory farms.[30] Congress did not renew the program and it was allowed to lapse on December 31, 1964. *The New York Times* editorial page cheered: "When wages and working conditions in the fields approach some minimum level of decency, there will be no shortage of American workers available to harvest the crops."[31]

Over the program's twenty-two years, over 5 million Mexican workers used it to find jobs inside the United States.[32] Even as the legal mechanism for Mexican farm workers to enter the United States ended, the farms still needed workers and the workers still needed jobs, so the seasonal migration networks continued as they had before, but no longer with any legal right to work.

Even as things calmed down at the border and immigration

slipped from the news in the early 1960s, the biggest change for the U.S.–Mexico border was in the works in Congress. Although the Border Patrol focused on patrolling for Mexicans in the United States, through 1965 there was no cap on Mexican immigration to the country. Mexicans were free to enter the United States as long as they passed through a point of entry, but many continued to cross the porous border without paying the border tax or submitting to embarrassing inspections, as they had since the 1920s.

In 1965, Congress passed the Hart-Celler Immigration and Nationality Act, which for the first time set a cap on immigration from Mexico. After the law went into effect in 1968, Border Patrol apprehensions soared and hundreds of cases questioning the constitutionality of the Border Patrol's stop and search authority made their way through the courts. After fifty years of operating in relative anonymity, the Border Patrol's authority to stop and search vehicles deep inside the United States would finally be reviewed by the Supreme Court of the United States.

Part II

The Supreme Court

7.

Law and Order

BY THE EARLY 1970S, THE IMPACT OF THE END OF THE Bracero program in 1964 and the signing of the Hart-Celler Immigration and Nationality Act of 1965 was becoming clear at the border. Although the demand for Mexican labor in the agricultural and manufacturing sectors remained, the legal pathways to enter the country and to work were rescinded. Mexican laborers continued to travel to the United States for the same jobs they had before, but now that migration was against the law and resulted in a surge of apprehensions by the Border Patrol. The Border Patrol apprehended only 40,000 people in 1965, but by 1974 it soared to over 570,000.

This dramatic increase led to many new cases in the courts contesting the Border Patrol's authority to stop and search vehicles in the border zone. The Border Patrol remained a small agency in the early 1970s—only 1,500 agents—and they primarily conducted immigration enforcement in the interior of the United States. The border line was long and difficult to guard in remote areas. Instead, the agents opted to search for immigrants away from the line at trails known to be used by smugglers and on highways that led away from the border into the United States. After the border zone was defined in 1947 as within one hundred miles of borders and coastlines, the agency set up interior checkpoints deep inside the United States to stop all vehicles to check the occupants' immigration status. They also routinely deployed agents on roving patrols on interior roads where they pulled over vehicles, without a warrant or any probable cause, to ask about their immigration status.

The Border Patrol's congressional authorization had remained largely unchanged since it was written in 1925 and allowed the agents to "board and search" vehicles without a warrant. A change in the wording in 1946 removed the need for the agents to have any belief that an individual was in the country without documents. Instead, the Border Patrol believed they had the authority to stop and search every single vehicle on American back roads and interstate highways up to one hundred miles from the border and coastlines.

The practices of the Border Patrol seemed to violate the basic protections against unreasonable searches and seizures that were guaranteed in the Fourth Amendment of the Constitution. The key cases that finally tested the constitutionality of the Border Patrol's expansive congressional authorization to make stops in the border zone reached the Supreme Court in 1973, 1975, and 1976. The first case, *Almeida-Sanchez v. United States*, considered whether the Border Patrol could search a vehicle twenty miles north of the border without any suspicion whatsoever. In 1975, the court heard the case of Felix Brignoni-Ponce, *United States v. Brignoni-Ponce*, whose stop was based only on his apparent Mexican appearance. In the same term, the court also heard three other Border Patrol cases, including *United States v. Ortiz*, about whether the Border Patrol could search vehicles at an interior checkpoint without a warrant. The final major Border Patrol case was *United States v. Martinez-Fuerte* in 1976, which considered whether the Border Patrol could set up interior checkpoints, which resulted in the brief detention of every single vehicle that drove through the checkpoint whether the driver was an American citizen or not. The decisions the justices made in these cases are still in force today and shape the lives of millions of citizens and noncitizens alike.

In the early 1970s, it was not yet clear on which side the court would rule. Would they focus on the text of the Constitution that protects individuals from unreasonable searches and seizures by the police? Or would they prioritize the Border Patrol's congressional authorization that waives the need for a warrant to stop and search vehicles for immigration enforcement purposes? Only time would tell.

What was clear as these cases made their way to the Supreme Court was that the political climate in the United States had changed. The liberal presidencies of John F. Kennedy and Lyndon Johnson in the 1960s were followed by a conservative resurgence and the election of Richard Nixon in 1968. One of Nixon's campaign pledges was to reverse the series of pro-defendant decisions by nominating conservative law-and-order justices to the Supreme Court. The legality of the Border Patrol's authority would be considered in this more conservative milieu, and one of Nixon's four nominees to the Supreme Court, Lewis Powell, would play a decisive role in all the major Border Patrol decisions of the 1970s.

Nixon's Conservative Supreme Court

Many politicians run a campaign promising bold changes, but Nixon was uniquely presented with the chance to achieve it in his first term. In his first four years in office, Richard Nixon had the unusual opportunity to select four new justices for the Supreme Court: Warren

Burger in 1969, Harry Blackmun in 1970, and Lewis Powell and William Rehnquist in 1971. In the process, liberal justices who had expanded Fourth Amendment protections in the 1960s were replaced by conservatives who all shared Nixon's focus on using the bench to impose "law and order."

Law and order can seem like an innocuous phrase. It draws on the belief that societies are governed by rules and that if someone breaks the rules, they should be arrested and locked up for their crime. In the late 1960s, this argument resonated with white voters as Nixon made it one of his campaign slogans. The demand for more rights for African Americans, combined with agitation against the Vietnam War, led to a sense on the part of many whites that the vision of 1950s American life was dissolving into chaos.

The civil rights and antiwar movements both relied on civil disobedience. Civil rights leaders led sit-ins to protest white-only policies and encouraged people to break morally unjust rules that protected racial segregation. This, however, violated some people's belief in the obligation to obey the law and led to fears about lawlessness. At the same time, the Supreme Court's rulings—for example, the *Mapp* and *Miranda* cases that created the exclusionary rule and required police to inform people of their right to remain silent and to have legal counsel— were described as limiting the ability of the police to enforce the law. Nixon used these threads to weave a story about the potential collapse of American society if law and order was not restored.

In Nixon's acceptance speech at the 1968 Republican National Convention in Miami, Florida, his primary theme was law and order. He began, "My friends, we live in an age of revolution in America and in the world." He argued that America's revolution in 1776 was based on both progress and order, saying that order is essential for that progress to occur. He continued, "Tonight it is time for some honest talk about the problem of order in the United States."

Nixon put the blame for the lapse in order on the Supreme Court under Earl Warren: "Let us also recognize that some of our courts, in their decisions, have gone too far in weakening the peace forces as against the criminal forces in this country." The audience broke into sustained applause. He concluded by saying, "And to those who say that law and order is the code word for racism, here is a reply. Our goal is justice, justice for every American . . . Just as we cannot have progress without order, we cannot have order without progress . . . And so as we commit to order tonight, let us commit to progress."

Despite Nixon's effort to defuse the charge of racism by acknowledging but not really addressing it, "law and order" functioned as a mechanism for reframing racial bias into a more palatable form. Richard Nixon rode the law-and-order platform to the presidency by campaigning against civil disobedience and the liberal Supreme Court under Earl Warren that weakened the position of the police. Nixon's victory would have a profound effect on the Supreme Court.

Nixon's first chance to appoint a new Supreme Court justice came at the start of his term when he selected Warren Burger to replace the retiring Chief Justice Earl Warren. Burger was involved in local Republican politics and helped deliver the Minnesota delegation to Dwight Eisenhower during the 1952 Republican convention. After Eisenhower's election, he was named assistant attorney general in the civil division of the Justice Department, where he worked under Attorney General Herbert Brownell Jr. In 1956, he was appointed to the D.C. Circuit Court of Appeals. In the 1960s, he spoke frequently about his concerns over how far the criminal justice system had swung toward protecting defendants, language that fit perfectly with Nixon's campaign focus on law and order. He was nominated as the chief justice on May 21, 1969, and he was confirmed by the Senate in a 74–3 vote. A retrospective on the Burger Court summed him up as "A conservative chief justice for conservative times."[1]

Burger looked the part of a chief justice, with the silver hair, height, and baritone voice to perform the role of authority. Behind the scenes, he was an adept manager, working to improve the conditions of the court building and the flow of work. However, as a jurist, he was not well regarded. His colleagues were often unhappy with his opinions, which they thought were not well argued or written, and they often had to write memos to him to suggest the arguments he should make. Court documents also show that Burger routinely argued against a particular outcome behind the scenes, for example in *Roe v. Wade*, but then joined the majority at the end so that he would not be seen as weak.

Only a few months into his term, Nixon got his second chance to nominate a new Supreme Court justice when Abe Fortas resigned on May 14, 1969, amid an ethics scandal. Fortas had signed a retainer with a financier who was under investigation for fraud that paid Fortas $20,000 ($140,000 in 2022, adjusted for inflation) per year for the rest of his life. After the House of Representatives began impeachment proceedings against him, Fortas resigned.

Harry Blackmun became Nixon's second appointment to the Supreme Court but, as Blackmun liked to joke, he was "old number three," since Nixon's first two nominees for the position, Clement Haynsworth and G. Harrold Carswell, were both withdrawn. Blackmun was really number four, because Nixon also offered the position to Lewis Powell, who privately turned it down. (Powell would join the court two years later.)

Blackmun happened to be a lifelong friend of Chief Justice Warren Burger. The two first met when they were five. Blackmun worked as counsel for the Mayo Clinic before becoming a judge on the Eighth Circuit Court of Appeals in 1959, after much encouragement from Burger to pursue a judgeship. Nixon nominated Blackmun on April 15, 1970, and he was unanimously confirmed on May 14. Initially, he was seen as a second vote for Chief Justice Burger, gaining the names "Minnesota Twin" and "Hip Pocket Harry." Later he strayed away from the conservative bloc, becoming a swing vote who eventually sided most often with the liberals from the early 1980s until he retired in 1994. He was perceived to be a slow worker by the other justices and got a small share of cases assigned to him. His most significant ruling was *Roe v. Wade*, which legalized abortion in 1973.

Nixon's good fortune with the Supreme Court continued in September 1971 when both Hugo Black and John Marshall Harlan, who were both ill, announced their retirements on September 17 and September 23 respectively. Black had a stroke two days after stepping down and died on September 25. Harlan had spinal cancer and passed away on December 29. With two more openings, Nixon decided to announce them together, hoping that the older, well-respected, and moderate Lewis Powell would draw attention away from the younger, brash, and conservative William Rehnquist.

Rehnquist worked as a meteorologist before using the GI Bill to enroll at Stanford University where he got a BA and MA in political science. After obtaining an MA in government from Harvard in 1950, he returned to Stanford for his law degree and finished first in his class. During his time at Stanford Law, he briefly dated another student, Sandra Day O'Connor, who would later be one of his colleagues on the Supreme Court. A 2018 biography of O'Connor said that he proposed to her, but she rejected him.[2]

Rehnquist was confirmed by the Senate on December 10, 1971, by a vote of 68–26. In his early years on the court, Rehnquist saw himself as an archconservative block of one, often finding himself in dissent, and he came to be known as the "Lone Ranger." His law clerks gave him a small Lone Ranger doll he kept on his office shelf. However, he was well liked by his colleagues and many people commented on his charming nature as well as his intelligence.[3] Rehnquist used his charm for behind-the-scenes maneuvering to ensure that even if he was on the wrong side of the ruling, it was still infused with the ethos of law and order. Rehnquist did precisely this in several of the Border Patrol cases that soon came before the court.

Lewis Powell

The Burger Court was meant to be a conservative revolution, particularly on crime, but it ended up not being quite as radical of a break as expected, and it largely upheld the rulings of the Warren Court. In many of its most high-profile rulings in the early 1970s, the court made liberal decisions. In addition to effectively ending the Nixon presidency in 1974 by unanimously ruling that he had to turn over tapes and other materials to a federal court, the court struck down capital punishment in *Furman v. Georgia* in a 5–4 ruling in 1972 and legalized abortion in *Roe v. Wade* in a 7–2 vote in 1973.[4] The Burger Court also allowed racial preferences in college admissions through affirmative action in *Regents of the University of California v. Bakke* in 1978.

In many of these surprising decisions, the decisive votes were cast by Lewis Powell, a southerner with deep roots in segregated Richmond, Virginia, and Nixon's final "law and order" addition to the Supreme Court. Powell's ancestor Nathaniel Powell was an original Jamestown settler and the acting governor of the colony. However, Lewis Powell did not grow up in the aristocracy of the South, but rather in a modest, middle-class family. He was a good student and athlete, but his wide ears bothered him growing up and he once tried taping them to the side of his head while he slept in a failed attempt to reshape them. While most boys from his private high school attended the University of Virginia, he instead chose the smaller and more remote Washington and Lee University, in hopes of continuing to play baseball, but he did not make the team.

Powell excelled at Washington and Lee, where he was student body president and graduated first in his law class in 1931. He received a Master of Law degree from Harvard University in 1932 but spurned high-paying offers at New York law firms to return to his roots in Richmond. After a few years, he settled at Hunton Andrews Kurth LLP, as the firm is currently known, where he would remain until he joined the Supreme Court.

Powell volunteered for World War II, where he became the American liaison to the top-secret Ultra project. A team of mathematicians and code breakers led by Alan Turing figured out how to decrypt messages sent by the Germans with their Enigma machine. The intelligence from the project proved invaluable for the Allies, but they were constantly worried that if they used too much of it, the Germans would realize their secret code had been broken. Consequently, officers with discretion, like Powell, were brought in to figure out how best to hide the sources of the intelligence when transmitting it to commanders in the field. The Ultra project remained secret until the early 1970s, when Powell, by then on the Supreme Court, was revealed to have played a role.

After the war, Powell returned to private practice with Hunton Andrews Kurth LLP, where he was particularly adept at bringing in major clients to the firm, including Philip Morris, Ethyl Corp, and the Colonial Williamsburg Foundation. He served on the board of directors for several of these corporations, including the tobacco giant Philip Morris from 1964 to 1969. He even tried to take up smoking to be in solidarity with the firm and would pose with a cigarette in hand for photos of the board.

Powell believed in the patriotic duty of citizens to serve, and he was frequently appointed to boards, committees, and task forces in the state of Virginia and eventually nationally. The most contentious position he held was chair of the Richmond School Board from 1952 to

1961, a period that included the momentous *Brown v. Board of Education* ruling and massive resistance to integration from politicians in the state. During Powell's tenure on the board, there were no Black students in white Richmond schools until 1960. When he resigned in 1961 to join the state school board, only 2 of 23,000 Black children went to white schools. John Jeffries, in his authorized biography of Powell, concluded, "What emerges from these details is a picture of local collaboration in maintaining segregated schools long after they were declared unconstitutional."[5]

Powell began to see his national profile rise after he was elected president of the American Bar Association in 1963. He used the position to update ethics rules and to push for better legal aid for the poor, but his focus in many of his speeches was what he saw as a weakening of the rule of law in the United States. In 1965, Lyndon Johnson asked him to chair the president's Commission on Law Enforcement and the Administration of Justice. He declined the role of chair, but agreed to serve on the committee, which produced a report entitled "The Challenge of Crime in a Free Society." Powell and several other conservative members of the committee were not completely pleased with the final report, so they authored a supplemental statement on "Constitutional Limitations" that was seen as a critique of the Warren Supreme Court.

Powell felt that recent Supreme Court decisions "unduly limit reasonable law enforcement activities" and that "pendulum may possibly have swung too far" in favor of defendants' rights.[6] He particularly disliked the exclusionary rule from the *Mapp* decision that dramatically expanded Fourth Amendment protections. In words that must have been music to the ears of Richard Nixon, he wrote that there was "an alarming increase in crime" and a "partial breakdown in law and order" that could be a "prelude to revolution." For Powell, recent Supreme Court decisions "render the task of law enforcement more difficult."[7] Although these positions were out of step with Johnson and other Democrats, they positioned him well if a more conservative Republican were to become president.

Just before his nomination to the Supreme Court, Powell authored what came to be known as the Powell Memorandum, a confidential memo to the U.S. Chamber of Commerce titled "Attack on American Free Enterprise System." The memorandum identified an effort by academics, media, activists like Ralph Nader, and celebrities to undermine the capitalist system of free enterprise. In the memo, Powell laid out a multipronged approach for conservatives to counter this threat by using many strategies that have become the modus operandi of the right: calling for equal time in media, funding right-wing speakers on college campuses, and most significantly establishing a conservative academic counterweight to universities in the form of think tanks. The Powell Memorandum spurred the creation of the Heritage Foundation, the Manhattan Institute, the Cato Institute, and efforts to lobby local governments for pro-corporate legislation, such as those pursued by the American Legislative Exchange Council.

Nixon first asked Powell to join the Supreme Court in 1969 to fill the seat that went to Harry Blackmun, but Powell said no, feeling he was too old. Powell did not accept the nomination immediately in 1971 either, taking a day to think it over. For one thing, the capitalist-minded lawyer would see a substantial drop in pay by leaving his firm for the court. Powell, at sixty-four, was also an unusually old nominee for the bench. However, he felt the obligation to serve and reluctantly agreed to the nomination. He was confirmed 89–1 on December 6, 1971. He is the fifth-oldest person to begin a Supreme Court position, and he ended up serving sixteen years, until his retirement in 1987.

When Powell arrived at the court, he was well prepared for the business-oriented cases, but he relied heavily on his clerks to get him up to speed on the dizzying array of other constitutional questions. His pragmatism and careful consideration of the facts in each case meant that he was often in the middle of the conservative and liberal blocs as he looked for compromise. The tendency to give his clerks substantial responsibility and his desire for a just and fair outcome based on the facts in each case resulted in a series of unexpected positions on abortion, capital punishment, and affirmative action.

Although Powell did not have any experience with the border or immigration, he found himself casting the critical votes in each of the Border Patrol cases. His decisions in these cases were among those that he agonized over the most and were some of the most surprising decisions of his career, beginning with the case of Condrado Almeida-Sanchez in 1973.

8.

Terrorists in Suits

JAMES CHANOUX WAS ALREADY FEELING ILL WHEN HE HEARD Chief Justice Burger call his name and ask him to proceed with his oral arguments for Condrado Almeida-Sanchez before the Supreme Court on Monday, March 19, 1973. Out in California, Felix Brignoni-Ponce was awaiting his first trial after his arrest on I-5 near San Clemente on March 11, completely unaware that another significant Border Patrol case was being heard at the Supreme Court, where his case would finally arrive two years later. Indeed, without some last-minute maneuvering by a clerk and an eleventh-hour change of heart by one of the justices, the *Almeida-Sanchez* case would have been decided differently and the *Brignoni-Ponce* case would never have made it to the Supreme Court.

Chanoux, a forty-year-old lawyer from San Diego representing Almeida-Sanchez, did not have the pedigree of a typical attorney arguing a case before the highest court in the land. He had been a probation officer in San Diego as he took classes to get his law degree from the University of San Diego. However, when he took on Almeida-Sanchez's case in his small private practice, he recognized that there were important Fourth Amendment constitutional questions in play.

Condrado Almeida-Sanchez was arrested while driving on California Highway 78 late at night in 1971. The road did not come directly from the border and instead was an east-west corridor that was at all points at least twenty miles north of the border. The Border Patrol agents did not see his vehicle cross the border but began tracking it in Calexico, the border town on the United States side. The Border Patrol agents had neither a warrant nor the probable cause required under the *Carroll* doctrine to stop the vehicle based on the belief that the vehicle was smuggling people or contraband. However, the Border Patrol regulations at the time said they did not need probable cause and could stop any vehicle in the one-hundred-mile zone for any reason.

The agents stopped Almeida-Sanchez to ask his citizenship and discovered he was a legal permanent resident of the United States. The Border Patrol had recently given agents a memo stating that smugglers were hollowing out back seats in cars to fit people inside, and one of the agents decided to check behind the seat of the car. He did not find any people, but he did find marijuana. Almeida-Sanchez was convicted of smuggling drugs. His lawyer, James Chanoux, appealed the original conviction to the Ninth Circuit Court of Appeals and eventually to the Supreme Court.

As he stepped to the lectern, Chanoux must have felt both proud to have risen this far and also awestruck by the surroundings he found himself in. The justices sat in black leather chairs at an imposing mahogany table with white Italian marble columns behind them and an ornate ceiling above. Despite its importance as the pinnacle of one of three coequal branches of the U.S. Government, the Supreme Court did not even have its own building until 1935. Prior to that, it used different parts of the Capitol building. The Supreme Court building was constructed during the Great Depression and, due to declining wages, actually came in under budget, something that is hard to imagine today. When it was completed, the Supreme Court finally had a building that symbolized its role. The white marble steps leading up to classical Corinthian columns are imposing and grave, setting the solemn mood for the proceedings inside.

From his first words, Chanoux seemed uncomfortable, perhaps feeling nerves as he stood in front of the nine justices at the pinnacle of the American court system for the first time in his life. He stumbled over the traditional "Mr. Chief Justice and may it please the court," saying instead, "May the, uh, court please." Chanoux spoke slowly and coughed every few words but soldiered on for several minutes, explaining his contention that the Border Patrol's regulations should be ruled unconstitutional on Fourth Amendment grounds. He coughed violently and said, "Excuse me, if the court please." He took a sip of water and tried to continue. While Chanoux collected himself, Justice Potter Stewart filled the silence by asking a question about airports.

Suddenly, Chanoux collapsed onto the table in front of him. Chief Justice Burger broke in and noted that Chanoux looked ill and asked an officer to help him, "Just let counsel sit down and we'll, uh, relax." Burger sent for the court's nurse and then decided to take a recess. As the nurse and paramedics arrived, it became clear that Chanoux had suffered a heart attack and was rushed to the hospital. Since Chanoux obviously could not continue, the Supreme Court rescheduled the oral arguments in the case for nine days later, on March 28.

James Chanoux survived the heart attack and recovered but was not able to represent Mr. Almeida-Sanchez in the rescheduled hearing.[1] The court quickly had to find someone to step in who was familiar with Border Patrol case law and experienced enough to argue before the Supreme Court. They turned to the Federal Defenders of San Diego and its executive director, John J. Cleary. Cleary was young, brash, and ultra-confident, which probably explains his quixotic decision to take the case with only a week to prepare.

The Federal Defenders of San Diego

John Cleary grew up on the streets of Chicago, the son of a police officer.[2] He went to the University of Chicago for his undergraduate and law degrees before joining the Army Special Forces. His law training allowed him to become the first Green Beret to serve as a Judge Advocate General. He left the army in 1964 and became the deputy director of the National Defender Project from 1964 to 1969, which had received a Ford Foundation grant to establish public defender offices across the United States. After briefly serving as the attorney in residence for the Illinois Law Enforcement Commission, Cleary moved to San Diego and became the executive director of one of the new public defender offices he had established, the Federal Defenders of San Diego.

One of his first hires was Chuck Sevilla, another young, confident lawyer who had recently returned to his native California from a stint in Washington, D.C., while his wife was getting a degree at George Washington University. Sevilla was blanketing defense attorney openings across the area with applications and was hired after one interview with Cleary, which started a lifelong partnership. Sevilla stayed at the Federal Defenders of San Diego for five years before moving to the state public defender office in 1976. The two reconnected in 1983 when they established their own private defense practice of Cleary and Sevilla in San Diego and remained partners until 2004.

Later in life, Cleary developed an interest in the Russian language and judicial reforms in Russia after the collapse of the Soviet Union. He wrote his 1998 PhD dissertation in Russian. After that, he spent time lecturing at Moscow State University and San Diego State University, establishing an exchange program where students from each city spent time in the other. An online course evaluation said, "Cleary was the most difficult strange but brilliant and caring prof around."[3] In 2018, Cleary briefly made the national news after he offered a course at the San Diego State Law School on impeaching Donald Trump.

With Cleary at the helm in the 1970s, the San Diego office became a model for other public defender branches around the country. Cleary was an aggressive attorney who gained nicknames of "Machine-Gun Cleary" and "the white phosphorus kid" for his incendiary tactics. Cleary wore suits in court, but always with his trademark army boots and his vintage seventies-era flowing hair. Sevilla and the entire office followed Cleary's lead, with a local magistrate referring to them as "terrorists in suits" as they aggressively filed motions and doggedly pursued cases on behalf of their poor clients. During a later Border Patrol case in front of the Supreme Court, *United States v. Martinez-Fuerte* in 1976, Chief Justice Burger lamented all the frivolous petitions the court had to deal with each week. Sevilla replied, "I've probably written a few, Your Honor," drawing laughter in the court.[4]

As the crackdown on immigration played out after the 1965 Immigration Act, Cleary and Sevilla found themselves on the front lines of new and novel legal questions about how the Fourth Amendment of the Constitution and the regulations for the Border Patrol should be balanced. The Federal Defenders of San Diego also gained the grudging respect of prosecutors and the courts. Cleary had already argued and won a case before the Supreme Court in *United States v. Campos-Serrano* in 1971, a statutory case about border identity cards, which was why the Supreme Court called him to step into the *Almeida-Sanchez* case.

Almeida-Sanchez v. United States was the first case to reach the Supreme Court that began to wrestle with the complicated racial and Fourth Amendment questions at the border. The issue at stake was fundamentally a constitutional one: What takes priority in the border zone, the Fourth Amendment protections against unreasonable searches and seizures or the congressional legislation authorizing the Border Patrol to search for undocumented people inside the United States?

"Nobody Is Protected"

When the oral arguments in *Almeida-Sanchez* were reheard on Wednesday, March 28, 1973, most of the country was focused on events in Vietnam as U.S. troops made their final exit. The last American combat troops left on the following day, March 29, but the famous images of helicopters evacuating the U.S. embassy in Saigon were still two years away, on April 29, 1975.

The oral arguments of the Supreme Court are held in the great room in two-week intervals on Mondays, Tuesdays, and Wednesdays throughout the term, running from the first Monday in October until late April. The arguments begin precisely at 10:00 a.m. as the court crier announces "The Honorable, the Chief Justice and the Associate Justices of the Supreme Court of the United States. Oyez! Oyez! Oyez! All persons having business before the Honorable, the Supreme Court of the United States, are admonished to draw near and give their attention, for the Court is now sitting. God save the United States and this Honorable Court." The justices, gathered behind the maroon felt curtains, simultaneously emerge between white marble columns and take their seats. The chief justice is at the center and the associate justices are arranged on either side, with the most junior at the ends. Early in his time on the court, Chief Justice Burger redesigned the bench to bend slightly at the ends so the justices could see each other.

John Cleary came ready to win his case even though the odds seemed very long. Straightaway, Cleary framed the case as not about the border and immigration but about the Fourth Amendment of the Constitution, which should apply equally to everyone in the United States. He said, "The issue in this case concerns the application of the Fourth Amendment to interior searches. More specifically the petitioner contends that the nature and extent of this search permitted by immigration regulation is in conflict with the Fourth Amendment, the *Carroll* decision, and the litany of precedent. Following that decision, basically can the government authorize a regulation that permits a search of an automobile on a highway without a warrant and more specifically without probable cause? That is the issue."[5]

As the Border Patrol cases made their way through the courts, it became clear that there were four distinct locations in which a stop might occur: a vehicle at the border itself, a vehicle that agents maintained continuous surveillance of after crossing the border, a vehicle not seen crossing the border that was stopped by a roving patrol, and a vehicle not seen crossing the border that was stopped at an interior checkpoint on a highway away from the border. In each location, the court needed to consider whether the agents could only ask questions or whether they could conduct a search. In the first two locations, at the crossing point and stops of vehicles under continuous surveillance after crossing, it was considered to be a border search that did not require a warrant because the individual had consented to the search by presenting themselves at the border.[6] The *Almeida-Sanchez* case considered the third location: a warrantless search of a vehicle by a roving patrol away from the border.

For Cleary, the key distinction was that the vehicle was not observed crossing the border, so the *Carroll* doctrine had to apply. Under the *Carroll* doctrine, police are required to have probable cause and exigent circumstance to search a vehicle without a warrant.

Chief Justice Burger asked, "Does not the regulation by its terms apply to border crossers?"

Cleary replied, "No, Your Honor. It applies to . . . it can search any vehicle, meaning it could be anyone's vehicle."

At the time, the Border Patrol's regulation had no requirement that the Border Patrol know that a person or vehicle had crossed the border. Cleary turned to his wit in his answer: "Your Honor's vehicle could be down the highway, and technically under this regulation, you could be stopped and not only are you questioned, but your vehicle is searched. And the trunk opened up. And, in the case we have, to show you how far they have gone, under the seat."

Cleary's point was clear. The regulation said the Border Patrol could stop and interrogate anyone about immigration status, including the chief justice of the Supreme Court. The agents were abusing this authority to do what Cleary contended were illegal searches for drugs. In Condrado Almeida-Sanchez's car, they found them.

Cleary moved on to the racially discriminatory nature of the regulation. He pointed out that the government brief stated that random stops were made based on nationality alone. His voice dripping with indignation, Cleary went on: "Well, I do not know how one can physically observe one's nationality other than to use certain racial or color characteristics and I think that—"

At that point, Justice Rehnquist broke in and asked Cleary a question, which meant that Cleary's view on racial profiling at the border would have to wait for a few more years until he was back in front of the court arguing the case of Felix Brignoni-Ponce in 1975.

As his time wound down, Cleary summed up his argument: "All we're asking for here is once a vehicle is in the interior, it's on the highways, should not the government be required to have at least probable cause?" Random stops on American highways could not be border searches, he argued, because "I only contend that a border search requires a border entry."

The U.S. government was represented by Assistant Solicitor

General Philip Lacovara, who explained that according to the regulation, the Border Patrol did not need to articulate any reason to make a stop within the one-hundred-mile border zone to inquire about immigration status.

Justice Thurgood Marshall asked, "They suspected that this man had an alien?"

Thoroughgood Marshall, later shortened to Thurgood, was born July 2, 1908, in Baltimore to parents who were both descendants of slaves. He graduated from Lincoln University with a BA in American literature and philosophy and was first in his class at the Howard School of Law. He founded the NAACP legal defense and education fund and argued thirty-two cases in front of the Supreme Court, winning twenty-nine, including *Brown v. Board of Education* in 1954. In 1961, John F. Kennedy nominated him to the Second Court of Appeals, over the objections of some southern senators, and Lyndon Johnson made him solicitor general in 1965. When Justice Tom C. Clark retired, Johnson nominated Marshall to the Supreme Court. He was approved by the Senate by a vote of 69–11 and joined the court on August 30, 1967.

Marshall was a key member of the liberal wing, voting consistently with William Brennan in favor of defendants and against restrictions on liberty. He saw the Constitution as a document that should protect everyone equally, and he pressed Lacovara over the claim that the government could violate everyone's Fourth Amendment protections in the border zone.

Lacovara responded "No" to Marshall's question about whether the agent suspected the car was carrying undocumented people. He continued, "It was conceded at trial that there was no particular reason to suspect that this car was carrying an alien."

Marshall asked, "Will they stop my car if I was driving through that?"

Lacovara clarified, "In that area?"

"Yes."

Lacovara said, "Yes, sir. Yes, what we are saying is the focus here as in—"

Marshall broke in, raising the stakes. "Could you stop the president's car?"

Lacovara paused for a second. "Well, if the car were marked as the president's car, they would be—"

Marshall got to the point. "If it was not, you could stop it?"

Lacovara agreed, "Yes, sir."

Marshall had made his point. "Nobody is protected."

Lacovara's time ended, and Chief Justice Burger called Cleary back up for the balance of his time. Burger began with an interesting point, starting with a critique of the imaginary nature of borders. "Mr. Cleary, we know of course that a border line is simply a hypothetical line, a thin line made by mapmaker with a pen." Given that, Burger asked, veering in an unexpected direction, would it not be reasonable for the government to set up a "cordon sanitaire," or buffer area, in the border zone and "require everyone in that area, day or night, twenty-four hours a day, to have a pass?"

Cleary was taken aback by the totalitarian nature of the suggestion and replied, "Well, Your Honor, I cannot speak to the law, but speaking as an American citizen, I think that smacks of something so gross, with our way of life, I cannot imagine Congress doing something like that."

Burger backtracked, acknowledging that was not what the case was about and saying, "We won't hold you to it." Afterward, the lawyers from the Federal Defenders marveled at the chief justice's outrageous comment, likening it to the tattoos that prisoners received in Nazi Germany to track them.[7]

After a few more questions, Burger ended the proceedings and thanked Cleary for appearing in front of the court on short notice and under such unusual circumstances. Cleary and the lawyers from the Federal Defenders of San Diego thought the oral arguments went well, but still knew that given the conservative composition of the court, a verdict in Condrado Almeida-Sanchez's favor was unlikely. All they could do was wait until the decision was announced.

9.

Change of Heart

Every Friday that the Supreme Court is in session, the justices meet for a conference to discuss the cases, take informal straw votes to determine where each justice stands, and assign who is in charge of writing the majority opinion. The conference is a unique space because it is only the nine justices in the room. No aides, no note takers, just the nine talking freely. The conference room is oak paneled with a mahogany table and a portrait of John Marshall, the first chief justice of the Supreme Court, looming over the proceedings. The justices arrive at 10:00 a.m. and shake hands before taking their spots. They discuss each case in order of seniority, beginning with the chief justice and moving down the table toward the junior justice, who in 1973 was William Rehnquist. The junior justice sits by the door and can occasionally open it to send a note in or out as the discussion continues.[1]

At the conference after the *Almeida-Sanchez* oral arguments, five of the justices, Warren Burger, Harry Blackmun, Lewis Powell, William

Rehnquist, and Byron White, voted to sustain the Ninth Circuit Court's ruling granting the Border Patrol the right to make the stop. Chief Justice Burger assigned the duty of writing the opinion of the court to Byron White.

As a young man, White had been an excellent football player. He finished second in the Heisman Trophy voting as a senior at the University of Colorado and was drafted by the Pittsburgh Pirates of the National Football League. White was the leading rusher in his first season in the NFL, then left for England to take up a Rhodes Scholarship at Oxford. He returned to Yale Law School and played football for the Detroit Lions. His legal career was shaped by his friendship with Robert and John F. Kennedy. White first met the future president in Europe in 1939 and their friendship continued in Washington, D.C., after the war, when Kennedy was a new congressional representative from Massachusetts and White was a Supreme Court clerk. White returned to Colorado to practice law and was tapped by Kennedy to help with his presidential campaign in the state in 1959. After Kennedy won the presidency, White became an assistant attorney general to Robert Kennedy.

When Charles Whittaker resigned from the Supreme Court on March 31, 1962, after suffering a nervous breakdown due to the stress, Kennedy nominated the forty-four-year-old White, who was quickly approved by the Senate in a voice vote. White did not have a rigid ideological position, but generally was on the conservative side of issues. He was strongly against communism and supported the police, as demonstrated by his dissent in the *Miranda* case. He also wrote an impassioned dissent in *Roe v. Wade*.

White began to write his opinion in *Almeida-Sanchez*, which would defer to the congressional authorization that allowed the Border Patrol to search any vehicle they wanted to in the border zone. His opinion was sure to retain the support of three of Nixon's law-and-order appointments, Burger, Blackmun, and Rehnquist. Lewis Powell also voted with the conservatives at the Friday conference.

Powell generally wanted to abide by precedent, but he thought Fourth Amendment protections were less important than other parts of the Bill of Rights. If the individual was innocent, then the search would not find anything and no harm would be done, but if they were breaking the law, then the search would demonstrate that.[2] Throughout his life, Powell always tried to do what was right, and he tended to believe others in positions of authority did the same. Consequently, his inclination was often to side with law enforcement and trust they would use their power fairly.[3]

One of Powell's clerks, however, felt strongly that the *Almeida-Sanchez* stop violated the Fourth Amendment.[4] Powell was an open-minded justice and carefully considered all possibilities before coming to a decision, particularly in areas outside his expertise in business law. Powell asked the clerk to write a memo making the argument and promised not to make a final decision on the case until he read it.

While White was writing the majority opinion allowing the searches, Potter Stewart was crafting a sharp dissent that decried the scope of the waiver of the Fourth Amendment. Stewart was a conservative justice who had been nominated to the court by Dwight Eisenhower in 1958, but he strove to make limited judgments based on the facts of individual cases, which reduced his influence and resulted in little scholarly attention to his work. He is perhaps best known for his concurring opinion in 1964 in *Jacobellis v. Ohio* about defining what counts as obscenity when he coined the phrase, "I know it when I see it."

Stewart also knew a violation of the Constitution when he saw it, and his draft dissent in the *Almeida-Sanchez* case was filled with righteous outrage. The first paragraph called the idea that the Border Patrol could stop any vehicle in the border zone a "gross violation of the Fourth Amendment" that gave the Border Patrol an "extravagant license to search." The next paragraph pointed out that since the one-hundred-mile zone was from coastlines as well, Washington, D.C., was also covered by the ruling: "A quick glance at a map of this country will indicate just how many populated areas are within 100 miles of an external boundary. It might come as a surprise to residents and visitors in the city of Washington D.C., for example, to learn that there are a statute and a regulation purporting to authorize federal agents to stop and thoroughly search their cars on the streets of this city at any time and with no probable cause, in alleged pursuit of illegally entered aliens."

Stewart also wrote, "This strikes me as an extraordinary piece of constitutional logic, and a complete abdication of the duty of judicial review . . . I thought it settled since *Marbury v. Madison*, that the insistence of a congressional enactment is only the starting point of constitutional analysis, not its conclusion." Essentially, he was asking, *Why do we even have courts if we are going to give the legislature carte blanche to invalidate the Constitution?*

Potter Stewart was Lewis Powell's closest friend on the court. Given their conservative but moderate judicial approaches, they tended to vote together on most cases. However, Powell was a more measured man. On his copy of Stewart's draft dissent, he underlined each of the above flourishes and even wrote "absurd" next to the line about Washington, D.C. In other places he scribbled "no" and "I can't go with this."

As the end of the term neared, Powell decided to join Byron White's majority opinion that allowed the search and sent White a memo confirming his vote. Powell's clerk who had concerns about the Fourth Amendment was furious and convinced Powell to reread the memo the clerk had written about the opinion.[5]

Powell considered the memo and then reread White's opinion. He wavered, then changed his mind. After thinking more about it, he decided he could not accept White's contention that the Supreme Court should defer to Congress on a constitutional question.

On June 8, 1973, just weeks before the end of the term, Powell sent another memo to White and Stewart, changing his vote on the case. Because the other justices were split 4–4, Powell's change of heart swung the majority to Stewart's opinion ruling that the Border Patrol's search without a warrant or probable cause was unconstitutional. Powell opted to concur with the result of Stewart's opinion, but not the reasoning. Nevertheless, he convinced Stewart to rewrite the contentious sections. In the end, none of Stewart's rhetorical flourishes quoted earlier ended up in the final opinion of the court.

The result was that the Supreme Court invalidated the Border Patrol's fifty-year-old practice of searching any car they wanted in the border zone. Instead, the Supreme Court found that the Border Patrol had to abide by the *Carroll* doctrine, which required probable cause and exigent circumstances to search a vehicle, just like every other law enforcement officer.

Supreme Court justices are always upset when they lose the majority for their opinion, and White was not happy to have the opinion taken away from him in the final days of the term. Powell and White already did not get along, with White often frustrated with Powell's careful desire to think through both sides. White once broke a pencil in Powell's face, saying he should "make up his damn mind."[6]

After White lost the majority in *Almeida-Sanchez*, he sent Powell a lighthearted memo that recounted the experience of a baseball player named Al Bumbry. Bumbry was on first base when the batter hit a fly ball. Bumbry thought the ball had no chance of being caught, so he eagerly ran all the way to home base. Only then did he realize that the fly ball was indeed caught, and he was easily thrown out at first base.

Powell read the memo from White, but although he had been a

baseball player as a young man, he did not know what to make of it. Was White complaining about all the lost work toward the opinion he thought was sure to be approved? Powell wrote back guardedly, "Although I may ask Harry to interpret for me the precise import of your parable of Bumbry's being caught off base by 95 feet, I take it that Potter's opinion will now become that of the court . . . I am a bit contrite at unwittingly causing you to classify yourself with Al Bumbry, although on the baseball diamond (at least) I would still consider this quite a compliment."[7]

When the 5–4 ruling was announced less than two weeks later on June 21, 1973, it was a resounding and unexpected victory for the upstart lawyer John Cleary and the Federal Defenders of San Diego. The ruling meant that the conservative Burger Court had overruled the more liberal Ninth Circuit and sided with a defendant against law enforcement. Powell and Richard Nixon's other three appointments had been meant to rein in the exclusionary rule, but instead Powell had expanded it. Condrado Almeida-Sanchez was released because the evidence from the illegal search was suppressed.

Stewart's final opinion for the court stated, "It is clear, of course, that no Act of Congress can authorize a violation of the Constitution." Stewart acknowledged that border crossings and their functional equivalent do afford the government more authority to conduct searches without a warrant: "But the search of the petitioner's automobile by a roving patrol, on a California road that lies at all points at least 20 miles north of the Mexican border, was of a wholly different sort. In the absence of probable cause or consent, that search violated the petitioner's Fourth Amendment right to be free of 'unreasonable searches and seizures.'"

Powell wrote an eleven-page concurrence that agreed that legislation from Congress cannot invalidate the Constitution, but also laid out his conflicted view that would shape his decisions in the Border

Patrol cases that would arrive before the court over the next few years. For Powell, while it is reasonable to search everyone at a border crossing point, it is not reasonable to do so in the interior of the United States. "One who travels in regions near the borders of the country can hardly be thought to have submitted to inspections."[8]

Instead, Powell suggested that the Border Patrol get warrants if it wanted to search in the interior of the United States. He suggested an "area warrant" that was not specific to an individual suspect but rather gave agents the authority to make stops in a particular location for a defined period of time. His concurring opinion listed factors that could be used to justify a warrant: "(i) the frequency with which aliens illegally in the country are known or reasonably believed to be transported within a particular area; (ii) the proximity of the area in question to the border; (iii) the extensiveness and geographic characteristics of the area, including the roads therein and the extent of their use, and (iv) the probable degree of interference with the rights of innocent persons, taking into account the scope of the proposed search, its duration, and the concentration of illegal alien traffic in relation to the general traffic of the road or area."

With the conspicuous absence of race, these facts presage, almost word for word, some of the articulable facts that Powell would use in his opinion in the *Brignoni-Ponce* racial profiling case the court would hear two years later, in 1975. Additionally, the Border Patrol would draw on Powell's concurrence to test out the idea of area warrants, which became one of the primary issues in the *Martinez-Fuerte* case that would reach the court in 1976.

In the end, the *Almeida-Sanchez* ruling opened up more questions than it answered. John Cleary, Chuck Sevilla, and the lawyers of the Federal Defenders of San Diego left the court ebullient. They had miraculously won the case and convinced the conservative Burger Court to rein in the Border Patrol.

Cleary and Sevilla redoubled their efforts and included motions to suppress evidence from all Border Patrol stops for their clients. By the fall of 1974, there was a new round of Border Patrol–related cases before the court, as the legitimacy of the regulation was suddenly up for debate. The *Almeida-Sanchez* decision resolved the issue of searches away from the border, but the issues of stops by roving patrols like in the *Brignoni-Ponce* case and of interior checkpoints like the one at San Clemente on I-5 were still not settled. Was it possible that Richard Nixon's law-and-order Supreme Court would decide to overturn those as well?

10.

Rank Racism

OVER THE SUMMER AND INTO THE EARLY FALL, THE Supreme Court faces the daunting task of deciding which of the thousands of cases that are appealed to the court should be heard that term. Prior to Lewis Powell's arrival on the court, it was the practice of each justice's chamber to review all the cases and decide which ones to grant a writ of certiorari to hear the case and which to deny. Powell realized that the majority of these were easy decisions, and it was a huge waste of time for each justice to put together their own summaries of the cases. Instead, he began a pool with other interested justices in which a clerk from one justice would provide a neutral summary of the case for the other justices to consider, freeing up clerks for other work.

The summary memo for the case of Felix Brignoni-Ponce was written by John O'Neill, who was a clerk for William Rehnquist. A few decades later, O'Neill would arrive in the national political spotlight as the primary spokesperson for the Swift Boat Veterans for Truth, a

group that opposed John Kerry's run for president and produced political ads questioning his military service in Vietnam. A number of the
other clerks involved in the 1974 term also went on to prominent ca-
reers: Joel Klein, who became the superintendent of the New York Public school system, was a clerk for Lewis Powell; Richard Blumenthal,
the U.S. senator from Connecticut, was a clerk for Harry Blackmun.

O'Neill's summary memo on September 17, 1974, describes the
facts of the *Brignoni-Ponce* case: the inclement weather that closed the
checkpoint near San Clemente, California; the positioning of Agents
Brady and Harkins's vehicle to shine headlights across I-5 into passing
vehicles; and the decision to stop Brignoni-Ponce's car based only on
the fact that the occupants looked Mexican.

Brignoni-Ponce was found guilty in his initial trial, but the Ninth
Circuit Court of Appeals had overturned his conviction after the
Almeida-Sanchez ruling. O'Neill summarized the Ninth Circuit decision, which found that the Border Patrol needed to have reasonable
suspicion to make a stop. The ruling stated: "Here, the border-patrol
agents who stopped Brignoni-Ponce's car did not possess facts which
constituted a founded suspicion that he or his passengers were illegal
aliens. All that they knew was that Brignoni-Ponce and his compan-
ions appeared to be of Mexican descent and were in a sedan traveling
north on Interstate 5, approximately 65 miles north of the border. This
is not enough." The unanimous Ninth Circuit Court concluded: "The
conduct does not become suspicious simply because the skins of the
occupants are nonwhite."[1]

The government's brief in the case was signed by Solicitor General Robert Bork, himself a later failed nominee for the Supreme
Court. Bork argued that the *Almeida-Sanchez* ruling said that only a
search by the Border Patrol required some form of reasonable suspicion, what the Ninth Circuit referred to as founded suspicion. A brief
stop for questions did not. Instead, the government argued that the

suspicion does not have to be particular to an individual or vehicle, but "It may be based, instead, upon knowledge of conditions in the area as a whole."

The brief goes on to refer to the congressional authorization for the Border Patrol, the language of which was largely unchanged since it was first written in 1925.[2] The first section of the authorization allowed stops anywhere in the United States if there is probable cause that someone is in the country illegally. The Border Patrol cases hinged on the third clause of the law, which was limited to the one-hundred-mile zone. The brief contended that the wording of the congressional authorization meant that a stop to "board and search" for undocumented immigrants by the Border Patrol does not require any cause or suspicion. Instead, *any stop* in the border zone, the government's brief emphasized, was permitted by the law.

O'Neill wrote that the government "states that many cases are pending in which this point of law will be crucial and that the uncertainty resulting from the split as to standards governing such stops has seriously undermined the Border Service's effectiveness."[3] In his copy of the memo, Powell underlined the point that many similar cases were pending. Given the conflict between the lower courts and the government's desire for clarity, O'Neill recommended that the court take it up. For a case to be heard by the court, four of the justices need to grant a writ of certiorari. For *Brignoni-Ponce*, eight justices granted it, with only Potter Stewart passing on it.

Penny Clark, one of Powell's new group of clerks, jotted a note to him on the memo: "Here is yet another Almeida-Sanchez issue, not mentioned in my Hendrix memo. It is another conflict between CA9 and CA10, this time over the application of A-S to stops rather than searches. Anticipating your view on the subject, I would recommend that this be granted to reverse CA9. But in any event, this should be discussed along with other A-S cases. As Ron [Ronald Carr, another of Powell's clerks who died in 1995] commented, 'Oh, what a tangled web we weave . . .' "

Penny Clark never thought of becoming an attorney.[4] She was one of the first in her family to go to college, but she excelled as a double major in English and Spanish. After graduating, she took a job at a legal aid society that was looking for a bilingual typist and quickly realized that she was fascinated by the law. Clark graduated first in her class at the University of Texas law school and clerked for Braxton Craven Jr. at the Court of Appeals for the Fourth Circuit before joining Powell's staff. Clark was Powell's first female clerk and, really, the first female lawyer he worked closely with. Powell's Richmond upbringing was traditional and there were not any women partners at his law firm. None of his associates at the firm was ever a woman either.

Clark's note to Powell also included a prescient assessment of the motivations of the Border Patrol and the solicitor general. It seemed to her that "the gov't is more interested in establishing a principle than in winning a case."[5]

The Oral Arguments

The *Brignoni-Ponce* case about stops based on racial profiling was heard along with three other Border Patrol cases, *Bowen v. United States*, *United States v. Ortiz*, and *United States v. Peltier*, on Tuesday, February 18, 1975. *Bowen* and *Peltier* were about whether the *Almeida-Sanchez* ruling that required probable cause for searches by the Border Patrol could be applied retroactively, while *Ortiz* considered whether *Almeida-Sanchez* also applied at the Border Patrol's interior checkpoints.

Seated in front of the justices, representing the government, was Andrew L. Frey, the deputy solicitor general of the United States. Frey had already argued eight cases in front of the court in previous terms, winning six and losing two, but one of those two losses was significant.

In the 1972–73 term, Frey lost in *Bronston v. United States*, which tightened the perjury standard in federal cases and required investigators to ask precise questions for the statute to apply. The ruling is still in effect and played a role in the exoneration of Bill Clinton in the impeachment trial in the Senate in 1999.

Felix Brignoni-Ponce was represented by John Cleary and Chuck Sevilla, who had won the *Almeida-Sanchez* case two years earlier. Cleary handled the oral argument for this case, while Sevilla argued the *Ortiz* case later in the day. A few weeks before the appearance, Sevilla had broken his leg playing basketball, so he hobbled in on crutches. When he told a friend that he was arguing his first case before the Supreme Court, the friend said, "Break a leg," to which Sevilla replied, "I already have."[6]

Oral arguments typically last one hour, with each lawyer given thirty minutes to make their case. The petitioner is asked to speak first, in this case the government appealing the Ninth Circuit Court's ruling in favor of Brignoni-Ponce. Chief Justice Burger initiated the session by calling on the government: "Mr. Frey, you may proceed." Frey stood and responded in the customary, "Mr. Chief Justice and may it please the court."

Frey was experienced in front of the court but he got off to a rocky start. Although oral arguments are dramatic and can help develop lines of reasoning that make it into the final opinion, many justices have already carefully read the case histories, the briefs of the parties, and the many amicus briefs submitted by outside parties in favor of one result or another. They have typically already decided where they stand on the issue and are instead looking to probe those arguments and draw out the litigants by testing their claims and, in the process, convincing the other justices. Consequently, they are not patient with lawyers who use their few minutes in front of the court recounting the details of the case or establishing the facts, which by this point everyone already knows.

Nevertheless, Frey fell into this trap. He began by summarizing the Ninth Circuit Court's reversal of Brignoni-Ponce's conviction and the government's position that the evidence from the stop should not be suppressed. Then, inexplicably, he began listing the facts of the case, all things the justices already knew. Finally, almost seven minutes into his remarks, Frey moved on to make the crux of his argument: in the border zone, the Border Patrol has the right to stop all vehicles, briefly, to inquire about citizenship.

Harry Blackmun asked, "Let's see if I follow you there, Mr. Frey. In other words, if this were in Chicago, you wouldn't be defending it?"

Blackmun's question indicates that some members of the court did not fully comprehend what the one-hundred-mile border zone meant in 1975. Although Potter Stewart's fiery first draft of his opinion in the 1973 *Almeida-Sanchez* case had pointed out that the one-hundred-mile zone also applied to coastlines and the Canadian border, in their deliberations in *Brignoni-Ponce*, the court seems to have only considered the implications at the Mexican border.

Frey said, "Well, we would have to look at the circumstances. We would not—we do not assert a right to stop cars on a random basis or without particularized suspicion in Chicago."

Despite Frey's assurance to the contrary, that is exactly what the government was defending. The Border Patrol considers Lake Michigan an international waterway, so Chicago was, and still is, in the border zone.

Stewart then asked Frey to explain how the government's position was different from the *Terry* decision, the stop-and-frisk ruling that said the police did have the right to stop and question pedestrians without a warrant if they had facts of reasonable suspicion. Frey noted that while *Terry* applied to pedestrians, the difference here was that they had to stop a vehicle to conduct the interrogation.

Frey said, "If he were a pedestrian, I think there would be a basis for arguing that you could go up to him and simply say 'I'm an officer of the immigration service and . . .'"

Stewart jumped in: "Did you see a man go by here in a white hat?"

Frey then completed the thought, as there were quiet chuckles in the room. "Or indeed, are you a citizen of the United States?"

Stewart agreed: "Or are you a citizen of the United States."

Byron White was not enjoying the light moment and returned the discussion to the key questions: "But you want to do more than that, don't you?"

Frey responded, "Yes."

White pushed further. "You're suggesting you can not only stop but you can hold them until you ask the question?"

Frey agreed. "That's correct."

Now nine and a half minutes into his time, a third of his total, Frey tried to state the core argument of the government. "We . . . When I get into the legal portion of the argument, we're suggesting that—"

But White wanted a clarification on the claim that the government could hold people without a warrant. He pressed Frey to explain where the government was saying they could stop and briefly detain vehicles. Frey responded that the border zone is what makes the difference, and they can stop and briefly detain anyone there, including citizens.

Until Powell's last-minute reversal in *Almeida-Sanchez* in 1973, the Supreme Court had been poised to say that the Border Patrol could search any vehicle in the one-hundred-mile zone. Now the question was whether they could even stop a vehicle and ask them a few questions.

Frey explained that Congress gave the Border Patrol the ability to stop any vehicle in the zone for a brief interrogation. "We say this is necessarily included within the power to search is the power to stop."

White then asked if that meant they could stop anyone randomly. Did they need suspicion?

Frey answered, "No. We say that we have the power to stop randomly."

At this point, the issue of race came to the front of the discussion. Harry Blackmun pointed out that Frey's argument "makes irrelevant in this case that they thought these looked like Mexicans, they thought they were Mexicans, or anything else?"

Frey agreed. "I think it's completely irrelevant. Now, I could picture a case in which the individual stopped was let us say a sixty-year-old lady who was alone in her car and who was clearly Anglo-Saxon, and her car was stopped for simply for the purpose of asking her about her citizenship and—"

Potter Stewart jumped in, ever the comedian. "She might be Norwegian . . ."

Frey continued, "She might be, that's true. But of course, the conditions in the Mexican border area that justify the power that we are asserting here and that we say make this case distinguishable from *Terry*'s articulated particularized suspicion requirement, it's applicable to Mexicans."

William Brennan asked, "You said earlier, you thought there might be a distinction between the old lady driving the car and these people, and I swear I don't understand this."

Brennan was nominated for the Supreme Court by Eisenhower and approved in early 1957 by the Senate, with only Senator Joseph McCarthy voting against him. Brennan served on the court until 1990 and was, according to Antonin Scalia, "probably the most influential justice of the century."[7] He wrote the second most opinions in the history of the Supreme Court, after William O. Douglas. Brennan was effective at influencing his colleagues, and he worked throughout his time on the court to expand individual rights, particularly those enshrined in the Bill of Rights. Consequently, he would be expected to be skeptical of the government's claim that they could stop any vehicle for any reason in the border zone.

Frey started to reply about what he would do if he were representing the old lady against the government, which drew rebukes from the bench because he was, of course, the government. Frey took a deep breath and then said sheepishly, "I'm trying my best."

White and Brennan were both impatient with the solicitor at this point and asked angrily, "What is the answer?"

Frey stammered, "The distinction is that—is that—it's not—I'm saying that we have a right to stop anybody."

The audience chuckled as Stewart joked again, "Those old ladies can very suspicious sometimes."

As Frey's time ended, Bryon White asked a question that caused Frey to stumble into another blunder. "But if they say 'go about your business, I don't want to answer a single question,' you're not supposed to hold them? Here, you say you can hold them to ask them questions, what is it?"

Frey tried to reply but went the wrong way. "Well, I'm—we say we can hold them here. I don't see that is fruitful really to get into the— we say that this is different."

White broke in: "Oh, it's fruitful, and it is so fruitful that the Ninth Circuit—"

Frey, rather than backtracking, dug in: "Well, now the reason the Ninth Circuit thought we were wrong unanimously, I believe was a product of a superficial analysis of the issues on their part, and the same superficial analysis it seems to me is contained in the respondent's brief."

Frey had called the unanimous decision by the full Ninth Circuit Court of Appeals "superficial." After another minute, he decided to stop. "I think I'd like to save a couple of minutes for rebuttal if I may."

"You Can't Use Race Alone"

Chief Justice Burger turned it over to John Cleary to speak on Felix Brignoni-Ponce's behalf. After the obligatory "Mr. Chief Justice and may it please the court," Cleary began with a quip about what Frey called his brief: "I don't mind having my brief called superficial if the *en banc* Ninth Circuit's reasoning is called superficial."

Pausing briefly so the justices could appreciate the point, Cleary then summarized the case law on the Fourth Amendment that made this particular stop unconstitutional. He concluded that the Supreme Court had ruled in 1968 in *Terry v. Ohio* that the police needed more than a hunch to stop and search someone. The Border Patrol did not have it in this case. After going through the legislation that led to the current border exception, he got to the point: "We're dealing with a fundamental right."

Potter Stewart asked, "The Ninth Circuit, it's now settled after this case I gather, requires what it calls a founded suspicion for a stop, is that it?"

Cleary replied, "That is the fact, Your Honor. It requires a founded suspicion to believe that there's illegal aliens . . . for any interdiction of highway traffic, there must be founded suspicion."

Cleary then proceeded to build up steam toward one of his strongest lines of the argument: "Can they say that a person who appears to be of Mexican descent in the area of Southern California contiguous with the Republic of Mexico constitutes some rational basis, reasonable suspicion that that person is an alien?" After pausing for effect to let his question sink in, he went on, "I would contend if such ever was the case that would be rank racism."

Stewart, taking in Cleary's point, noted that the statute does not say there has to be a rational ground for the belief an individual is undocumented but simply the belief on the part of the officer. Surely, they would not make the stop if they did not believe it.

Cleary argued that the belief needed to be based in articulable facts, not a hunch, and there needed to be more than one fact. This mirrored Powell's concurrence in *Almeida-Sanchez* two years before and, with what Cleary said next, would inform Powell's eventual decision in this case.

Cleary said, "There must be at least two criteria. One, suspicious circumstance, and two, objective articulable facts, and we contend that the Ninth Circuit's construction is consistent with the statute, that implements the statute and at the same time gives validity to the Fourth Amendment. The more important thing is that the hunch of the officer can be used and abused. In this case, we make note of that because here, the only articulable basis given in cross-examination was that the person appeared to be of Mexican descent."

Cleary outlined for the first time how the case could be decided. He advocated strongly for his client, Felix Brignoni-Ponce, but not necessarily all people of color at the border. He argued that in this specific case the only factor used by the agents was the perceived Mexican appearance of the passengers in the car, and based on the case law, that was insufficient grounds to make a stop. However, he also hinted at the compromise position that he returned to at the end of his time. With multiple facts of reasonable suspicion, the Border Patrol had more than a hunch and could make a stop.

Cleary explained, "It's our contention that you can't use race alone," but "possibly as one of many factors it can be used. It might be used in many other things."

At this point, the young conservative justice William Rehnquist joined the questioning, perhaps having seen the opening he was looking for. "Well, Mr. Cleary . . . what factors does he use in reaching his initial determination of believing a person to be an alien? I mean, what would you suggest?"

Cleary suggested a multiplicity of factors. When Rehnquist pushed him to be specific, he hedged and began to backtrack a bit, arguing that race and appearance might not be useful factors. Cleary noted the government brief said that Mexicans are thinner than Americans, to which he said, "How many fat aliens have I represented? You can test because they have coarse hands, that they wear coarse clothes. They have their hair cut in a certain way." He added with an audible grunt of disgust, "I've had my hair cut once or twice in Tijuana."

It was a funny line, but the damage was done. Cleary had suggested a way for the court to rule in favor of his client in this specific case, but at the same time to establish the principle that the government was seeking in relation to the Border Patrol, which Powell's clerk Penny Clark had surmised was the entire reason they appealed the case to the Supreme Court. Cleary's oral arguments identified a middle ground that required multiple articulable facts of reasonable suspicion in order for the Border Patrol to stop a vehicle. Just one factor, the Mexican appearance of the driver, was not enough, but paired with other factors, race could contribute to the decision to make a stop. The court adjourned and now the decision was in the hands of the nine justices.

11.

Mexican Haircuts

AT THE FRIDAY CONFERENCE ON FEBRUARY 19, 1975, THE justices discussed the *Brignoni-Ponce* case and took a straw vote, which split 4–4. William Brennan, Thurgood Marshall, Lewis Powell, and Potter Stewart would affirm the Ninth Circuit ruling in Felix Brignoni-Ponce's favor, while Harry Blackmun, Warren Burger, William Rehnquist, and Byron White would reverse and rule in favor of the Border Patrol's right to stop all vehicles in the border zone for brief questioning. William O. Douglas missed the Friday conference—he was convalescing after suffering a massive stroke while on vacation in the Bahamas on New Year's Eve. The stroke paralyzed Douglas's left leg and forced him into a wheelchair. However, he did not want to retire.

Douglas is the longest-serving Supreme Court justice and believed in liberal activism from the bench, often dissenting based on principles that were outside the mainstream at the time. His focus on principles, not practical politics, frustrated his ideological allies. President

Lyndon Johnson once remarked to him "Liberty and Justice . . . that's all you apparently think of. And when you pass over the last hill, I suppose you will be shouting 'Liberty and Justice.'" Douglas replied, "You're goddamn right, Mr. President."[1]

In the spring of 1975, as he recovered from his stroke, Douglas was determined to continue his work, but he was not able to attend many of the oral arguments or participate fully in the affairs of the court. The other justices had doubts about his ability to continue and agreed among themselves that they would try to avoid any 5–4 ruling in which Douglas would be the deciding vote.[2]

On February 27, Douglas wrote a memo on the *Brignoni-Ponce* case indicating that he would also affirm, placing five votes on that side. Lewis Powell was assigned the case and set about working on what he hoped would be a consensus argument that would draw in the support of his more conservative colleagues, thereby avoiding the problem of the incapacitated Douglas's deciding vote.

Fits and Starts

At the beginning of the term, Powell assigned a roughly equal number of cases to each of his clerks. David Boyd was assigned *Brignoni-Ponce*. Boyd produced a thirty-page memo summarizing the issues in the cases, which dwelled on the sensitive racial questions. He wrote: "I continue to be quite troubled by the palatability of an opinion that rests exclusively on the racial characteristics of the occupants of the automobile . . . such an opinion would be a disaster." For Boyd, "the preferable approach is to indicate that the officer's ability to stop rests on a combination of factors, of which the racial characteristics of the occupants is only one."[3] It was an approach that would be "more acceptable 'politically.'" However, Boyd became bogged down with other opinions, so Powell asked Penny Clark to take over the *Brignoni-Ponce* case.

Powell focused his interest on the idea of a judge or magistrate issuing an area search warrant that would allow for brief stops in the border zone, an idea he proposed in his concurrence in the *Almeida-Sanchez* decision in 1973. In his own summary memo produced in preparation for the oral arguments, Powell wrote, "Although there is obvious force to the government's reluctance to endorse a general area-type warrant or specific checkpoints, I am not yet persuaded that this procedure is not feasible—especially if we laid down some fairly broad guidelines."[4] At the oral arguments, Powell asked John Cleary a question about area warrants and jotted in his notes, "Responding to my Q, Cleary expressed view that a warrant procedure for checkpoints is 'conceptually feasible.'" Unbeknownst to Powell, the Border Patrol had begun to use area warrants at the San Clemente checkpoint, and at that very moment, the Ninth Circuit Court in San Francisco was considering a case brought by the Federal Defenders of San Diego about area warrants.

As Clark worked on a draft of the *Brignoni-Ponce* opinion, she struggled to find the key to it. She expressed doubts about general area warrants in a memo to Powell on May 8: "I am still fairly uncomfortable with it, and I will outline my current thoughts about its weak points. I have tried to write as strong a case as I can for the area probable cause and search warrant theories, but the more time I spend on them, the less I am convinced."[5] She pointed out that parts of his current opinion would appeal to each faction, but also possibly lose all of them.

Instead of the area warrant, Clark suggested the court emphasize the difference between a stop and a search, which would harmonize the rules for both roving patrols and the checkpoints and would represent a middle path between the government's claim that they could stop everyone and the Fourth Amendment's ban on unreasonable searches and seizures. Clark proposed that a search would require consent or probable cause, as the court's opinion in *Almeida-Sanchez* held in 1973 for roving patrols and for checkpoints. However, she proposed that for a short stop with questions by a roving patrol, a lesser standard of reasonable suspicion might be sufficient. Clark ended the memo by suggesting that

Powell might have a better chance at a majority if he went with that line of argument.

Even before Clark wrote her memo, Powell had expressed his personal concerns about the Border Patrol cases in a memo to the other justices after the Ninth Circuit Court released its decision in the area warrant case about the interior checkpoint at San Clemente. In *Martinez-Fuerte*, the Ninth Circuit invalidated almost every stop at the interior checkpoints, extending the logic of *Almeida-Sanchez* to stops as well as searches. Additionally, the Ninth Circuit decision also had several pages criticizing Powell by name for his area warrant idea.

Powell immediately saw that the court would have to address the issue of the interior checkpoints as well. Since he was already struggling with the border cases and because he was worried about the possibility of a 5–4 split with the ill Douglas casting the deciding vote, Powell suggested to his colleagues that they postpone their decision until *Martinez-Fuerte* reached the court the following term. He wrote, "If a court cannot be assembled, the cases presumably should be set for reargument early next fall."[6]

However, a few days later, on April 1, Powell was presented with another important fact that changed his mind again. Chief Judge John Brown of the Fifth Circuit Court, which covered Texas, Louisiana, and Mississippi, called Powell and told him there were almost twenty border cases pending at that court and two hundred more at the prosecutors' offices waiting for resolution. Consequently, Judge Brown was hoping for a decision on at least some of Border Patrol issues that term.[7] Powell went back to work.

"Dear Fellow Losers"

As the justices draft their opinions on cases, they send short memos back and forth to each other stating where they stand. Powell circulated his latest version of the *Brignoni-Ponce* opinion, which removed his un-popular area search warrant idea and instead pursued Penny Clark's idea of reasonable suspicion based on articulable facts for stops, which was alluded to in Powell's concurrence in *Almeida-Sanchez* and in John Cleary's oral arguments before the court.

Powell was disappointed when the responses came back 5–4, in the same configuration as *Almeida-Sanchez*. Brennan, Marshall, and Stewart signed onto the ruling, and the ill Douglas planned a con-currence that agreed that Mr. Brignoni-Ponce should be released but did not go along with the lower reasonable suspicion standard for the Border Patrol.

Powell was frustrated to find himself with a majority of five that was dependent on the incapacitated Douglas's fifth vote, despite his efforts to appease the more conservative bloc. Powell was particularly disappointed in the chief justice's position, who he had hoped would also not want a 5–4 decision with Douglas as the deciding vote and would therefore sign on to the latest draft.

Chief Justice Burger, however, was not swayed. He wrote on June 6 that he was "glad you now avoid the 'area search warrant' approach but I fear we may not have found the key I need to the resolve the problem."[8]

Powell wrote a personal note back to Chief Justice Burger on the same day, expressing his surprise and disappointment that the chief justice was not a vote in favor of his revised opinion in *Brignoni-Ponce*. Powell said he had "devoted more time to the study of these cases than to any assignment you have given me this year." He pointed out that his current draft "can be said that I have departed somewhat from prece-dent. In Brignoni-Ponce, I proposed 'reasonable suspicion' standard for random stopping and questioning of occupants of vehicles by roving patrols. This affords more leeway to law enforcement officers than any prior Fourth Amendment case with which I am familiar."[9] Powell then noted that he was working with Rehnquist on changes to limit the

REECE JONES

ruling to the Border Patrol. Powell's point was that this was already a generous ruling for the Border Patrol and likely the best the conservatives could get, given the court's current makeup.

The chief justice wrote back a few days later on June 9, 1975.[10] Burger began the letter with an apology—"I'm sorry to 'let you down' on the Border Search cases"—but he could not overlook the connection between the border and social problems in the United States. Burger placed some of the blame on Court's previous decision in the *Almeida-Sanchez* case, in which Powell cast the deciding vote. Burger suggested, "And the vexing aspect of the plurality opinion in *Almeida-Sanchez* is that it has been followed by an unemployment figure exceeded only by the number of illegal aliens reliably estimated to be in the United States." For Burger, rising unemployment and crime were caused by immigrants, "With a shocking rise in crime, . . . Here, as elsewhere, the key lies in the irrational, monolithic, mechanical application of the Suppression Doctrine [the rule from *Mapp* that forbade improperly obtained evidence from being used in court] . . . You have my vote on the Border cases if you link it with a sane, selective use of exclusion—as in England, Israel, and every other civilized country in the world save ours!" The exclamation point was added later by pen, with some emphasis.

With Powell frustrated by the lack of conservative support for his draft opinion, Rehnquist made his move on June 10. Seeing that there was a 5–4 majority in favor of exonerating Felix Brignoni-Ponce, but unease about how to allow the Border Patrol to do their work, Rehnquist penned a memo to the other three holdouts, Chief Justice Burger, Byron White, and Harry Blackmun.

Rehnquist began the letter "Dear Fellow Losers" and pointed out that they had two choices.[11] They could continue to dissent, which would likely allow the cases to be held over to the following term. Alternatively, they could offer up some revisions and pledge that if Powell made the changes, they would agree to vote in favor of the opinion. Rehnquist concluded, "I think the second choice has much to be said for it for at least two reasons." First, even if they dissented, the current formulation would become law. As it was written at that moment, Rehnquist felt that the Fourth Amendment protection of "the interest of innocent citizens in using the highway" was trumping the need for law enforcement to make brief stops and inquiries. Given the dynamic, he instead proposed a series of changes in the opinion that would dismiss the charges against Felix Brignoni-Ponce but also give law enforcement the latitude it needed to make stops based on reasonable suspicion in the future.

The gambit worked. Powell, who was conservative by nature and always sought consensus and compromise, quickly rewrote the text to include Rehnquist's changes. These were a line that confirmed that agents with reasonable suspicion could stop vehicles and language that limited the ruling to roving Border Patrol stops. Rehnquist insisted that the ruling explicitly state that Border Patrol checkpoints, and other police checkpoints, were still allowed.

On June 16, Powell then wrote to the other more liberal justices, who had already indicated their agreement with the earlier draft, to tell them about the changes. Powell wrote that the changes were minor and did not alter the basic formulation of the decision. However, he was pleased to see the possibility of a broad consensus opinion on the border cases. He concluded: "In sum, I think we have a chance now to bring these cases down. We will have settled conclusively the 'search' issue at fixed checkpoints as well as by roving patrols; we also will have settled the 'stop' issue with respect to roving patrols. These decisions will go far toward resolving the doubt which now overhangs the entire Border Patrol operations."[12]

Given the late-term rush to finish opinions and the fact that the outcome remained the same with the release of Felix Brignoni-Ponce, it is not clear how closely the bloc of liberal justices reviewed the new draft. Penny Clark surmises that William Brennan may not have given the revisions careful scrutiny because he was pleased that it would be a unanimous ruling in favor of the defendant.[13] By June 26, all the justices signed on to the revised opinion.

"The Characteristic Appearance of Persons Who Live in Mexico"

As the author of the opinion, Lewis Powell announced the decision in *Brignoni-Ponce* on the last day of the term, June 30, 1975. After establishing the basic parameters of the case, Powell got to the point: "[B]ecause it was a mere stop, the questioning about citizenship is less intrusive than a search, we hold that the standard of probable cause is not required. But even random stops for questioning anywhere near the Mexican border could subject law-abiding citizens to potentially unlimited interference with their use of the highways. We therefore hold that Border Patrol officers on roving patrol may not stop a private vehicle unless they have reasonable grounds to suspect that it contained aliens." Therefore, the stop based solely on the perceived Mexican appearance of the people in the car did not rise to this standard, and the court unanimously upheld the Ninth Circuit's ruling in Felix Brignoni-Ponce's favor.

The decision was another victory for John Cleary, Chuck Sevilla, and the Federal Defenders of San Diego. The charges against Brignoni-Ponce were dropped and he was released. The ruling made clear that unlimited stops in the border zone would violate the Constitution. A superficial reading of the decision would make it seem to be another confounding example of the supposedly law-and-order Burger Court coming down on the side of the defendant and undercutting law enforcement further, this time unanimously.

However, the votes by the conservative justices suggest the ruling was not exactly as it appeared. After Rehnquist's late intervention, the details of the ruling were favorable to the Border Patrol.

The ruling finds that unlimited stops and stops based only on the race of the occupants of a car are not allowed. However, it recognizes a legitimate need for the Border Patrol agents to make stops: "In this case as well, because of the importance of the governmental interest at stake, the minimal intrusion of a brief stop, and the absence of practical alternatives for policing the border, we hold that when an officer's observations lead him reasonably to suspect that a particular vehicle may contain aliens who are illegally in the country, he may stop the car briefly and investigate the circumstances that provoke suspicion."

In order to make a stop, the Border Patrol agents need specific, articulable facts that give them reasonable suspicion that a particular vehicle contains someone without documents. Although Clark is sure that Powell never thought of it this way, the Border Patrol has interpreted the ruling to mean that a single fact is not sufficient, but two is enough.[14]

In some of the most remarkable text in a Supreme Court decision still in force, the opinion laid out what might constitute the necessary facts for reasonable suspicion. These include (quoted verbatim from the ruling, but with citations and case law removed):

1. The characteristics of the area in which they encounter a vehicle
2. Its proximity to the border
3. The usual patterns of traffic on the particular road
4. Previous experience with alien traffic are all relevant
5. Information about recent illegal border crossings in the area
6. The driver's behavior

7. Erratic driving

8. Obvious attempts to evade officers

9. Aspects of the vehicle itself

10. Certain station wagons, with large compartments for fold-down seats or spare tires

11. The vehicle may appear to be heavily loaded

12. It may have an extraordinary number of passengers

13. The officers may observe persons trying to hide

14. The characteristic appearance of persons who live in Mexico, relying on such factors as the mode of dress and haircut

15. Previous experience with aliens

Most of these facts individually could seem like reasonable reasons for a Border Patrol agent to stop a vehicle. In constructing the first draft of the list, Clark drew from past Border Patrol cases to demonstrate the types of factors that are reasonable.[15] However, in totality, they create a broad range of possible reasons to stop someone, so broad that virtually any stop can be justified.

The final two examples about race and the agents' previous experience with what undocumented people look like are the most troubling. In the oral arguments, John Cleary mocked the idea that clothes or haircuts could be used to identify foreigners as "rank racism," but the opinion allows precisely that. The result of Powell's opinion is that the Border Patrol can use racial profiling to make a vehicle stop as long as race is combined with one other articulable fact of reasonable suspicion, such as fact 2, driving on a road near the border. Although Cleary and the Federal Defenders of San Diego won the individual case for their client, they opened the door for racial profiling across the border zone.[16]

The *Brignoni-Ponce* opinion focuses exclusively on the Mexican border, which makes clear that the justices did not realize that their decision would also authorize similar racial profiling stops based on the lower standard of reasonable suspicion, not probable cause, within one hundred miles of coastlines and the Canadian border. The opinion mentions the possible intrusion of these stops in American cities, but only lists San Diego, El Paso, and the Brownsville-McAllen area in the Rio Grande Valley. It is surprising that neither the court nor any of the lawyers saw that the case was not just about the Mexican border, but also all the other areas where the Border Patrol operates.

Despite these far-reaching implications, the *Brignoni-Ponce* decision was treated as a minor case at the time. The only time the term *Brignoni-Ponce* has ever appeared in the entire history of *The New York Times*, the newspaper of record in the United States, was in a short roundup of Supreme Court decisions on the following day. The *Times* noted that the court "Ruled that law enforcement officers on roving border patrol cannot stop vehicles and question occupants about citizenship solely on the grounds that the occupants appear to be Mexican (No. 74-114, *United States v. Brignoni-Ponce*)."

As the court recessed for the summer and Lewis Powell retreated to his home in Richmond to read and visit with his grandchildren, the only Border Patrol issue that remained was brief stops at Border Patrol checkpoints. The case of *United States v. Martinez-Fuerte*, which the Ninth Circuit had ruled on in April just as Powell was trying to find a consensus on *Brignoni-Ponce*, was sure to be added to the docket. The court's opinion in the case would resolve the final questions about the authority of the Border Patrol to make stops in the one-hundred-mile border zone, and Powell would make one more unexpected decision.

12.

A Sixth Sense

JOHN CLEARY AND CHUCK SEVILLA DID NOT IMMEDIATELY see the broader implications of the *Brignoni-Ponce* ruling. They were elated, and blinded, by the fact that they won a unanimous verdict for their client, which followed on their win in the *Almeida-Sanchez* case two years earlier. They also won a unanimous verdict in *United States v. Ortiz*, which was announced the same day as the *Brignoni-Ponce* decision. The *Ortiz* case was argued by Sevilla and the decision written by Justice Lewis Powell. In *Ortiz*, the court followed the precedent of their decision in *Almeida-Sanchez*, finding that the Border Patrol needed to have the higher standard of probable cause to search a vehicle at an interior checkpoint.

Cleary and Sevilla thought they had the wind at their backs as they continued to defend clients stopped by the Border Patrol over the summer and into the fall of 1975. In the previous three cases, the court had ruled that all Border Patrol searches, whether by a roving patrol or at an interior checkpoint, required probable cause or consent. Additionally, even a brief stop by a roving patrol required multiple facts of reasonable suspicion.

The only question that remained was whether the Border Patrol could make brief stops at interior checkpoints without a warrant or reasonable suspicion. Cleary and Sevilla had what seemed like a favorable decision in *Brignoni-Ponce* that would force the court to rule that all interior checkpoints violated the Fourth Amendment of the Constitution. If the Border Patrol needed reasonable suspicion to stop a single vehicle when conducting roving patrols, then surely, Cleary and Sevilla contended, they needed at least reasonable suspicion to stop every single vehicle on a major interstate highway.

The lawyers had the perfect case to test that theory—and, they hoped, to get the Supreme Court to decide that the Border Patrol's interior checkpoints throughout the border zone were unconstitutional. *United States v. Martinez-Fuerte* was the Ninth Circuit ruling that came just as Justice Lewis Powell had been wrestling with his *Brignoni-Ponce* decision the previous term. Despite seeming to have momentum on their side, Cleary and Sevilla's final moment of triumph would not go as planned, and Powell would again write the decisive opinion of the court.

The San Clemente Interior Checkpoint

On June 24, 1974, Amado Martinez-Fuerte was driving two women north on I-5, the main interstate highway that connects two of California's largest cities, San Diego and Los Angeles. The women paid a smuggler in Tijuana $200 ($1,050 in 2022, adjusted for inflation) for fake documents to cross the border. He told them to proceed through the border checkpoint and then go to the San Diego bus station, where he would meet them. They crossed without incident at San Ysidro, the busiest border checkpoint in the world, then found the same man waiting for them at the San Diego bus station. He took back the fake documents and then walked the women to a car, where Martinez-Fuerte was waiting at the wheel. They got in and Martinez-Fuerte drove off without even asking where they wanted to go.

The skyscrapers of San Diego faded in the distance as they headed north on I-5. The sun set over the Pacific Ocean as they passed the last beach towns of Carlsbad and Oceanside and sped past the rugged hills and grassy coastline before they reached the southern suburbs of Los Angeles.

Martinez-Fuerte knew that the last barrier for the women to pass was the Border Patrol's checkpoint at San Clemente, sixty-six miles north of the border. The Border Patrol had operated a checkpoint along this stretch of highway since its founding in 1924. At first, it was closer to Oceanside, but after I-5 was opened in 1968, it was set up at its current location.[1] The San Clemente checkpoint was the same spot where Felix Brignoni-Ponce had been arrested a year and half before, except on that rainy evening the checkpoint was closed due to the inclement weather.

Martinez-Fuerte was transporting the women on a warm and cloudy Monday evening, so he knew the checkpoint would probably be open. He hoped to pass through with only a cursory glance from the agents on duty. On average, 1,200 vehicles passed through the checkpoint every hour in 1974, over 10 million per year. Less than 1 percent of those were diverted to secondary inspection for more thorough questioning.

As Martinez-Fuerte and his two passengers approached the checkpoint at 8:00 p.m., they saw a large sign with flashing yellow lights that indicated that the checkpoint was in operation. It warned, ALL VEHICLES STOP AHEAD, 1 MILE.[2] As they got closer, another sign spanned the highway itself: WATCH FOR BRAKE LIGHTS. When they reached the checkpoint, flashing red lights lit up a sign that instructed all vehicles to STOP HERE—U.S. OFFICERS. Orange traffic cones funneled the vehicles into two lanes for the inspection. Two Border Patrol agents stood on the road below the flashing lights, and Border Patrol vehicles were parked sideways on the shoulders of the interstate to prevent efforts to evade the checkpoint. As the sun slipped below the horizon over the Pacific Ocean to their left, the floodlights that lit up the checkpoint at night had just been turned on.

Unbeknownst to Amado Martinez-Fuerte, he arrived at the San Clemente checkpoint just as the Border Patrol was experimenting with a new way of justifying the stops of all the vehicles traveling on the interstate. After the string of Ninth Circuit and Supreme Court rulings limiting their ability to make stops without a warrant, the Border Patrol decided to ask a magistrate for an area warrant for the checkpoint.[3] The first area warrant was granted by magistrate Edward Infante two days earlier, on June 22. The warrant stated: "I am satisfied that there is probable cause to believe that mass violations of the immigration laws of the United States have been or are being committed at a point known as the Border Patrol checkpoint on the northbound lanes of Interstate Highway Route 5, approximately five miles south of San Clemente, California."[4]

The area warrant allowed for "routine inspections," which the Border Patrol interpreted to mean cursory searches of trunks and interior spaces of vehicles. The warrant was limited to a ten-day period, but it was continuously renewed twenty-six times in a row. In effect, it was permanent. The area warrant was an idea that Lewis Powell had proposed in his concurrence in the 1973 *Almeida-Sanchez* ruling. He also worked with his clerk Penny Clark on a draft of the *Brignoni-Ponce* ruling that relied on area warrants, but abandoned the idea after Clark convinced him that the rest of the justices would not support it. Now it was being used for stops at interior checkpoints.

The area warrant required the Border Patrol to collect and report data on its implementation at the San Clemente checkpoint. For the ten days of the first area warrant in June 1974, 145,960 vehicles passed through the checkpoint. Most vehicles only came to a fleeting stop as the officers quickly looked at the driver and passengers before waving them through. However, if the agent saw something that "broke the pattern" of normal vehicles, then they sent it to secondary inspection for more scrutiny.

During the first ten-day period, only 820 vehicles, less than 1 percent of the total traffic, were diverted to secondary inspection for actual questioning about immigration status and citizenship. Of those, 202 were searched after the occupants' initial answers were not satisfactory to the agents; 169 of those were found to have undocumented people inside the car "in plain view." In two more instances, they found undocumented people hidden in the trunks of vehicles. That resulted in a total success rate of 0.12 percent of the 145,960 vehicles that made fleeting stops at the checkpoint.[5]

Amado Martinez-Fuerte and his two passengers were among the 820 vehicles sent to secondary inspection. As the agents questioned the passengers, Martinez-Fuerte supplied them with his identification documents. He was not a citizen but was legally in the United States as a permanent resident. The two women, however, admitted they were from Mexico and lacked documents to be in the United States. Martinez-Fuerte was charged with transporting illegal aliens and taken to the San Clemente Border Patrol station with the two women. Like Felix Brignoni-Ponce the year before, Martinez-Fuerte's case was heard in the court of Judge Howard Turrentine and he was convicted of the charge by a jury. His lawyer, Chuck Sevilla, appealed to the Ninth Circuit Court of Appeals in San Francisco.

The Ninth Circuit was not impressed with Judge Turrentine's decision to accept the evidence gathered from the stop. Instead, they saw a clear violation of the Fourth Amendment and ruled that the checkpoint operations had to stop. They wrote: "The requirements of the Fourth Amendment apply with full vigor at immigration checkpoints. A stop, even a fleeting stop, is subject to Fourth Amendment protections. . . . The Border Patrol must have a founded suspicion to stop a vehicle at a checkpoint and probable cause to search it. As the government concedes, under our decisions and absent a valid warrant, the Border Patrol cannot continue its checkpoint operations."[6]

The Ninth Circuit considered the area warrant, Powell's pet idea and the fact that made this particular case novel, but was not convinced. "We recognize that the seeds of this argument were sown by Mr. Justice Powell in his concurrence in *Almeida-Sanchez*, but we nevertheless reject the proposed analogy to the administrative inspection cases." The ruling went on for two pages criticizing Powell's concurrence: "[W]e conclude that Justice Powell's premise and the government's corollary themselves are unsatisfactory."[7] Another paragraph began, "What troubles us most about the administrative inspection analogy, proposed by Justice Powell . . ."

The Ninth Circuit concluded that in order to justify such an intrusion on an individual's constitutional rights, there had to be a legitimate and significant reason. In the case of the San Clemente interior checkpoint, they ruled there was not a legitimate reason for its location. The checkpoint was too far from the border, and the benefit of finding one car with an undocumented immigrant did not outweigh the brief, but unreasonable, seizure of the other 999 vehicles. Just as the Supreme Court ruled in the *Carroll* case in 1925 that officers could not stop every vehicle to search for alcohol, the Ninth Circuit ruled that the government could not stop every vehicle to look for immigrants.

Chuck Sevilla and the Public Defenders of San Diego had another resounding win, which invalidated all interior checkpoints across the border zone in California. However, as expected, the government appealed the case to the Supreme Court. Sevilla went into the oral arguments extremely confident, but the paradoxical ruling in *Brignoni-Ponce* the year before should have given him pause. Additionally, the Ninth Circuit's ruling included a broadside against Powell and his idea of area warrants, a fact that was sure to rankle the justice. The outcome of the final Border Patrol case was less certain than it seemed.

"The Complexion, I Suppose, of the Driver"

As they prepared for the oral arguments in Powell's chambers, one of his new group of clerks, Christina Whitman, wrote a detailed memo analyzing the case. Whitman was Powell's second female clerk and would go onto become a law professor at her alma mater, the University of Michigan Law School, as a scholar of feminism in law. Whitman and Powell disagreed on most political and legal questions, but they remained close throughout their lives, as Powell became a mentor and second father to Whitman.[8]

Whitman began her memo by stating that she recognized that her view probably diverged from Powell's, but she recommended affirming the Ninth Circuit ruling that freed Martinez-Fuerte. For her, the problem was not the checkpoints or the area warrants specifically, but rather that they were being used too far from the border and in a way that would affect millions of citizens with no connection to the border whatsoever.[9] This would inevitably have a racial component: "I am sure as a practical matter those who appear to be Mexican are singled out more frequently than others (this is unfortunate but, I think, inevitable)." While it might be annoying for most travelers to have to slow down and stop at the checkpoint "for a citizen who looks Mexican and is detained every time he passes the checkpoint, the annoyance must reach really frustrating proportions." She also expressed "fear that the area warrant in reality will become a mere rubber stamp," since it was renewed twenty-six times in a row.[10]

The oral arguments for *United States v. Martinez-Fuerte* and a similar case, *Sifuentes v. United States*, were held jointly on Monday, April 26, 1976. Justice William O. Douglas, incapacitated after his stroke on December 31, 1974, had attempted to continue to serve on the court but had finally retired on November 12, 1975. He was replaced by John Paul Stevens on December 17. By the time Stevens retired in 2010 as the third longest serving justice in the history of the court, he was consistently the most progressive justice. However, Stevens was nominated to the court by Republican president Gerald Ford. In his early years, Stevens, already sporting his signature bow tie, tended to vote with the conservative bloc of justices. Consequently, the two remaining progressives, William Brennan and Thurgood Marshall, found themselves even more isolated on the court.

Assistant Solicitor General Mark Evans was familiar with the Border Patrol checkpoints, having argued and lost the *Ortiz* case about searches at interior checkpoints in the previous term. For Evans, the Fourth Amendment's protection against unreasonable searches and seizures depended on the balance of law enforcement needs and the imposition it placed on citizens. Therefore, the checkpoint stops differed from the roving patrols adjudicated in *Brignoni-Ponce*, because "it is, we think, at once the single most important aspect of the traffic checking program and the least intrusive."[11]

It was a formulation that resonated with Lewis Powell, who always wanted to protect the ability of law enforcement to do their work, but in a way that had the least intrusion on the lives of citizens.

During the term, Powell was pulled over for speeding on I-95 while driving back to Richmond for a weekend.[12] When he recounted the story to his clerks the following Monday, he told them how impressed he was with the professionalism of the officer, who was polite and just gave him a warning. For Powell, it confirmed his belief that police were reasonable and friendly in most interactions. He did concede to the clerks that he had showed the officer his Supreme Court credentials. The clerks marveled at how Powell failed to understand how his position as a distinguished white male Supreme Court justice would mean that his interactions with the police could be any different from anyone else's.

As Evans stood before the nine justices in their black robes, he argued that because the stop was so short and fleeting, it did not require any evidence against the driver at all: "A checkpoint officer has only a brief second or two to look at an oncoming car and the decision simply cannot, in most instances, be made that there is something suspicious about the car."

Consequently, Evans conceded, the agents did not even have facts that would constitute a reasonable suspicion about a particular vehicle. He continued, "It may not rise to a reasonable suspicion, that's right. They are trained and many of them are very experienced, and, they, they tend to call it a sixth sense."

The claim that agents did not need any particular suspicion and could use their "sixth sense," or a hunch, went against all previous Supreme Court precedents regarding the Fourth Amendment. In *Terry v. Ohio*, the 1968 case that established the lower standard of reasonable suspicion for brief stops such as stop-and-frisk encounters, the court dismissed hunches. The *Terry* opinion said, "in determining whether the officer acted reasonably in such circumstances, due weight must be given not to his inchoate and unparticularized suspicion or 'hunch,' but to the specific reasonable inferences which he is entitled to draw from the facts in light of his experience."[13] Four of the justices on the bench on this day in 1976, Brennan, Marshall, Stewart, and White, had signed onto the majority opinion in *Terry* eight years before.

Surprisingly, none of the justices questioned Evans's assertion that the Border Patrol agents had a "sixth sense" that allowed them to spot undocumented immigrants. However, Stewart asked a question about race. Stewart wrote the 1973 opinion in *Almeida-Sanchez* and at the time was outraged by the violation of the Fourth Amendment it represented. Now he wondered exactly what the agents' "sixth sense" could detect: "Among many other things, the complexion, I suppose, of the driver?"

Evans acknowledged that race was definitely a factor for the agents. "I think it necessarily enters into it. . . . I think it would affront common sense to say that—if they are looking for illegal Mexican aliens that they should ignore the facial features of the occupants of the vehicle."

The *Brignoni-Ponce* ruling allowed race to be one of the factors when agents make a roving patrol stop, but here Evans suggested that it could perhaps be the only factor when deciding which vehicles needed to go to secondary inspection at the interior checkpoints. Evans went on to argue that if the court were to require reasonable suspicion in order to stop a vehicle, "they would have to be closed down because they simply couldn't be operated in any effective way," as the Ninth Circuit had ruled the previous year.

"It Is Going to Be a Race"

That was exactly what Chuck Sevilla argued should happen when he stepped to the lectern. As with all the Federal Defenders of San Diego appearances before the court, Sevilla's arguments were forceful with an edge of righteous indignation.

He began by scoffing at the claim that the checkpoint on I-5 was a minor inconvenience that amounted to a fleeting stop. He reminded the court of all the flashing lights, the series of signs prior to the checkpoint, the Border Patrol vehicles blocking the shoulders, and armed agents standing in the middle of the interstate. It was an intense experience.

Sevilla noted that the *Brignoni-Ponce* stop from the previous term occurred at precisely the same location as the San Clemente checkpoint. If in that case the officers needed reasonable suspicion to stop a vehicle they observed while sitting on the side of the highway, then surely they also needed reasonable suspicion to stop a vehicle when standing beside traffic in exactly the same location.

Then he moved on to the government's apparent position that the stop at the checkpoint, which everyone agreed amounted to a brief seizure on the part of the Border Patrol, did not require any evidence or suspicion at all. Sevilla listed previous Court precedents that held that the Fourth Amendment requires "a factual predicate for a seizure," without which "it is arbitrary, capricious, and unconstitutional." This was particularly true in this case, when the large majority of the people passing through the checkpoint did not have any connection to the border at all.

Inevitably, Sevilla argued, the stops would inordinately affect people based on their race. He continued: "After all, there are a lot of legal citizens and residents of brown skin who have a right to proceed northward. If we are talking about the right to have these fleeting stops, what is going to be the factor that the officer grasps on to [to] decide whether to waive someone to secondary? It is going to be a race." Sevilla pointed out that every single individual caught up in the dragnet at the checkpoint was of Latino/a descent. "The names on these cases says something about what goes on at the checkpoint."

Lewis Powell asked Sevilla if he thought that a driver's license checkpoint by state police was unconstitutional.

Sevilla said no, and then proceeded to use the example to explain what he saw as the differences. First, a driver's license was required to drive on the road. In that case, the check was directly related to the location, similar to an immigration check at the border itself. However, an immigration document was not required to drive on the highway, so the checkpoint location on I-5 was inappropriate. Second, driver's license checkpoints are temporary, often deployed for a few hours at a particular location. The San Clemente checkpoint location was used intermittently by the Border Patrol since 1924, but had been in almost continuous operation for thirty-six years at that point. Finally, there were no other locations to check for driver's licenses, but there were many other ways for the Border Patrol to enforce immigration rules— for example, at the border line itself.

Drawing on the Ninth Circuit's ruling, Sevilla argued that even though it might be more difficult or cost more, the border line was where immigration enforcement should happen. In 1976, the Border Patrol reported that they had only thirty people patrolling the U.S.– Mexico border with California on a typical shift, for over one hundred miles of border. Sevilla concluded: "I do not think that we should dilute the protections of the Fourth Amendment to solve a law enforcement problem which Congress has control over but has not deemed fit, at this point, at least to try to solve it."

Sevilla and his colleagues left the oral arguments feeling good about their prospects because none of the justices had really challenged their points. However, their optimism turned out to be misplaced.

13.

Free to Stop Any and All Motorists

WHEN THE JUSTICES MET AT THEIR CLOSED FRIDAY CON-
ference to take a straw vote and assign the writing of the majority opinion in the case of *United States v. Martinez-Fuerte*, the vote was 7–2
in favor of the Border Patrol. The conservative, pro–law enforcement
slant of the court began to show, with Warren Burger, Harry Blackmun,
Lewis Powell, William Request, John Paul Stevens, and Potter Stewart
voting to reverse the Ninth Circuit's ruling. Only William Brennan and
Thurgood Marshall voted in favor of Martinez-Fuerte. Chief Justice
Burger assigned the opinion to Powell based on his experience with the
previous Border Patrol cases.

Powell gave the *Martinez-Fuerte* case to clerk Carl R. Schenker Jr.,
who would go on to be a partner at the D.C. firm O'Melveny & Myers
before he passed away in 2012. Powell regularly hired clerks with political and legal views that differed from his own, and he was usually open to
their arguments for different outcomes in particular cases. When Powell

joined the court, he felt confident in business cases but often relied more on the judgment of his clerks in other areas. In *Almeida-Sanchez* in 1973, a clerk had convinced Powell to change his mind and switch his vote at the very last minute.

By 1976, Powell had several years of experience and was more confident in different areas of the law, particularly regarding the border and the Fourth Amendment, about which he had already written several opinions. Consequently, he was less persuadable than he had been in earlier terms. Powell was kind and supportive of his clerks, leaving notes on their desks thanking them for their work and even sharing memos they wrote with the other justices, crediting them by name for their good work. However, Schenker did not have the same sort of relationship with Powell.[1] In his first memo to the justice at the beginning of the term, Schenker had proposed that Powell take a progressive position on a case that even Brennan and Marshall thought was too liberal. After that, Powell just did not seem to trust Schenker and was less open to considering his arguments. The lack of success made Schenker angry throughout the term, as he had to write conservative opinions he loathed.

After Schenker completed the first draft of the *Martinez-Fuerte* opinion, Powell wrote a long memo with the changes he thought should be made. He offered some praise to Schenker, but the length and tone of the memo made clear he was not particularly happy with the draft. He said Schenker should "take his time" on making the corrections for the next draft. These included condensing it substantially, but also removing any mention that implied that the location of the San Clemente checkpoint could be questioned.

Powell was convinced that the Border Patrol should decide the location of the checkpoint and that the inconvenience to most motorists was slight. Assistant Solicitor General Evans's line about the checkpoints being the most effective and least intrusive method became the crux of Powell's opinion.

Schenker finished the revision and Powell circulated the draft opinion to the other justices. By early June, the justices had signed onto the opinion with the same 7–2 majority as the straw poll in the Friday conference. Rehnquist offered two small edits, and Powell agreed to both. Brennan wrote a dissent, after which Powell added two footnotes to the opinion in response, one of which reminded Brennan that the year before, he had signed on to the *Brignoni-Ponce* opinion that had similar language about race.

The opinion was announced on Tuesday, July 6, 1976, along with the seven other cases that remained on the final day of the term. The week before, the court had announced a series of controversial cases that dealt with the use of the death penalty in the United States. The court reversed its 1972 ban and allowed states to recommence capital punishment. On the final day of the term, there were a series of Fourth Amendment cases, which were announced together with *Martinez-Fuerte*.

As soon as Lewis Powell began to read his explanation of the *Martinez-Fuerte* decision, it was clear which way it was headed. The first thing he emphasized was the substantial problem of people crossing the border from Mexico, suggesting that many did so clandestinely along the long and mostly open border line, even though the two women in the case actually crossed with forged documents at the official crossing point. Powell then minimized the intrusion of a checkpoint, comparing it to tollbooths and agricultural checks. He said these sorts of stops were familiar to all motorists and that the "[i]ntrusion on privacy and the limitation on freedom of movement in these situations are minimal."[2]

Although his clerk, Christina Whitman, tried to convince Powell that the checkpoints were unreasonable because they were so far from the border, his opinion made the case that they had to be quite distant. His reasoning was that many areas around the border are densely populated, so checkpoints needed to be farther away, in rural areas with fewer roads.

Additionally, since the 1950s, Mexican citizens have been eligible for Border Crossing Cards, which are valid for unlimited entries to the United States for a period of ten years. However, the cards are meant only for short-term trips. The cards are only valid for travel within twenty-five miles of the border in Texas and California, fifty-five miles in New Mexico, and seventy-five miles in Arizona. Consequently, Powell wrote, the checkpoints needed to be beyond these zones of free travel for Mexican citizens.

The opinion conceded that the stops, even if they were fleeting, "are 'seizures' within the meaning of the Fourth Amendment." However, because "the resulting intrusion on the interests of motorists [is] minimal" and the need for stops is "legitimate and in the public interest," the court held "that the stops and questioning at issue may be made in the absence of any individualized suspicion at reasonably located checkpoints."

The lawyers from the Federal Defenders of San Diego were stunned. The Supreme Court had found that a seizure without any individualized suspicion was reasonable.

Even after a year to consider the implications of the racial profiling that was allowed in the *Brignoni-Ponce* ruling, the majority of the court reiterated that the race of the individual was a legitimate factor for the agents to consider. The opinion continued: "We further believe it is constitutional to refer motorists selectively to the secondary inspection area at the San Clemente Checkpoint on the basis of criteria that would not sustain a roving-patrol stop. Thus, even if it be assumed that such referrals are made largely on the basis of apparent Mexican ancestry, we perceive no constitutional violation. As the intrusion here is sufficiently minimal that no particularized reason need exist to justify it, we think it follows that the Border Patrol officers must have wide discretion in selecting the motorists to be diverted for the brief questioning involved."

It was the first loss for the Federal Defenders of San Diego before the Supreme Court. After three previous victories in *Almeida-Sanchez*, *Brignoni-Ponce*, and *Ortiz*, which limited the Border Patrol's authority to stop and search vehicles in the border zone, the *Martinez-Fuerte* decision was a complete and total defeat. Chuck Sevilla had hoped that the court would affirm the Ninth Circuit's ruling that invalidated the checkpoints altogether. However, at minimum, even if they allowed the checkpoints, it seemed logical that they would use the same standard of reasonable suspicion for stops at checkpoints, as they had required for stops on roving patrols in the *Brignoni-Ponce* decision the previous year. The court's final decision that the Border Patrol did not need any reason at all to stop a particular vehicle at interior checkpoints was an unexpected and shocking result.

"The Continuing Evisceration of the Fourth Amendment"

In the previous year, the court's progressive wing had signed on to the *Brignoni-Ponce* decision that legalized racial profiling as one of the multiple factors that could be used by Border Patrol to decide whether to stop a vehicle during a roving patrol. In that case, the conviction of Felix Brignoni-Ponce was overturned, which perhaps led them to overlook the implications of the rest of the opinion. In *Martinez-Fuerte*, William Brennan did not make the same mistake again. He wrote an angry dissent, which was joined by Thurgood Marshall, blasting the weakening of the Fourth Amendment of the Constitution and the legalization of racial profiling by the Border Patrol.

After the retirement of William O. Douglas in November 1975, Brennan and Marshall found themselves outnumbered. As conservative opinions came one after another in 1976, Brennan's dissents became more and more biting. At a Friday conference at the end of the term when they were discussing *Martinez-Fuerte* and Powell's other Fourth Amendment cases, Brennan and Powell got under each other's skin. Powell said, "I'm ready, but I don't know if Bill Brennan is ready. He may have some more dissenting to do." To which Brennan responded, "I don't know why you even have to ask me. I take it you don't feel you have to read my dissents or respond to them anyway."[3]

Brennan's *Martinez-Fuerte* dissent was sharp, coming on the final day of a frustrating term. He first took aim at the hollowing out of the constitutional protection against unreasonable searches and seizures: "Today's decision is the ninth this Term marking the continuing evisceration of Fourth Amendment protections against unreasonable searches and seizures [. . .] the Court's decision today virtually empties the Amendment of its reasonableness requirement by holding that law enforcement officials manning fixed checkpoints stations who make standardless seizures of persons do not violate the amendment."[4]

Brennan argued the *Martinez-Fuerte* opinion was not in concert with the recent decisions in *Almeida-Sanchez*, *Brignoni-Ponce*, and *Ortiz*. Courts have set various standards in different situations, but "Conduct, to be reasonable, must pass muster under objective standards applied to specific facts." In his view, the Border Patrol's ability to stop a vehicle should always be based on at least reasonable suspicion. As Chuck Sevilla said during the oral arguments, it is illogical that reasonable suspicion should be required to stop a single vehicle but not required to stop every vehicle on the highway. Therefore, the opinion amounts to the "defacement of Fourth Amendment Protections."

Brennan was even more surprised at Powell's suggestion that the interior checkpoint was a minor inconvenience. If you added up all the inconveniences experienced by over 10 million motorists per year, it was a far different story. He wrote: "[C]heckpoints, unlike roving stops, detain thousands of motorists, a dragnet-like procedure offensive to the sensibilities of free citizens." The suggestion that the highways represented the easiest place for the Border Patrol to check for undocumented immigrants was preposterous, as both the Ninth Circuit and Sevilla argued. Brennan extended that argument: "There is no principle in the jurisprudence of fundamental rights which permits constitutional limitations to be dispensed with merely because they cannot be conveniently satisfied."

Brennan then turned his ire toward the racial profiling that the Supreme Court sanctioned in both *Brignoni-Ponce* and *Martinez-Fuerte*: "[C]heckpoint officials, uninhibited by any objective standards and therefore free to stop any or all motorists without explanation or excuse, wholly on whim, will perforce target motorists of Mexican appearance. The process will then inescapably discriminate against citizens of Mexican ancestry and Mexican aliens lawfully in this country for no other reason than that they unavoidably possess the same 'suspicious' physical and grooming characteristics of illegal Mexican aliens."

This would mean the clear and obvious infringement on the constitutional rights of American citizens. "Every American citizen of Mexican ancestry and every Mexican alien lawfully in this country must know after today's decision that he travels the fixed checkpoint highways at the risk of being subjected not only to a stop, but also to detention and interrogation, both prolonged and to an extent far more than for non-Mexican appearing motorists." Brennan concluded: "Today's decision would clearly permit detentions to be based solely on Mexican ancestry."

In the end, William Brennan belatedly realized what he and Thurgood Marshall had voted for the previous year: the Supreme Court had legalized racial profiling by the Border Patrol. The combined result of these cases was the formal approval of the Supreme Court for interior operations for the Border Patrol in the one-hundred-mile border zone that includes the homes of two-thirds of the United States population.

John Cleary and Chuck Sevilla did succeed in reining in the Border

Patrol's authority to search vehicles. In *Almeida-Sanchez* in 1973 and *Ortiz* in 1975, the Supreme Court ruled that the Border Patrol needed probable cause to search a vehicle during a stop by roving patrol or at an interior checkpoint. However, in *Brignoni-Ponce* in 1975 and *Martinez-Fuerte* in 1976, the court established guidelines that made it possible for the Border Patrol to stop virtually any vehicle in the one-hundred-mile border zone and to use racial profiling in the decision. *Brignoni-Ponce* said that the agents needed only two facts of reasonable suspicion to pull over a vehicle. The opinion listed a wide range of possible facts for a stop, which means that in practice virtually any stop could be justified, including stops based on the race of the occupants. *Martinez-Fuerte* went even further by allowing the Border Patrol to establish interior checkpoints that stop every single vehicle on an American road without any cause or suspicion whatsoever. Furthermore, the agents could use the race of the occupants to decide whether to send a particular vehicle to secondary inspection for more thorough questioning. All this was allowed within an area that the congressional legislation said should be a reasonable distance of the border, but which the Department of Justice decided in 1947 was one hundred miles from borders *and coastlines.*

The true implications of the Supreme Court's Border Patrol rulings would become clear on highways across the border zone over the ensuing decades. The results were as bad as William Brennan and Thurgood Marshall had feared.

Part III

The One-Hundred-Mile Zone

14.

America's Frontline

JUST AFTER 11:00 P.M. ON WEDNESDAY, OCTOBER 10, 2012, José Antonio Elena Rodríguez finished a game of basketball at a church near his house in Nogales, Sonora, Mexico.[1] After saying goodbye to his friends, the sixteen-year-old walked to a convenience store on Calle International, where his brother Diego worked, to grab a snack before heading home for the night. He lived a couple of blocks away.

Calle International runs along the border wall that divides the Mexican city from its smaller American counterpart, also named Nogales. The dual cities, often referred to as Ambos Nogales, "both Nogales," have an official combined population of 270,000 people, with 250,000 of those living on the Mexican side. Crossing between the cities used to be easy and common, but new security measures after the terrorist attacks of September 11, 2001, dramatically lengthened queues at the border. In the years that followed, the two cities started to seem less like a cohesive whole. In 2011, a shorter wall between the two downtown areas was replaced with a taller and more secure bollard-style barrier. Border Patrol agents prefer this kind of construction because the gaps between the bollards allow them to monitor activity on the other side. The design is relatively easy to climb, but in the downtown area of Ambos Nogales, the wall also had solid plates at the top meant to keep people from making it over. Nevertheless, people still do every day.

A few minutes before José Antonio turned the corner onto Calle International, the Nogales (Arizona) Police Department received a call about suspicious activity on International Street, the road that runs parallel to Calle International but on the U.S. side. Quinardo Garcia, a Nogales (Arizona) police officer, arrived on the scene and saw two men carrying bundles that he suspected were marijuana. He called for backup as he watched the men run into a dark yard on the U.S. side. The dispatcher called additional police officers as well as the Border Patrol. Within a few minutes, several Nogales police officers, in black uniforms with gold patches on their shoulders, and Border Patrol agents, in forest green uniforms accented by yellow badges on their chests, arrived on the scene.

Garcia and the other officers and agents spotted the two men again farther west, where the border wall and International Street climb up a hill. The men had ditched the large bundles and had apparently decided to return to Mexico. They were still on the U.S. side of the wall but were quickly scaling it to make their escape. The Nogales police officers and Border Patrol agents instructed the two men to climb back down. (For safety reasons, the agents do not try to climb the wall themselves.)

As they watched the two men climb and continued to speak with them, the police officers and Border Patrol agents heard what they thought were rocks land on the ground around them, apparently coming from the Mexican side. According to the Border Patrol's use of force guidelines, rocks are among the projectiles considered life-threatening to agents and can be countered with deadly force. The officers and agents on the scene did not initially respond with force, instead looking for cover and trying to figure out where the rocks were coming from.

José Antonio, the sixteen-year-old basketball player, walked onto Calle International at this moment and was likely startled by the commotion. Red and blue lights from the Border Patrol and police cars refracted through the gaps in the wall. Although the border wall and the road went up the hill on the U.S. side, on the Mexican side, Calle International did not. From where José Antonio was standing, there was a twenty-five-foot rock face and then the twenty-foot-high wall on top of it. José Antonio was on the sidewalk on the far side of the street, another twenty-five feet away from the border itself. He was in front of a single-story building with faded yellow paint, chipped and peeling, as he listened to the agents yelling at the two men.

Suddenly, gunshots rang out. José Antonio turned to run, but ten bullets pierced his body. He died on the spot.

On the U.S. side, there was shock and confusion over what had just occurred. Officer Garcia and the Border Patrol agents on the scene had been scrambling to take cover from the rocks when another Border Patrol truck pulled up. Agent Lonnie Swartz, with a red crewcut and mustache, jumped out of the vehicle. Without consulting the officers and agents on the scene, Swartz ran to the border wall and peered through a gap in the bollards. Then he pulled out his gun and fired all twelve rounds in the magazine into Mexico.

The violence that took José Antonio's life was perpetrated by a Border Patrol that in 2012 had changed substantially from the one that existed in the 1970s, when Lewis Powell and the other Supreme Court justices were deciding how much authority to give the agents. In 1975, there were only 1,500 Border Patrol agents, but by 2012, there were 21,394. Additionally, the agency had a wide array of new technologies to facilitate their work that would have been unimaginable in 1976. Nevertheless, despite the huge increase in agents and budget, apprehensions in the border zone had declined. In 1976 alone, 696,939 people were apprehended by the Border Patrol; in 2012, it was only 364,078. The counterintuitive decline in apprehensions occurred because fewer people made the trip. Those who were already in the United States, who in past decades might have traveled back and forth to visit family, largely opted to remain in the United States to avoid the increasingly dangerous and fraught journey.

The changes in the size and the approach of the Border Patrol had occurred in two phases, the first in the mid-1990s in response to political pressure after the NAFTA agreement, and the second in the mid-2000s after September 11 brought the border into debates about homeland security.[2] Both of these periods of change resulted in rapid hiring of new agents and contributed to the culture of violence that tolerated agents like Lonnie Swartz.

Prevention through Deterrence

Starting in the late 1980s, the southern border saw an increase of drug smuggling due to a shutdown of routes through the Caribbean, ones previously favored by Pablo Escobar and the Colombian cartels. They had to shift their distribution networks to Mexico, and in response, the Border Patrol took on a drug interdiction role that was not previously part of their mandate. While most migrants were not dangerous, drug smugglers presented a different type of threat.[3]

At the same time, the presence of undocumented Mexicans became a political issue in California and across the United States. An article in *The New York Times* in August 1993 explained the change. The article began, "Rich and poor, legally or not, they came to Southern

California by the millions over the last decade, foreigners in search of a better life or political refuge. The immigrants were mostly welcome at first." It continues, "But today the welcome has worn out. Immigrants are now widely perceived as an economic drag on taxpayers, sucking up health, school, police and other services while spreading crime, dirt and disease. With its economy struggling through the worst slump since the Great Depression, its cities battered, its government services breaking down, California, and particularly Southern California, has begun to say 'no' to more immigrants." A Republican politician is quoted as saying, "Illegal immigration is the hottest issue in the state. We've got to say to the Federal Government, 'if you don't close the border, we will.'"[4]

The anti-immigrant sentiment in California meant that the Border Patrol once again felt the pressure of political attention being paid to its work, just as it had before Operation Wetback in 1954, the last major crackdown at the border. Since the Border Patrol was established, it operated based on the assumption that there were not enough agents or resources to patrol the border line itself. Instead, the agency focused its attention on the border zone, using trails, roads, and chokepoints to locate people after they crossed the border but before they could blend into the U.S. population. This was the logic behind the roving patrols and interior checkpoints that the Supreme Court approved in the Border Patrol cases in the 1970s.

In the early 1990s, the Border Patrol needed to take action to placate angry politicians in California, so it tested a different strategy. The Border Patrol still recognized that it could not completely control the border. Instead, it decided to close down the easier-to-cross locations in order to deter people from attempting the journey. This "prevention through deterrence" strategy posited that if crossing the border became more difficult and dangerous, fewer people would try it.

The 1994 Border Patrol Strategic Plan described the anticipated impact of prevention through deterrence. "The prediction is that with traditional entry and smuggling routes disrupted, illegal traffic will be deterred, or forced over more hostile terrain, less suited for crossing and more suited for enforcement."[5] The Border Patrol's own prediction was that their policy of blocking easier migration routes would result in more deaths in the hostile terrain of remote deserts that comprised the border zone.

The prevention through deterrence strategy was tested in 1993–94 through several operations: Hold-the-Line in El Paso, Gatekeeper in San Diego, and Safeguard in Nogales. In these cities, the Border Patrol built short sections of wall in the urban areas and then posted a large deployment of agents directly on the line itself in a show of force.[6] In the areas where the operations were carried out, border crossings dropped substantially. However, none of the operations seemed to have an impact on total crossings in the sector. Smugglers and migrants simply moved to more rural and remote areas to cross. Nevertheless, the Border Patrol trumpeted the operations as successes, which they argued demonstrated that if they had more agents and resources, they could control the border.[7]

Over the rest of the 1990s, the prevention through deterrence strategy played out in the border zone. Congress increased the Border Patrol's budget and the agency doubled in size, from 4,287 agents in 1994 to 9,212 in 2000. Migration did not stop but was diverted to ever more remote locations. Additionally, cartels and smugglers became more dominant in the border zone, which the Border Patrol included as an indicator of the success of prevention through deterrence. Whereas in the early 1980s anyone could sneak across the border relatively easily, after the expansion of the Border Patrol, the cartel-controlled smuggling routes became the primary option for migrants headed to the United States. The new strategy also resulted in a humanitarian crisis and a sharp rise in migrant deaths as people were forced to cross through the parched deserts of Arizona. A decade into the new policy, morgues in southern Arizona documented a tenfold increase in deaths in the remote and dangerous deserts of the region.

The Department of Homeland Security

Even as the Border Patrol doubled in size from 1994 to 2000, it was poised for more growth in the first decade of the twenty-first century. The shock of 9/11 resulted in a broad reconsideration of how the United States conducted security inside its borders, leading to the creation of the Department of Homeland Security in 2003 to consolidate internal security operations. The sprawling department includes a wide array of agencies involved in different aspects of security, including the Coast Guard, the Federal Emergency Management Agency, and the Transportation Security Administration.

DHS also became the home to all the border, customs, naturalization, and immigration-related agencies. Immigration and Customs Enforcement (ICE) was established to arrest and deport people suspected of immigration violations in the interior of the United States. Citizenship and Immigration Services (USCIS) became the agency that handled citizenship tests and green card applications. The Border Patrol and the Customs Bureau were combined into a new agency, Customs and Border Protection (CBP). The Border Patrol, in their green uniforms, patrols between crossing points. Customs was renamed the Office of Field Operations; its agents, in blue uniforms, work at crossing points and in airports. Agents of a third unit of CBP, Air and Marine Operations (AMO), wear brown uniforms and manage the agency's aircraft and ships. AMO's authorization in the U.S. code differs from the Border Patrol in that it does not include any geographical limits, so they are able to operate anywhere in the country.[8]

For the first time, all the federal agents involved in border protection were in the same department of the U.S. government. The idea of this consolidation was first proposed all the way back in 1930 by Undersecretary of the Treasury Ogden Mills in the hopes of reining in what he saw as inappropriate actions of Border Patrol agents. When this consolidation finally happened, there was no discussion of reining in the Border Patrol. Instead, they were unleashed as the front line against terrorist infiltrations into the country.

The 2020 budget for DHS is over 51 billion dollars. The huge appropriations for national security allowed the agencies in DHS, such as the Border Patrol, to hire thousands of additional agents and purchase the latest military and surveillance gear developed for the wars in Afghanistan and Iraq. This has included the construction of a substantial tactical infrastructure, including over 700 miles of border wall, a network of cameras and sensors, and new buildings and holding facilities at permanent checkpoints along the Mexican border. To a lesser extent, the Border Patrol also constructed new facilities and deployed more agents to other areas, including to South Florida and the Gulf Coast, and along the Canadian border.

Terrorism prevention became the priority. The rebranding was based on the recognition of new vulnerabilities, but was also calculated, because framing the agency through the lens of national security was a sure path to increased appropriations.

Although the vast majority of the Border Patrol's work has remained the same as in previous eras, that fact is often not evident from the Border Patrol's website or promotional materials. For example, the Border Patrol's Official Ethos is all about terrorism and does not mention immigration at all:

We are the guardians of our Nation's borders.
We are America's frontline.

We safeguard the American homeland at and beyond our
borders.

We protect the American people against terrorists and the
instruments of terror.

We steadfastly enforce the laws of the United States while
fostering our Nation's economic security through lawful
international trade and travel.

We serve the American people with vigilance, integrity, and
professionalism.[9]

The focus on terrorism changed the mentality of the agents in the
field. Rather than thinking of themselves as primarily a policing organization, the agency shifted to treating everyone they encountered as a
potential terrorist threat.

A segment on the National Geographic television show *Border
Wars*, which for five seasons followed Border Patrol agents on duty,
illustrates how the terrorism focus changed daily interactions. In an
episode that aired in 2010, Border Patrol Agent Pittman gets a call that
a sensor was set off on a remote road near Nogales. Pittman and two
other agents on ATVs quickly locate two fifty- to sixty-year-old men
of apparently Mexican ancestry, walking on the dirt road. The men
are wearing nice, clean clothing and carry themselves in a dignified
manner. Despite their appearance, Agent Pittman carefully searches
and interrogates them. First, he inquires if they have weapons or drugs.
They respond, "No." Then he asks if they are terrorists. Again, "No."

Agent Pittman explained his concerns, "They look like unarmed
immigrants but the rule is never assume. It's dangerous—anything
that can be made into a weapon like toothbrushes, combs, and pens,
we'll take. Lighters, perfumes, that's flammable. We don't know who
we are dealing with. They may be just looking for an opportunity to do
something to harm you. We don't know their history, their criminal

records, until they get processed. You'd be surprised; we can't relax on these individuals because a lot of them do have criminal records."[10]

Although the Border Patrol describes itself as a front line against dangerous terrorists, being a Border Patrol agent is much less dangerous than other law enforcement jobs. Since 2003, the majority of on-duty agent deaths are due to medical emergencies or car crashes. In that period, only three agents were killed in violence perpetrated against them while on duty. The agency's data shows that Border Patrol agents face fewer assaults than regular police officers or even National Park Service police.[11]

An investigation by *The Intercept* found that even the low rate of reported assaults against Border Patrol agents are likely based on inflated statistics. In one instance in 2017, seven agents were assaulted by six men using rocks, bottles, and tree branches. Rather than recording the event as seven instances of assault, the Border Patrol data included 126 assaults from that single incident. They reached that inflated figure by multiplying seven agents by six men by three types of weapons.[12]

Despite the relative safety of the job, the Border Patrol has a culture of violence and abuse that mirrors the behavior of the early agents who cut their teeth in frontier law enforcement. Police brutality in the United States has become a major issue in part due to the ubiquity of camera phones that allow civilians to record the actions of police that would have previously remained hidden. By contrast, the Border Patrol operates in remote and sparsely populated areas where there are no witnesses to their actions, which leads to abuse. In August 2021, the Border Patrol decided for the first time to require some agents to wear body cameras.[13]

A 2013 survey found that 11 percent of migrants said they were assaulted by agents during or after their apprehension. The majority of these alleged assaults are not formally reported. Filing an abuse report is a daunting process for most migrants because many never interact with anyone other than the agents that abused them. Additionally, until 2015, complaints had to be filed in English, an insurmountable barrier for many poor migrant workers. The American Immigration Council reviewed all the complaints that were actually filed against Border Patrol agents from 2009 to 2015, during the Obama administration. The report documented accusations of agents committing sexual assault in detention facilities, running over people with ATVs, and beating people with the butts of their rifles. The researchers found that no action was taken against the accused agent in over 95 percent of abuse reports.[14]

A Deadly Weapon

The killing of sixteen-year-old José Antonio Elena Rodríguez on Calle International in Nogales was one of the few cases in which action was taken against the agent. The other police officers and Border Patrol agents on scene had reported rock throwing prior to the shooting, which at the time was a justifiable reason for an agent to use deadly force if they thought their life was in danger. However, investigators thought it was very unlikely that José Antonio was throwing rocks. He was standing at least twenty-five feet from the border line. Below the twenty-five-foot cliff and the twenty-foot wall on top of it, he would have had to throw a rock over fifty feet up in the air to even get it to the U.S. side. It was a difficult if not impossible throw. A Border Patrol official who investigated the scene concluded he could not have done it "even if he were a major-league baseball pitcher."[15] Furthermore, José Antonio was not involved in the smuggling attempt; he was playing basketball at a church. After the coroner's report found that all but two of the bullets hit him in the back, it was evident that José Antonio was running away from the scene.

Despite all the evidence, it still took three years for charges to be brought against the agent. In September 2015, Lonnie Swartz was indicted by a grand jury in Tucson for second-degree murder. It was the first time a Border Patrol agent was prosecuted for an on-duty killing in the history of the agency.

The reason so few Border Patrol killings were prosecuted was the broad use of force guidelines. The killing of José Antonio, along with several other similar shootings, put pressure on the Border Patrol to analyze its procedures. The agency commissioned an independent study of its use of force by the Police Executive Research Forum, a group composed of police chiefs from around the United States.[16] When the report was finished, the Border Patrol did not release it publicly until it was leaked to the press a year later.

The findings suggested many problems, including the frequent use of deadly force in response to rock throwing. From January 2010 to October 2012, there were twenty-nine instances of agents firing their weapons in response to rocks.[17] The report also identified numerous instances of agents shooting at vehicles that did not pose a threat. The report found that in some cases, agents had intentionally stepped in front of the vehicles in order to produce a justification to fire.

The Police Executive Research Forum report concluded that agents should be prohibited from firing their weapons against rock throwers or vehicles unless the agent's life was in serious jeopardy. Throwing rocks from a distance or a vehicle attempting to escape did not justify the agent discharging their weapon. The report recommended training in rock-throwing scenarios to "emphasize pre-deployment strategies, the use of cover and concealment, maintaining safe distances, equipping vehicles and boats with protective cages and/or screening, de-escalation strategies, and where reasonable the use of less-lethal devices." After this very critical report, the Border Patrol revised its use of force guidelines in 2014. However, the new guidelines still include rocks as a deadly weapon that could be used to justify deadly use of force in response.

The killing of José Antonio occurred when the previous looser regulations were in effect. The case against Agent Swartz was heard twice in 2018. In both instances, the juries reported that they were initially deadlocked but eventually delivered not guilty verdicts on two different charges. The second jury remained deadlocked on a voluntary manslaughter charge, but the U.S. Attorney declined to bring a third prosecution.[18] While the actions of Agent Swartz were violent and aggressive, the juries decided that they were justifiable under the Border Patrol's use of force regulations at the time.

José Antonio's family filed a civil suit seeking damages from Agent Swartz, a tactic that many of the families of the other victims of Border Patrol shootings were attempting. In 2020, one of the other cross-border killing cases made it all the way to the Supreme Court. Fifteen-year-old Sergio Hernández Guereca was killed by a Border Patrol agent in 2011 in El Paso in another cross-border rock-throwing incident. The court ruled 5–4 that claims against federal agents could not be made if the killing did not happen on American soil.[19]

The result is a Catch-22 for victims of cross-border shootings. If the agent was in Mexico, they could be charged in Mexican courts. If the victim was in the United States, they could sue in American courts. However, if the Border Patrol agent is in the United States and the victim in Mexico, there is no recourse.

In some respects, today's Border Patrol, with tens of thousands of agents using sophisticated military technologies, looks completely different from the early twentieth-century Border Patrol, which was tiny and underfunded. However, in other respects, nothing has really changed. Just as there were no consequences in 2012 for Border Patrol Agent Lonnie Swartz shooting across the border into Mexico and killing a teenager, in the 1920s there were no consequences for Agent Jack Cottingham, who went to the Rio Grande and randomly killed anyone he spotted on the Mexican side in retaliation for a smuggler injuring his brother. In the past decade, there have been at least six fatal cross-border shootings by the Border Patrol, none of which has resulted in legal consequences for the agents involved.[20]

The vast majority of deaths in the border zone, however, are not directly at the hands of Border Patrol agents, but rather are caused by their presence in the border zone. As easier migration routes through urban corridors like Tijuana–San Diego and Ciudad Juárez–El Paso were closed, most migrants were forced to rely on smuggling operations run by cartels. These routes often involve arduous days-long treks through the hot and dry deserts of the Southwest, a journey that has been deadly for untold thousands of people.

15.

Hostile Terrain

On the morning of January 17, 2018, the humanitarian aid group No More Deaths released a report that documented Border Patrol agents impeding the efforts of volunteers to provide humanitarian assistance to people in distress in the deserts of Arizona. The report included photos of destroyed water containers with knife slashes in them and videos of Border Patrol agents pouring out water at desert aid stations while smiling at the camera. The report also blamed the Border Patrol and its "prevention through deterrence" policy for forcing migrants into the deserts in the first place. The report was shared across social media and in newspapers around the world, including *The Guardian* and *The Washington Post*.[1]

Within a few hours of the release of the report, the Border Patrol arrested Dr. Scott Warren, one of the leaders of No More Deaths, and charged him with two felonies for harboring undocumented immigrants. He faced twenty years in prison if convicted.

No More Deaths was established in 2004 as residents of southern

Arizona became concerned about the increase in migration through the dangerous deserts of the region. The group is affiliated with the Unitarian Universalist Church in Tucson, and for many of the volunteers the motivation for their work can be found in the religious obligation to provide aid to those in need. In the Gospel of Luke, Jesus tells the parable of the Good Samaritan. A Jewish traveler with no clothes is left for dead on the side of a road. Two other travelers encounter the dying man but do not provide aid. The third man to arrive is a Samaritan, a group that was in conflict with Jews at the time. Nevertheless, the Good Samaritan provided aid for the injured man.

In the border zone, the No More Deaths volunteers play the role of Good Samaritans by leaving water, food, socks, blankets, and other supplies at aid stations on migrant trails in the desert. They also offer first aid to those in distress, both when they happen upon people in the desert and at properties in towns in the border zone, including a building in Ajo, Arizona, known as "the Barn." For the volunteers of No More Deaths, the identity or immigration status of the people dying in the deserts of Arizona is immaterial. They feel obligated to provide care for those in need.

The Border Patrol does not see it that way. Max Granger, a longtime volunteer with No More Deaths, explained, "The Border Patrol is a militarized law enforcement organization and they consider us an enemy." He continued, "They consider No More Deaths a smuggling organization that aids and abets terrorists. That is basically their perspective."[2]

The Border Patrol first raided a No More Deaths medical facility in Arivaca, Arizona, on June 15, 2017, when they arrested the undocumented people receiving medical treatment but did not arrest the American volunteers.[3] In the months before Warren's arrest, a Border Patrol agent named John Marquez had begun to surveil some of the No More Deaths volunteers. He texted with Fish and Wildlife Service

(FWS) employees to get information on who had requested permits to hike in the Cabeza Prieta National Wildlife Refuge, an area where No More Deaths volunteers regularly dropped water and searched for the remains of people who died in the desert. The FWS employee gave Marquez several names.

Marquez also determined that another FWS employee lived beside "the Barn," the property in Ajo that was a staging location and medical facility for No More Deaths. Marquez texted descriptions of the vehicles driven by No More Deaths volunteers, including Warren's truck, to that FWS employee. Marquez even sent Warren's home address. The FWS employee monitored the Barn and would text Marquez about the vehicles he saw on the property.[4] In a court filing by Warren's legal team, they described Marquez as "actively tracking NMD members, and, based on the tone of the exchanges, was doing so with a kind of relish not reflective of proper law enforcement motives."[5]

On the morning that the No More Deaths report was released, Marquez decided to surveil the Barn along with two other agents, Brendan Burns and Alberto Ballesteros. The Barn is a small building at the end of a residential street on the western edge of Ajo that has a ramshackle appearance, with each side made of different materials. A gate at the edge of the property is decorated with two wagon wheels and opens to a worn gravel parking area surrounded by saguaro cactus. A hand-painted white sign above the door says THE BARN. Ajo is forty-three miles north of the border.

Throughout the day, the agents texted back and forth, documenting who was coming and going from the Barn. In the afternoon, Burns spotted two young Latino men at the facility, whom he immediately assumed were undocumented. He texted the other agents, "2 toncs at the house," using a racial slur common in the Border Patrol to refer to undocumented people. Ballesteros replied "What!?!?!?!?!?! Nice!" As they made their plans, Marquez texted with the FWS employee who lived beside the Barn. "Yup. We are gonna be live soon. Ha." The text messages demonstrate that the Border Patrol agents did not yet have any evidence of undocumented people at the Barn because they did not request a search warrant for the property. However, their excitement reveals that their real target were the leaders of No More Deaths, specifically Scott Warren.

Warren, tall with straight brown hair pulled back in a ponytail and a perpetual five o'clock shadow, has a PhD in geography and taught classes at Arizona State University in Phoenix. As a No More Deaths volunteer, he was regularly out in the desert restocking aid stations and searching for remains. He would also lead student groups on service learning trips into the desert, including a group from a high school in Flagstaff that resulted in a profile in local newspaper in February 2017. The profile recounted how during the hike, Warren and the high school students stumbled upon two men fleeing the Border Patrol. The men told Warren that one of their friends had died nearby, and Warren was able to locate the body as the stunned teenagers waited. Warren told the newspaper that being a witness to what was happening in the desert "feels like one of the most important and almost sacred things that we do. Just being present for somebody."[6] Agent Marquez first learned about Warren after reading the article, which prompted him to begin his surveillance of the No More Deaths volunteers.

On that January 2018 afternoon, Border Patrol agents Marquez and Burns observed Warren gesturing to the north while talking to the two Latino men at the Barn in Ajo. They decided to enter the property to conduct a "knock and talk," a maneuver in which police who lack probable cause to get a warrant enter a property to knock on the door and ask a few questions to see if they can gather more evidence. As soon as the agents passed the wagon wheel gate at the entrance, Warren informed them they were on private property and asked them to leave if they did not have a warrant. They told Warren that they did not have a warrant but they asked if Warren was the property owner, which they already knew he was not. Since it was not his property, the Border Patrol agents told Warren they wanted to knock on the door to see if they could find the owner. When they got to the door, Marquez said that he saw the two Latino men inside the Barn through a window, along with several other No More Deaths volunteers. The agents decided this was enough evidence to continue their investigation.

Once they determined that the men were undocumented, they arrested them. Unlike previous raids on No More Deaths facilities, they also handcuffed and arrested Warren on charges of harboring the undocumented men. Prosecutors later added a conspiracy charge. The Border Patrol agents did not arrest any of the other No More Deaths volunteers on the site, a fact that Warren's lawyers interpreted as evidence that the arrest was retaliation against Warren, one of the leaders of the group and an outspoken critic of the Border Patrol.

As the case went to trial in 2019, no one disputed the basic facts that Warren and the other No More Deaths volunteers were providing medical aid and supplies to people in need as they walked through the deserts of the American Southwest. The only question for the jury was whether Warren provided "food, water, beds, and clean clothes," as the charges stated, with an intent to hide the two men from the Border Patrol, or simply as humanitarian assistance to people in need in a dangerous situation. The jury was asked to decide if being a Good Samaritan was a crime.

Left to Die

The deserts of southwestern Arizona are a stunning landscape dotted by stately saguaros and red mesas that glow during the sunset. The rugged beauty masks the dangerous reality that water is almost impossible to find in an area where summer temperatures routinely pass 110°F. The region was historically populated by the Tohono O'odham, who moved seasonally following water and animal migrations in an extended area that is now bisected by the border. Beyond the Tohono O'odham lands, much of the rest of the Sonoran Desert is managed by the federal government as nature preserves and military testing grounds. These include the Organ Pipe Cactus National Monument on the border itself, the Cabeza Prieta National Wildlife Refuge around the small town of Ajo, and the Barry M. Goldwater Range, a huge military bombing range that is larger than the state of Connecticut.

All these places have become graveyards in the aftermath of the Border Patrol's "prevention through deterrence" strategy.[7] The Border Patrol implemented prevention through deterrence in 1994 with a goal of forcing immigrants over "more hostile terrain, less suited for crossing and more suited for enforcement."[8] By the time Scott Warren was arrested in 2018, the consequences of this policy were clear. There was a decline in overall apprehensions from a high of 1.6 million in 2000 to just over 400,000 per year in the 2010s. However, the rate of migrant deaths in the deserts and remote sections of the border skyrocketed.[9] Whereas in the 1990s, the Tucson morgue handled on average fewer than twenty dead bodies from the border zone each year, by 2010, that number had increased tenfold, to over two hundred per year. In total, the Border Patrol reported 7,805 migrant deaths from 1998 to 2019.[10] These numbers are certainly an undercount—many bodies go undiscovered in the sparsely populated deserts. A *USA Today* analysis estimated that the true death toll could be as much as three times higher.[11]

As "prevention through deterrence" funneled people to the deserts of Arizona, the local residents found themselves at the center of a humanitarian crisis. The deaths are the result of a grim calculus. In order to reach the interior of the United States, migrants and their guides need to cross not only the border itself but also the interior checkpoints the Border Patrol operates on highways up to one hundred miles north of the border. Consequently, the trek through the desert often involves walking sixty or seventy miles in the parched and inhospitable landscape. In these conditions, the average person needs six or seven liters of water per day, and the migrants may be in the desert up to a week. Few are able to carry enough water, leaving many in life-threatening situations in remote locations, far from roads and even cell phone service.

People living in towns dozens of miles north of the border suddenly had sick and injured people knocking on their doors looking for water and medical care. Groups like No More Deaths were established by local residents to train their neighbors on the basics of wound care, sunstroke, and rehydration so they could help people while they waited for first responders to arrive.

Other organizations such as Coalición de Derechos Humanos, which previously worked on the needs of the local community, began to find much of their attention turning toward the crisis in the desert. As early as 1995, their office in Tucson began receiving calls from concerned family members of people who became stranded in the desert. Their loved ones were missing and they did not know who else to call. Over the years, the number of calls increased to the point that they trained their staff to receive missing-person reports. They eventually established the Missing Migrant Crisis Line as a dedicated call center, staffed twenty-four hours a day to provide assistance for panicked family members as well as people in distress in the desert. The number for the crisis line is widely posted in hostels and migrant staging areas in Mexico, so that people entering the desert have at least one lifeline to call if they get in trouble.

In February 2021, No More Deaths and Coalición de Derechos Humanos released a report about the Border Patrol's failure to carry out search and rescue missions to locate people missing in the border zone.[12] The report was the third in a series called "Disappeared," following a 2016 report about how the Border Patrol's apprehension tactics scatter groups, causing people to flee alone into the desert, and the 2018 report, released just hours before Scott Warren's arrest, on how the Border Patrol destroys water and other supplies left in the desert by volunteers.

The 2021 report includes an appendix that lists 457 emergency calls received by the Missing Migrant Crisis Line from 2015 and 2016 with a brief description of the reason the person was in distress. The first call: cannot walk. The second: chest pain, cannot walk, alone and afraid, no water.

> Third: lost, no food or water for three days
> Fourth: no water, no food, cannot walk, traveling companion
>   unconscious
> Fifth: no water, no food, cannot walk, traveling companion
>   unconscious
> Sixth: three to four days walking, lost
> Seventh: ill, cannot go on, alone
> Eighth: four days alone in the desert, disoriented, exhausted
> Ninth: bad physical condition, lost in the middle of the
>   mountains
> Tenth: lost and alone
> Eleventh: lost, traveling companion cannot walk, is vomiting

The list continues like that until the 457th entry: unable to continue walking, lost in the desert.

Despite its role in funneling people to these dangerous crossings as part of their "prevention through deterrence" strategy, the Border Patrol presents itself as the primary humanitarian aid provider in the border zone. They established a Search, Trauma, and Rescue unit (BORSTAR) in 1998 to aid missing and injured migrants, and their press office often focuses on the humanitarian work of the agency. For example, a press release on March 16, 2021, titled "Border Patrol agents rescue man missing for eight days," celebrates the rescue of a man who was reported missing by the Mexican consulate.[13] The BORSTAR agents searched for him for just one afternoon, but did not locate him. Four days later, he was found by chance by different agents on patrol. At that point, BORSTAR agents were called in and administered aid.

Pima County, Arizona, transfers all distress calls involving presumed undocumented people to the Border Patrol, over 1,500 calls per year, or 4.5 per day.[14] The No More Deaths analysis of the search and rescue call logs determined that the Border Patrol routinely declines to search for people reported missing. No More Deaths found that it was unclear if the Border Patrol conducted any search at all in 63 percent of referrals. In many cases, the Border Patrol said the information on the missing person was not specific enough to warrant a search.[15] They also claimed that some of the calls were fake and were meant to waste their time by directing their attention away from a planned smuggling attempt. When the Border Patrol does conduct a search, it is often short and cursory, like the BORSTAR search that lasted for only one afternoon.

On other occasions, the dispatchers could not even get in touch with the Border Patrol's search and rescue team. Although the Border Patrol celebrates the BORSTAR unit, its budget is only $1.3 million per year, a minuscule fraction of the agency's overall budget of over $4 billion. Furthermore, from 2007 to 2015, Pima County 911 operators had only a single cell phone number that belonged to one BORSTAR agent as the contact for all search and rescue referrals. Sometimes the agent was in a remote area outside of cell phone coverage. At other times, the phone was turned off when the agent was not on duty.[16]

In addition to failing to properly search for missing people in the border zone, the Border Patrol also actively disrupts efforts by humanitarian agencies. Beyond the destruction of water drops and aid stations, they often refuse to provide location information to other rescuers, deny access to interview people in Border Patrol custody who were with the missing person, and harass search teams in the border zone.[17]

As No More Deaths volunteer Max Granger explained, "The agency itself is causing the deaths and disappearances. Any response, even if it is a more robust response, is going to be inadequate. Their entire overarching prevention through deterrence policy paradigm requires death and suffering to work. They are not invested in saving people's lives."[18]

"An Apostle of Humanitarianism"

By the time Scott Warren's first trial began in May 2019, the prosecution of a humanitarian aid worker was international news. The United Nations released a report urging the United States to drop the charges against Warren, stating, "[P]roviding humanitarian aid is not a crime."[19] An online petition calling for the charges to be dropped was signed by over 139,000 people.[20] The *Washington Post* published an op-ed by Warren about the dangerous precedent his arrest set.[21] As the opening arguments began, the seats in the courtroom were full of Warren's supporters along with media from around the world.

The federal prosecutors alleged that Warren was actively harboring the two men. The prosecutors argued that the men were not in distress at all, but rather resting at the equivalent of a smuggling stash house. One critical piece of evidence for the prosecution was the moment that the Border Patrol agents observed Warren talking with the two men outside the Barn and pointing to the north. The prosecutors said he was instructing the men on how to evade the Border Patrol by making their way around the interior checkpoint north of Ajo. Warren testified that he was simply pointing out a mountain that they could use as a landmark to avoid accidentally stumbling into the nearby active military bombing range. He was also informing them of the location of roads, so if they became disoriented or in distress, they would know how to make their way out of the desert. Warren said his actions were shaped only by his religious obligation to provide aid for those in need: "an apostle of humanitarianism," as *The Washington Post* called him.[22]

After eight days of testimony, the case went to the jury, which deliberated for three days, but reported that they could not reach a verdict. There were eight jurors in favor of acquittal, but four held out for a conviction on the harboring charges. The judge declared a mistrial based on the hung jury. Warren was free to go, but the prosecutors could decide to retry him.

After a few weeks, the prosecutors opted to drop the conspiracy charge, but retry Warren on the harboring charges that had received at least some support on the first jury. Warren's second trial was held in Tucson in November 2019. This time the jury acquitted him, finding that the prosecutors did not prove that his intent was to harbor rather than simply aid the two men.

On the same day that District Judge Raner Collins presided over Warren's acquittal in his second trial, he also read the verdict in a separate case in which Warren, along with several other No More Deaths volunteers, were charged with trespassing in a protected area and littering. These charges stemmed from the aid group's efforts to leave water and supplies on migrant trails in the desert, including in the Cabeza Prieta National Wildlife Refuge. Judge Collins found that the prosecutors proved their case on both counts but ruled that the volunteers were protected from prosecution on the littering charge based on the Religious Freedom Restoration Act of 1993. This law is meant to ensure that First Amendment rights to freedom of religion are not infringed, even by laws that seem to be religiously neutral. It says the "government shall not substantially burden a person's exercise of religion even if the burden results from a rule of general applicability." Judge Collins ruled that because the aid to migrants was done based on the religious beliefs of the volunteers, the government was infringing on their First Amendment rights by prosecuting them for littering.[23] In early 2020, the convictions for trespassing were also reversed on appeal and the prosecutors decided to drop all the charges against all the volunteers.[24]

Although the arrest and prosecution resulted in two extremely stressful years for Warren and the other No More Deaths volunteers, the end result was a validation of their original belief that humanitarian aid to people in need was not a crime. Now they had a legal precedent that backed them up.

The verdicts, however, did not change the relationship between No More Deaths and the Border Patrol. Agents continue to harass volunteers when they are dropping off supplies in the desert, and they searched No More Deaths aid facilities twice in 2020. In both instances, they had warrants that allowed them to carry out armed SWAT-style raids with an armored tank, helicopters, and dozens of agents. During the raids, the agents smashed windows, broke down doors, and destroyed the first aid supplies at the site. However, they did not arrest any of the American volunteers, only the people receiving aid.[25]

Despite the efforts of No More Deaths and Coalición de Derechos Humanos to provide aid to people in distress in the deserts, the death rate has continued to climb. The highest number of migrant remains ever discovered in the Arizona deserts was recorded in 2020. The Border Patrol, whose tallies are criticized by humanitarian groups as under counts, reported 557 deaths at the U.S.–Mexico border in the 2021 fiscal year, which was the highest number ever.[26]

In the 1970s, the Supreme Court accepted the Border Patrol's argument that internal patrols and fixed checkpoints up to one hundred miles inside the United States were necessary because the agency did not have the resources to stop immigration at the border line itself. However, the court was clear that that authority was limited to immigration enforcement. In the decades since, the Border Patrol has expanded its mission beyond immigration to countering drug cartels and terrorism prevention. Despite the massively increased capacity to control large stretches of the border itself, the Border Patrol has not ended internal checkpoints and patrols. Today, it operates well over one hundred interior checkpoints throughout the border zone. The Supreme Court authorized these internal checkpoints because it was convinced they were the most effective and least intrusive method for the Border Patrol to do immigration checks inside the United States. However, the experiences of millions of American citizens who have to pass through the checkpoints suggest neither justification was correct.

16.

Checkpoint Nation

GROWING UP IN NEW ENGLAND, TERRY BRESSI COULD NEVER have imagined that most of his adult life would be shaped by a feud with the Border Patrol.[1] He joined the Coast Guard out of high school and became fascinated with the stars after he was taught celestial navigation. After five years on ships, mostly stationed in Anchorage, Alaska, Terry enrolled at the University of Arizona to study astronomy. The transition from frigid Alaska to the deserts around Tucson was jarring, but he settled in and never left. He is now the chief engineer for the Spacewatch program at the University of Arizona's Lunar & Planetary Lab. Even in middle age, Terry has a youthful, clean-cut appearance, almost like a prototypical white male astronaut of the 1960s.

Terry's office is on the main campus in Tucson, but his engineering work often takes him to the Kitt Peak National Observatory, a fifty-six-mile drive to the southwest. Terry started making regular trips to Kitt Peak in the 1990s, as many as fifty times per year. The

trip takes about an hour, as the suburbs of Tucson quickly give way
to the mesquite and occasional saguaro that line State Route 86 as it
leads toward Ajo. After a left on Route 386, the drive to the observatory climbs up through Tohono O'odham lands to a height of 6,887
feet (2,096 meters). For Terry, the drive there and the work on the
telescopes are routine. The problems start on the trip back.

There was no Border Patrol checkpoint on SR 86 in the early years,
but Terry noticed that the number of Border Patrol agents increased
every year after the area was designated a high-intensity enforcement
zone. Agents would aggressively pull up behind his official University of Arizona truck when he was on remote roads on the way back
from the observatory. It irritated him. The increased Border Patrol
presence also rankled Jim Kolbe, a moderate Republican who represented southern Arizona in the House of Representatives from 1985
to 2007. In 1999, Kolbe added a provision to the Omnibus Consol-
idated and Emergency Supplemental Appropriation Act: "No funds
shall be available for the site acquisition, design, or construction of any
Border Patrol checkpoint in the Tucson sector." The Tucson sector is a
Border Patrol zone that covers most of the state of Arizona except the
far western area around Yuma.

The Border Patrol hated the provision and looked for ways to get
around it. One strategy they tried was to piggyback on other types
of checkpoints used by local or tribal police. Terry Bressi's first major dispute was at a drunk driving checkpoint set up by the Tohono
O'odham Nation in December 2001. On his way back to Tucson from
the observatory, Terry sensed that the checkpoint was not really about
drunk driving because there were more Border Patrol vehicles than
tribal police cars. After refusing to answer the officer's questions, Terry
was forced to lie on the ground in the dirt for thirty minutes while
they searched his truck. The whole ordeal lasted three hours. He filed
a lawsuit against the Tohono O'odham police officers at the scene that

day and finally won a $210,000 settlement in 2011. It was the first of his many protests at checkpoints.

In 2005, the Border Patrol tried another strategy to get around the ban on checkpoints in the Tucson sector. They began to set up temporary checkpoints on SR 86 that would be in place for only a few days. Then they would disassemble the checkpoint and move it a few miles up or down the highway. By 2007, the Border Patrol was running these "temporary" highway checkpoints on a continuous basis.

That same year, Representative Kolbe retired and was replaced by Democratic Representative Gabrielle Giffords. Giffords had much stronger border security views, and she immediately set out to reverse the ban on checkpoints in southern Arizona. She held town halls around the state jointly with representatives of the Border Patrol and she asked the General Accountability Office (GAO) for an assessment of checkpoint effectiveness. Even though the GAO report was critical of checkpoints, Giffords pushed ahead with her plans to remove the ban on checkpoints in the Tucson sector. After 2008, the Border Patrol stopped having to move the checkpoints around to comply with Kolbe's ban. The checkpoint on SR 86 has operated 365 days a year since then.

Bressi was offended that even though he had not left the country—not even been within twenty-five miles of the border—he had to answer questions every time about his citizenship status. Instead, he refused to comply. Even he could not have foreseen how many contentious Border Patrol interactions the ensuing years would bring.

Checkpoints

Since the Border Patrol was established in 1924, the agency has used interior checkpoints as a "second line of defense" against unauthorized entries into the country. The interior checkpoints are justified based on the Border Patrol's congressional authorization, which says that in the border zone agents can "board and search" all types of vehicles "for the purpose of patrolling the border to prevent the illegal entry of aliens into the United States."[2] In the *Martinez-Fuerte* case in 1976, the Supreme Court considered and approved the Border Patrol's use of interior checkpoints on highways and interstates within one hundred miles of borders and coastlines, as long as the location served an immigration policing purpose and did not overly interfere with other motorists.

The GAO conducted a 2017 review of the interior checkpoints, which found that the Border Patrol operated thirty-four permanent fixed checkpoints and 103 additional tactical checkpoint locations in the southern border zone. The Border Patrol does not operate any permanent interior checkpoints on the northern border with Canada, but does have many tactical checkpoint locations where they conduct periodic checks. These northern checkpoints were used much more frequently in recent years, expanding border enforcement into northern communities unaccustomed to the practice.

As the Border Patrol's budget expanded, the fixed checkpoint facilities in the southern border zone have become elaborate. They include permanent offices and holding facilities on the side of the road as well as multiple lanes of traffic with covered booths for the agents. The Border Patrol uses automated license plate readers tied to a Drug Enforcement Agency (DEA) database to run checks on every vehicle that enters the checkpoint. They also regularly deploy dogs to search for drugs and even radiation sensors to look for dirty bombs. In 2012, Raul Castro, the ninety-six-year-old former governor of Arizona, was forced to stand in the sun for thirty minutes on a 100°F day after his recent treatment for cancer set off a radiation sensor at a checkpoint on I-19, north of Nogales.[3]

In 1976, the Supreme Court understood the purpose of checkpoints to be narrowly focused on immigration violations and said, "Our holding today is limited to the type of stops described in this opinion." The

Martinez-Fuerte opinion is quite specific on what types of inspections the agents can do: "Neither the vehicle nor its occupants is searched, and visual inspection of the vehicle is limited to what can be seen without a search."[4] Drugs and other contraband are not mentioned in the ruling. Nevertheless, the Border Patrol uses the checkpoints for all kinds of inspections not explicitly authorized by the Supreme Court's decisions. The dogs, license plate readers, and radiation sensors are not primarily for immigration detection.

For example, Customs and Border Protection, the parent agency that includes the Border Patrol and the Customs Bureau, describes the purpose of the Falfurrias (Texas) checkpoint between McAllen and Houston, about ninety miles from the border itself, as primarily about terrorism prevention, while also mentioning drugs from the border. According to the CBP website, "The station's primary responsibility is to maintain traffic check operations to detect and apprehend terrorists and/or their weapons of mass effect as well [as] to prevent the passage of illegal aliens and/or contraband from the border area to major cities in the interior of the United States via U.S. Highway 281." Despite the focus on terrorism, the checkpoint has never caught a terrorist. Neither have any of the other interior checkpoints. Instead, while they do catch some immigration violations, the primary purpose of the interior checkpoints has become drug interdiction.

In the 1976 *Martinez-Fuerte* case, the government lawyers convinced the justices that the permanent checkpoints were "the most important of the traffic-checking operations."[5] However, the Border Patrol's own data in the decades since does not support that assertion. The 2017 GAO report showed that 9.4 percent of the Border Patrol's staffing time was spent at interior checkpoints but only produced 3.1 percent of apprehensions.[6] The data showed that patrols deep inside the one-hundred-mile zone were ineffective and instead showed that 85 percent of apprehensions occurred within twenty miles of the southern border. Fifty-eight percent of apprehensions occurred within one mile of the border. In 2013, nine of the Tucson sector's twenty-three checkpoints did not result in a single arrest of a "deportable subject" in the entire calendar year.[7]

The checkpoints did have a meaningful impact on drug seizures, but not necessarily from across the border. Sixty-eight percent of the Border Patrol's drug seizures occurred more than ten miles from the border, almost exclusively at the interior checkpoints.[8] Additionally, the size of the seizures and the citizenship of the person in possession of drugs varied dramatically based on the location. At the interior checkpoints, 40 percent of all seizures were from American citizens with less than one ounce of marijuana: citizens who had not traveled abroad, who were found with a small, recreational amount of a drug that is legal in many parts of the country. By contrast, seizures closer to the border at non-checkpoint locations were typically large amounts of smuggled drugs. Seventy-five percent of non-checkpoint seizures of marijuana were over fifty pounds. In the majority of these cases, there was no arrest at all because the smugglers simply dumped the load after being spotted. American citizens account for 83 percent of marijuana seizures at checkpoints. At all other locations, only 6 percent of marijuana seizures involve American citizens.[9]

"The Primary Purpose of the Action Was Detection and Seizure of Drugs"

Jesse Drewniak spent the last Sunday of August 2017 fly-fishing near the picturesque Profile Lake in central New Hampshire. The thirty-seven-year-old white man, with a full beard and brown and white baseball cap, was an avid outdoorsman who made upward of fifty trips per year from his home in Hudson, near the Massachusetts state line, up I-93 to the White Mountains. He would forage, hike, and swim in the

summer and even make several trips a year to ice fish on Lake Winni-
pesaukee in the winter.

After a full day soaking in the views of the forests around the
lake on that August day, Jesse and two friends packed up their gear
in the early evening and began the return trip to Hudson, which normally took just under two hours. However, fifteen minutes into their
journey, they encountered vehicles backed up on I-93 just outside of
Woodstock. A sign warned motorists of federal agents ahead. As they
approached the checkpoint, which was situated ninety miles south of
the border with Canada, another sign said IMMIGRATION CHECK-
POINT, HAVE YOUR LICENSE READY.

When they finally reached the temporary Border Patrol checkpoint, an agent holding a machine gun asked if they were U.S. citizens.
All three men were and responded, "Yes." They also provided their
driver's licenses as the sign suggested. Jesse figured he had nothing to
worry about. He had not been to Canada that day, or ever in his life.
He had only left the United States once before, on a short vacation to
the Bahamas when he was eight.

As Jesse and his friends answered questions about their citizenship,
Mark Qualter, a Border Patrol K-9 Agent, walked around the checkpoint with Marian, a drug-sniffing dog. As Marian reached Jesse's car,
she sat down, signaling to Qualter that there was contraband in the
vehicle. Qualter informed the first agent, who directed the vehicle to
secondary inspection. At the secondary inspection, Agent Qualter told
the three men to get out of the car, which they did. They left the doors
open. Agent Qualter then took Marian around and through the vehicle. She jumped in the trunk, climbed inside on the seats and sniffed
around, and circled the vehicle six or seven times. After fifteen minutes, Qualter finished the search but Marian did not locate any drugs.

At that point, Qualter got angry and began yelling at the men,
"Where's the fucking dope?" As he got right up in their faces, Jesse

finally admitted there was some in the center console. Qualter screamed again, telling him to retrieve it from the vehicle. Jesse climbed in the front seat and pulled out a plastic container with a small amount of hash oil he used occasionally when vaping.

Jesse's problems with the Border Patrol at an interior checkpoint, despite never leaving the United States, places him in good company. Rapper Lil Wayne's two tour buses were driving north on highway 281 from McAllen, Texas, toward San Antonio on December 18, 2009, when the Border Patrol discovered a pound and a half of marijuana at the Falfurrias checkpoint. Singer Willie Nelson was on his tour bus headed east on I-10 on the Friday after Thanksgiving, November 26, 2010, when he was stopped at the Sierra Blanca, Texas, checkpoint with six ounces of marijuana. Rapper Snoop Dogg was driving east on I-10 on January 7, 2012, headed to San Antonio to watch his son play football in the Eastbay Youth All-American Bowl. He had a medical marijuana license for migraines and blurred vision when the Border Patrol found two ounces of marijuana in his car. Singer Fiona Apple had four ounces of hashish when she was driving east on I-10 in her tour bus on her way to concerts in Austin and San Antonio on September 19, 2012. Al Reinert, the screenwriter of the film *Apollo 13*, had two marijuana buds in a vial in his shaving kit when was driving east on I-10 in 2013.[10]

The most serious celebrity arrests at Border Patrol interior check-points were of the rapper Nelly, who was driving east on I-10 in his tour bus on October 10, 2012, and two football players, Greg Robinson and Jaquan Bray, who were driving from Los Angeles to Louisiana on I-10 on February 19, 2020. On Nelly's tour bus, Border Patrol agents found a loaded .45 caliber handgun, thirty-six small bags of heroin, and ten pounds of marijuana. Nelly's bodyguard, Brian Keith Jones, took responsibility for the items. Nelly denied any knowledge of the drugs and berated his bodyguard on Twitter for taking these risks. Greg Robinson, the second overall pick in 2014 NFL draft, who played tackle for the Cleveland Browns, and Jaquan Bray, who played for the Indianapolis Colts, had 157 pounds of marijuana in their SUV.

From 2005 to 2011, at the Sierra Blanca checkpoint on I-10, where all these celebrities were arrested except Lil Wayne, there were 2,500 drug arrests per year, or 7 per day. Of those arrests, 80 percent were American citizens and 88 percent were for small amounts that were minor possession charges. Federal prosecutors in Texas have long opted not to prosecute small drug possession cases. Consequently, the Border Patrol would call up the local sheriff in Sierra Blanca and turn the cases over to them. Sierra Blanca, however, is not a major metropolis that can house and prosecute over 2,000 drug cases per year. The town has no stoplights and a population of only 764 people. Instead, Arvin West, the Hudspeth County Sheriff, would allow the individual to plead guilty to a drug paraphernalia charge, thus not admitting to actually possessing any drugs. The citation only included a fine of several hundred dollars. Willie Nelson, Snoop Dogg, Al Reinert, and thousands of other unsuspecting motorists paid up and were back on their way within a few hours.[11]

Back in New Hampshire, the Border Patrol knew that the U.S. Attorney's office, which handles federal prosecutions, would not prosecute drug possession charges for small amounts like those that Jesse Drewniak had. Rather than just not search for small amounts or ignore it if they found it, the Border Patrol again turned to the local police. Prior to the checkpoint operation on I-93, the Border Patrol emailed local New Hampshire officials in order to ensure officers were on hand for small amounts of drugs: "When we do the checkpoint we will probably have some personal use seizures. Our federal attorney will not prosecute that amount of marijuana. Do your guys or local police still ticket for this type of thing?"[12]

The Woodstock Police Department did ticket for this type of thing and stationed officers at the checkpoint with the Border Patrol.

As Jesse's case went to trial, the police department said the officers were not there simply to cite for small drug seizures. Instead, in the court filings they claimed the department stationed officers at the checkpoint in case someone "has a heart attack" or "if there is a child that needs to be delivered."[13] These contingencies did not occur, but the Woodstock police did make many drug possession arrests. In total, the Border Patrol's three-day operation in August 2017 resulted in thirty-three drug citations, all but two of which were for small amounts. The Border Patrol made twenty-five immigration-related apprehensions, mostly for people overstaying legal visas. These sorts of immigration violations are not under the purview of the Border Patrol, whose authorization is for stopping people who recently crossed the border clandestinely. None of the individuals apprehended for immigration violations at the Woodstock checkpoint had crossed the border from Canada.

Jesse's case, along with over a dozen of the other small drug seizures from the Woodstock checkpoint operation, was taken up by the American Civil Liberties Union of New Hampshire. Gilles Bissonnette, the ACLU lawyer handling the cases, thought the use of the dogs was absurd: "They claim [the dogs] are designed to detect human smuggling when really what they do in practice is detect for drugs. That's what this case is about at the end of the day. It is really the Border Patrol using the so-called immigration authority as a ruse to do drug enforcement, which we think violates the Fourth Amendment."[14]

Bissonnette and the ACLU successfully argued that the searches were illegal under New Hampshire law and the evidence was suppressed. The judge handling the case found that, "while the stated purpose of the checkpoints . . . was screening for immigration violations[,] the primary purpose of the action was detection and seizure of drugs."[15] The judge ruled that any evidence from Border Patrol checkpoints produced by drug-sniffing dogs was inadmissible in New Hampshire because it violated a state law prohibiting the random use of dogs.

The Border Patrol claims that the dogs are trained to locate people hiding in trunks. However, in Jesse's case in New Hampshire, the Border Patrol dog handler admitted that in his entire seventeen-year career, none of his dogs had ever found a concealed human in a car. Only drugs. Jenn Budd, a former senior Border Patrol agent, said that in her six years on duty she never saw a dog hit on a vehicle for humans. "They have nothing to do with immigration. A dog can't tell you if the person in the back seat is legally here or not. They can't tell you that, so I don't understand why we use them."[16]

In August 2020, the ACLU and Jesse decided to sue to the Border Patrol and the agents involved for violating his Fourth Amendment rights. The new filing emphasized that the 1976 *Martinez-Fuerte* ruling did not authorize unlimited interior Border Patrol checkpoints. Instead, it authorized checkpoints when specific conditions were met, which required that the Border Patrol demonstrate that the route was used by people who had crossed the border and were headed to the interior. Additionally, the Border Patrol needed to show that the efficacy for immigration checks outweighed the violation of Fourth Amendment rights. Bissonnette explained, "They need to be able to prove efficacy here and they need to prove they are actually stopping people crossing the border to get into the interior of the country. I just don't think they'll be able to prove that."

Refusing to Comply

Terry Bressi, the University of Arizona astronomer, pulled into the Border Patrol's interior checkpoint on SR 86 at 5:12 p.m. on Monday April 10, 2017, on his way home to Tucson from the Kitt Peak Observatory. It was the 383rd time Terry had been stopped at the checkpoint.

After his 2001 experience with the tribal police, Terry decided that he had to record every interaction at the checkpoint. He stopped driving the university vehicle and added cameras to his own truck. By 2017, he had cameras in place on all four sides, recording every trip through the SR 86 checkpoint. He promptly posts the videos online.[17]

On that Monday evening, Terry's silver pickup truck settled into the queue behind a man riding a Harley with a black bandana and red and black plaid shirt. As they proceeded toward the checkpoint, Terry filled the time with a commentary about the relationship between the Border Patrol and the local Pima County Sheriff's Office. Just as they enlisted the Woodstock Police Department for the checkpoint in New Hampshire, the Border Patrol also regularly worked with the Pima County sheriff in Arizona. However, in Arizona, the relationship was more formal and used a national Department of Homeland Security funding program called Operation Stonegarden to pay the salaries of the deputies while they were stationed at the checkpoint.[18] Funding from the program can be used for overtime, travel, per diem, and vehicle rentals but only to supplement, not replace, the local police budget. From 2008 to 2017, $541.5 million was awarded to local police in twenty-two states and territories through the program.[19] The 2019 fiscal year allocation was $90 million.

In the April 10, 2017 video, Terry explained that Stonegarden was just another example of how the Border Patrol expanded the purpose of the checkpoints beyond simply immigration into general law enforcement stops, which they were not supposed to do. Terry had no way of knowing that his point was about to be proved.

As Terry nears the checkpoint, orange barriers come into view along with several Border Patrol vehicles parked on either side of the road. The Harley rider pulls to the front of the queue, awkwardly maneuvering his bike over the speed bumps the Border Patrol has installed on the highway. Terry points out a Pima County Sheriff's deputy

vehicle parked among the Border Patrol vehicles, indicating a local police officer is working at the checkpoint that day. Having been through
the checkpoint so many times, he knows many of the agents and they
know him. The *Martinez-Fuerte* ruling said, "Motorists whom the officers recognize as local inhabitants, however, are waved through the
checkpoint without inquiry," but Terry's experiences showed that was
not always the case.

The biker seems to be having a problem with the agent, and he
is gesticulating wildly as he explains what brought him to that place.
Terry notes that it is Agent Lopez conducting the interrogation. Lopez
stands in the center of the road under a small shelter with a corrugated
metal roof. After about fifteen seconds, Agent Lopez is apparently not
satisfied with the biker's answers and waves him into secondary inspection on the side of the road. Lopez, who would have recognized Terry
and waved him through, follows the biker over to secondary.

Terry waits for a new, unfamiliar agent to cross the road and staff
the checkpoint. Terry pulls up to the stop sign but does not roll down
the window. The new agent, young and trim in his green uniform with
sunglasses and slicked-back hair, nods his head and leans in toward the
window. He says, "U.S. Border and Immigration checkpoint, how you
doing?"

The agent waits for an answer, but Terry does not say anything.
The *Martinez-Fuerte* decision only said that the Border Patrol could
set up the checkpoint and ask questions about citizenship. It did not
say that the individual has to answer them. The Fifth Amendment of
the Constitution protects the right to remain silent in interactions with
law enforcement. For Terry, this strategy has produced mixed results.
It is up to the agent to decide if they have articulable facts of reasonable suspicion to send Terry to secondary inspection or if he is free to
go. A source in the Border Patrol sent Terry a 2012 policy memo that
went to agents at the checkpoint that said, "A subject's 'bad attitude' or

refusal to answer questions, without more, does not constitute 'reasonable suspicion' and does not justify 'detention.'" However, just as Terry is irritated about the fact that he has to stop, the Border Patrol agents are often irritated that Terry challenges their authority by refusing to roll down his window or answer questions. Sometimes the agents just wave him on. However, on other occasions, they hold him for minutes or even hours while they decide what to do.

The young Border Patrol agent appears uncomfortable as he sways back and forth while glancing in Terry's back seat. The agent looks down as he says, "Hey, mind pulling over there for a second?" The agent finds a little resolve and points toward secondary inspection. "Pull over there for a second."

Terry responds, "I do mind."

The agent looks surprised and puts his hand to his ear as he leans closer to the car and says, "Excuse me?"

Terry looks at the agent's nametag and says, "I do mind, Agent Frye."

Although Agent Frye has literally just asked if Terry minded or not, he says, "I didn't ask if you mind. Can you pull there for a second?" He keeps his arm pointed toward secondary inspection. "U.S. Border and Immigration checkpoint. Are you a United States citizen? Can you pull over there please?" The agent's face is close to Terry's camera. There are old acne scars on his cheeks. "Mind pulling over there, you are blocking traffic here." Frye points to cars lined up behind Terry at the checkpoint.

Terry is amused. He replies, "You're the one blocking traffic. Let me know when I am free to go, Agent Frye."

Frye still has his hand pointed toward secondary as he says, "You are free to go when you answer my questions. It's an immigration checkpoint and I am seeing if you are a United States citizen."

Terry asks, "What law requires me to answer your questions, Agent Frye?"

Frye grimaces, looks down, and then again points to secondary. "Can you please pull over there?"

Terry is well known at the checkpoint. Typically, at this point a supervisor who recognizes him would give the junior agent a signal to cut him loose. Anticipating this, Terry turns his camera toward the larger shelter on the side of the road, but there is no supervisor there. There is only a Pima County Sheriff's deputy in a brown uniform, with his hands on his hips.

Agent Frye steps to the front of Terry's truck and calls over to the deputy, "Where did the supervisor go?" Agent Frye nervously shifts his weight back and forth and sighs as he waits for an answer. Instead of finding the supervisor, the middle-aged deputy, slightly rotund and bald with a generous mustache, makes his way over to join Agent Frye.

The deputy arrives at the driver's side window with a bemused grin. The young Border Patrol agent, seemingly relieved not to be in charge, steps back and puts his hands in his pockets. Terry does not give the deputy a chance to ask any questions. Instead, he asks the deputy, whose name is Ryan Roher, if he is working with the Border Patrol on a Stonegarden grant, which pays him overtime to be stationed at the checkpoint.

Roher says, "Yes, I am." Roher then confers with Agent Frye and then says to Terry, "OK, I need you to pull into secondary or answer his questions."

Terry replies, "Why's that? Who is detaining me right now?"

Roher says, "I am."

Terry chuckles and says, "So you are operating at this federal Border Patrol immigration checkpoint?" Roher steps in closer, looks back and forth, and sighs. Agent Frye steps farther back. Terry asks, "You have jurisdiction to enforce federal immigration laws?"

Roher says, "I'm not going to argue with you. You understand you are blocking the roadway, correct?"

Terry points toward to Border Patrol Agent Frye and says, "He's blocking the roadway. I'm ready to go."

Roher grimaces and says, "OK, sir, I'll let you go."

Terry says "Thank you" and starts to pull away.

Behind him, Deputy Roher trots across the road and jumps into his patrol car. Terry slowly leaves the immediate checkpoint area and then pulls over to the side of the road as Roher's patrol car pulls in behind him. Trucks passing on the highway slow down to get a look at what is going on. Roher parks and then comes to Terry's window and tells Terry to step out of the car.

Terry asks, "Why?"

Roher gets angry and yells, "Sir, step out of the car!" Terry does.

Roher asks for his driver's license. Terry is indignant and keeps asking questions. Roher finally says, "Driver's license, sir, or you're going to end up in handcuffs and go to jail." Terry hands him the license. By that point, several of the Border Patrol trucks have pulled in behind Roher's patrol car and the agents are observing the interaction. Roher asks Terry a series of questions and Terry does not respond to any of them. Roher then says, "OK, I'm going to ask you to turn around and put your hands behind your back please." Terry complies as Roher puts on handcuffs and asks Terry to sit on the hood of the car. Terry instead sits on the ground as a cloud of dust kicks up around him.

As Roher calls in the arrest to dispatch, Terry starts to talk to the Border Patrol agents. He stands up to have the conversation, and Border Patrol Agent Lopez grabs him by the arms and tries to get him to sit again. Eventually Lopez relents as Terry explains that Deputy

Roher asked him to sit on the hood in the first place. Terry tells the Border Patrol agents that was assault.

Roher returns and says, "So, Mr. Bressi. The reason you are in handcuffs right now is you were blocking the checkpoint. OK?" Roher has a habit of smirking and sticking his neck out each time he says "OK?" He continues, "It is a public road. OK? I gave you a lawful order."

Terry interjects, "It is a federal immigration checkpoint and I was being detained by federal officers for federal immigration purposes. Not Pima County purposes."

They banter back and forth before Roher finally sticks his neck out and says, "This is outstanding. I've never met you before." Roher continues, "So right now, you are under arrest. You're going to go to jail. OK? You're blocking a roadway and you cannot do that. The Border Patrol agents are friendly. You come through here every day."

Roher starts to smile.

"I know you do. I've seen your videos. And they're awesome, by the way. But the bottom line is you can't block the roadway."

Terry says, "Thanks for admitting you've seen my videos."

Roher says, "Absolutely. It is impressive. I have no problem with what you do. But the bottom line is you can't block the roadway."

"You Can Go Out and Stop as Many Cars as you Want"

Terry's arrest by Deputy Roher at the Border Patrol checkpoint on SR 86 raises the issue of why local police are even present at what is supposed to be a federal checkpoint limited to immigration enforcement. Since 2005, Terry has been stopped at the Border Patrol's interior checkpoint on SR 86 a total of 574 times. In none of those 574 stops has the Border Patrol charged him with anything. The arrest in April 2017 by Deputy Roher was the fourth time Terry was cited by a local police officer at the checkpoint, but the first time he was hand-cuffed for a criminal charge. The previous three were civil traffic in-fractions that were dropped by the courts.

In the process of discovery for the April 2017 arrest, Deputy Roher submitted to a deposition. It did not go well for him. Roher stated that he loved being stationed at the checkpoints because he was paid overtime for the work and he could do his favorite thing: give citations to motorists. The lawyer asked if the Border Patrol ever gave him any direction about what he was supposed to cite for, since it was an immi-gration checkpoint, after all.

Roher said no. "I don't know that I've ever received any specific training or anything like that." Instead, he said, "So, the way I have understood it is our goal is to go out and do as much, do as many traffic stops as possible. Do enforcement as needed. Do—go find drugs, go find people, go find money." He continued, "Now, because I'm a traffic deputy and I enjoy stopping cars and doing enforcement, Stonegarden is kind of natural for me. So, if somebody says to me 'Hey, you can go out and stop as many cars as you want,' woo-hoo!"

Later in the deposition, Roher bragged, "I can stop as many cars as I want. And so part of Stonegarden for me is just the, the part of the joy of being able to do that." He said his personal record was thirty citations in a single shift at the immigration checkpoint.

After Roher's deposition, Pima County dropped the charges against Terry for blocking the roadway. Additionally, but not directly related to Terry's case, the Pima County Board of Supervisors decided in 2020 to withdraw from Operation Stonegarden and stop taking funding to do immigration enforcement.[20] Terry filed a civil rights complaint against Deputy Roher, Agent Frye, the Border Patrol agent who initially detained him at the checkpoint, and Agent Lopez, who manhandled him while he was in handcuffs on the side of the road. The case is ongoing.

What connects Terry's case with Jesse Drewniak's, the New Hampshire litigation about drug-sniffing dogs, is the question of whether the checkpoints continue to serve a legitimate immigration policing purpose. In *Martinez-Fuerte*, the Supreme Court decided that the specific checkpoints they considered did. However, Border Patrol interior checkpoints have evolved into something else entirely, accounting for only a small fraction of immigration apprehensions but the majority of drug busts for the agency.

In 2000, the Supreme Court ruled in *City of Indianapolis v. Edmond* that general checkpoints "whose primary purpose is to detect evidence of ordinary criminal wrongdoing" are not allowed. Instead, the court found that checkpoints need a specific stated purpose that limited them to tasks like immigration policing or drunk driving prevention.

Although the Border Patrol checkpoints are officially about immigration, in practice they seem to operate as exactly the type of general law enforcement checks that were banned by the Supreme Court in 2000. The internal Border Patrol checkpoints are used for drug interdiction, DEA license plate checks, radiation searches for dirty bombs, and by local police officers like Deputy Roher who want to give as many citations as possible for traffic infractions. This is not what Lewis Powell and the Supreme Court authorized in the 1976 *Martinez-Fuerte* case.

There have been congressional efforts to move the checkpoints closer to the border. Vermont senator Patrick Leahy was stopped at an interior Border Patrol checkpoint in 2008 and in the years since has attempted to pass legislation to restrict checkpoints and roving patrols to within twenty-five miles of the border. The smaller border zone was part of the comprehensive immigration reform bill that passed the Senate in 2013 with bipartisan support, but was never brought to a vote in the House of Representatives. Leahy continued to introduce bills to reduce the size of the one-hundred-mile zone every year since.[21] Only time will tell if the Congress or the Supreme Court will decide to re-visit the Border Patrol's checkpoints and their continued hollowing out of the Fourth Amendment protections against unreasonable searches and seizures.

In many ways, however, Patrick Leahy, Terry Bressi, and Jesse Drewniak were lucky. They experienced the authority of the Border Patrol to operate deep inside the United States, but they did so as white, male, American citizens. For millions of Brown or Black Americans, their experiences with the Border Patrol can be far worse.

17.

Somebody Speaking Spanish

Ana Suda and Martha "Mimi" Hernandez were chatting as they waited in line at the Town Pump convenience store in Havre, Montana, in the late evening of May 16, 2018. Both women were certified nursing assistants at the Northern Montana Care Center. They would often go to the gym together in the evening after their children went to bed and would regularly stop afterward at the store to pick up some groceries.[1]

Havre, a small farming town thirty miles from the Canadian border, has a population of fewer than 10,000 people, 81 percent of whom are white. Native Americans make up the second largest group, with 13 percent. The Latino/a population is only 4 percent, or about 400 people.[2] Havre was founded in the 1890s as a stop on the Great Northern Railroad that linked Minneapolis with Seattle. The town has a network of underground businesses that were dug over one hundred years ago as a refuge from the biting winter winds. The underground mall, which is marked at street level by purple tiled skylights, once held a bar, a

Chinese laundry, and a bordello, but is now a tourist attraction. Despite its small size, Havre is the hometown of two former governors of Montana, Stan Stevens (1989–1993) and Brian Schweitzer (2005–2013), as well as Montana's Democratic senator, Jon Tester (2007–present). Jeff Ament, the bass player in the rock band Pearl Jam, is also from Havre.

Ana and Mimi were speaking to each other in Spanish when Border Patrol agent Paul O'Neill walked into the store. O'Neill, with a thick brown mustache and crisp green uniform, was immediately suspicious because he thought no one spoke Spanish in Havre. He got a water from the cooler and then stood in line behind the two women in order to eavesdrop on them.

Havre is a small town where everyone knows each other, and people often greet each other in stores. Mimi turned to O'Neill and said, in English, "Hi, how's it going?"

Agent O'Neill said, "Hi." Then he commented on how strong her accent was and asked, "Where are you from?"

Ana and Mimi were surprised. They said, "We're from Havre."

Both women were American citizens born in the United States. They had moved to Havre in the previous decade, Ana in 2014 for her husband's job and Mimi in 2010 because she fell in love with the area after a visit. As longtime Havre residents, they did not recognize O'Neill and were actually wondering where he was from. The women continued their conversation in Spanish.

Agent O'Neill flashed a knowing smile and then said, "Yeah, okay, but where were you guys born?"

The women were annoyed at this point. "Seriously?" they asked.

Agent O'Neill noted their confrontational tone and said, "I'm very serious, actually."

Ana told him she was born in Texas; Mimi, California. O'Neill was not convinced, particularly because he could not believe that Mimi would speak accented English if she was born in California. He asked for their IDs and both women gave him valid Montana driver's licenses.

Agent O'Neill knew that driver's licenses were not citizenship documents and continued to harbor doubts that Ana and Mimi were in the country legally. He decided to detain them and took them out to the parking lot beside his white and green Border Patrol truck to continue his investigation. He also called for backup, and several other agents quickly arrived, including a supervisory agent. Other shoppers at the Town Pump gawked at the spectacle of the cluster of Border Patrol trucks and the two detained women in the normally quiet town.

Ana and Mimi decided to record the interaction. On camera, they asked O'Neill why he targeted them.

He responded matter-of-factly, "Ma'am, the reason I asked for your ID is because I came in here and saw that you guys are speaking Spanish, which is very unheard-of up here." The women decided not to remind the agent that *Montana* itself is a Spanish word.

The women turned to the supervisor and asked if they would have been detained if they were speaking French.

The supervisor shook his head. "No, we don't do that."

After being held for forty minutes, they were released. At no point during the detention did Ana mention that the reason she moved to Havre was because her husband was one of their colleagues who worked for Customs and Border Protection as a field operations agent at the port of entry on the Canadian border.

In 2019, the ACLU filed a lawsuit on behalf of the women, asking for damages for the violation of their Fourth and Fifth Amendment rights. The residents of Havre, however, blamed the women.[3] They were yelled at and harassed in public and Ana was even pushed by a man who confronted her. Their children were called racial slurs in school. Both women were forced to move away to avoid the harassment. Ana went back to El Paso, even while her husband continued to work as a CBP agent in Havre, and Mimi moved to Great Falls, Montana.

As the case made its way through the courts, the ACLU obtained a series of damaging documents about Agent O'Neill specifically and the conduct of the Border Patrol in Havre generally. As part of the investigation of the incident, the supervisory Border Patrol agent who arrived as backup for Agent O'Neill at the Town Pump store partici-pated in an interview with Border Patrol internal affairs officials.[4] The supervisor thought that Agent O'Neill's actions were routine and well within the norm for agents in Havre. The supervisor even recounted a story about himself when he was at the local mall in Havre with his family on his day off. He was eating at a restaurant when he looked up and saw "two Mexicans" at a nearby store. He debated about whether he should report it to his on-duty colleagues and after a few moments of observation decided to make the call. As he reached for his phone, he realized he was too late. He noticed another off-duty Border Patrol agent with his cell phone to his ear, following the two people about twenty feet behind them. He chuckled, "Really, it's like that if there is somebody speaking Spanish down here, it's like all of the sudden you've got five agents swarming in."

The supervisor went on to explain, "It is a small place and we have a lot of agents here. And nobody really has much to do." The supervisor said he was surprised when he found out that Ana was from El Paso. He felt like she should understand that racial profiling is the norm for non-white people in the border zone. He shrugged and laughed as he said, "What are you complaining about? You're from El Paso, you do this every day."

Racial Profiling in the Border Zone

The Border Patrol denies that they use racial profiling as a normal prac-tice in the border zone. They collect data only on arrests, not on all stops or interactions, so they do not have data to prove their claim. However, their training documents give agents an overview of the 1970s Border Patrol cases and expressly allow for racial profiling. The 1981 version of the training materials summarized the articulable facts of reasonable suspicion from the *Brignoni-Ponce* case but expanded the wording beyond the "Mexican appearance" in the ruling. It lists "characteristic appearance of persons who are from foreign countries" as an example of an articulable fact.[5] The 1999 Laws of Search Manual says agents can use "appearance of the occupants, including whether their mode of dress and/or haircut appear foreign." By 2012, the explicit references to race were removed from the training manuals, but they still said that appearance could be a fact of reasonable suspicion, including if someone looked "dirty."[6]

Complaints by individuals targeted by the Border Patrol and studies by outside groups have shown that racial profiling is a common practice both in roving patrols like the one that targeted Ana and Mimi and at the interior checkpoints. In an analysis of Border Patrol arrests in Ohio in 2010 and 2011, 85 percent were of Latino/a descent even though they make up only 3 percent of the state population. Although ostensibly the patrols in the northern border region should be targeting entries from Canada, the country across the border, less than one quarter of 1 percent of those stopped by agents were Canadian.[7]

Geoffrey Alan Boyce and the ACLU of Michigan found a similar pattern when they analyzed the Border Patrol's apprehension and arrest records in Michigan. Although the Border Patrol's authorization is to stop clandestine entries into the United States, only 1.3 percent of people apprehended in Michigan had crossed from Canada. The majority were longtime residents stopped by the local or state police for a traffic infraction. The Border Patrol was then called when the officer suspected the individual was in the country without authorization. The average person had resided in Michigan 7.36 years at the time of their apprehension.[8]

The Michigan analysis also demonstrated how easy it was for agents to manufacture reasonable suspicion under the guidelines the Supreme

Court established in *Brignoni-Ponce*. No matter what an individual did when they encountered a Border Patrol agent, it was perceived as suspicious. If they drove too fast or drove too slow, that could result in suspicion. If they stared at the agent, that was suspicious in some cases, but in others it was suspicious if they averted their gaze. The records also confirmed that the agents were relying on racial characteristics in their decisions to make stops. In essence, the *Brignoni-Ponce* guidelines for reasonable suspicion were so broad that the agents could stop any vehicle they wanted.[9]

In Arivaca, Arizona, local residents were frustrated with the Border Patrol's constant interference with their daily lives. Although the *Martinez-Fuerte* decision stated that "Motorists whom the officers recognize as local inhabitants, however, are waved through the checkpoint without inquiry," the residents of Arivaca have found this is not the case.[10] The Border Patrol tries to prevent agents from establishing roots in the local community because they believe it makes them susceptible to corruption and smuggling. Instead, agents are typically rotated through different postings every few months, before they can become familiar with the local population. The residents of Arivaca formed an organization called People Helping People, initially to provide humanitarian aid, but later they began to monitor the Border Patrol's activities in town and on the highways nearby.

Arivaca is a tiny town with a population of only 700, about eleven miles north of the U.S.–Mexico border. It has a post office, a restaurant, and a small grocery store along with a few blocks of irregularly spaced homes. There is only one road that passes through town, the two-lane Arivaca Sasabe Road. To the east, it is a thirty-minute drive to Interstate 19, which connects Tucson and Nogales. To the west, the road winds through the Buenos Aires National Wildlife Refuge for twelve miles before it hits Route 286, the north-south road that connects the border town of Sasabe with the western suburbs of Tucson. No matter which way they go, residents of Arivaca have to pass through at least one Border Patrol checkpoint to drive to any other part of Arizona.

Rather than refusing to comply with the Border Patrol's requests like Terry Bressi, the University of Arizona astronomer, People Helping People instead started to simply show up at the checkpoints and observe what was happening there.[11] They would bring folding chairs, cameras, and notebooks to monitor the activities of the agents. From their perspective, it was a public road so they were free to sit on the shoulder for as long as they wanted.

The Border Patrol did not see it that way. On the first day of observation, the Border Patrol threatened to arrest the monitors and called the local police. The Border Patrol tried to prevent them from observing at all and then expanded the size of the checkpoint so the monitors were forced to sit far from where the stops occurred. The agents parked vehicles in front of them to block their view and left the engines running for hours with the exhaust pointed at the observers so they had to breathe in the noxious fumes. The Arivaca residents filed a lawsuit against the Border Patrol on First Amendment grounds, which is ongoing.[12]

In 2014, People Helping People released a report on their observations of the Amado checkpoint, to the east of Arivaca toward I-19. Between February 26 and April 28, 2014, People Helping People volunteers counted 2,379 vehicles that were forced to stop by the Border Patrol at the checkpoint. They found that cars with only Latino/a occupants were twenty-six times more likely to be asked to show ID and twenty times more likely to be referred to secondary inspection compared to vehicles with white occupants. The report also raised serious questions about the efficacy of the Amado checkpoint. During the entire one hundred hours of observation, the Border Patrol did not make a single immigration apprehension or drug seizure.[13]

Racial Slurs

The discovery process for Ana and Mimi's lawsuit in Montana revealed numerous racist text messages from Border Patrol agent O'Neill, who detained them for speaking Spanish in the convenience store. In one thread, a friend texted Agent O'Neill, "Haha hey man what's going on?" O'Neill texted back, "Busy working to the max.. thank God for Trump the national constipation has been relieved were back to doing some good numbers.. quit harassing little beaner girls.. 😂 😂 😂." In another, a friend wrote, "Yeah what is he doing if he isn't with you guys?" O'Neill wrote back, "Idk. Talking about killing tonks with a machine gun instead of the wall to some dude standing behind me." The friend replied, "That sounds like him."[14]

The violent and racially charged culture of the Border Patrol is not limited to a few bad actors like Agent O'Neill. Instead, evidence suggests that it is pervasive across the agency, from the lowest field agents to the highest echelons of leadership.

Jenn Budd was a Border Patrol agent from 1995 to 2001 and witnessed the racism firsthand. Budd, with reddish blonde hair and blue eyes, graduated from Auburn University with a BA in criminal law but without a clear plan for what she wanted to do. She thought about law school, but then heard from a friend that the Border Patrol was hiring. Growing up in Alabama, she had no idea what the Border Patrol did, but when the recruiter explained that agents were tasked with stopping criminals from entering the United States, she signed up. She was one of four women in her class at the Border Patrol Academy at the Federal Law Enforcement Training Center in Glynco, Georgia.

During Budd's training at the academy, a Latino language instructor explained the different terms agents use for migrants. He told her that in Texas, they call them *wets*, a shortened version of *wetback* that was commonly used by the Border Patrol for decades. However, in

California, they do not use *wets* because migrants have not crossed the Rio Grande. Instead, they use *tonks*.

Budd asked what it meant.

"For the outside, to the press, you say it means 'Temporarily Out of Native Country,'" the instructor told her.

"Okay," Budd said, "but what does it really mean?"

The instructor responded, "It's the sound our flashlight makes when we hit them on the head. *Tonk*."

Budd explained to me that using terms like *tonk* was just part of the culture at the agency. She said, "If you have a problem saying the word *tonk*, you can't be a Border Patrol agent." She continued, "I knew it was a racist term. . . . Yet, at the same time, it was also taught to me and reinforced. Those who don't use the *tonk* word are looked down upon and seen as threats."

In 2018, Hector Regalado, a retired senior Border Patrol agent, started a new business selling Border Patrol–themed T-shirts. Prior to his retirement, Regalado was a special operations supervisor, which is the third highest-ranking position at a Border Patrol station. In his new career as a T-shirt maker, Regalado's marketing materials made light of the common racial slurs used by Border Patrol agents. One shirt had a large flashlight and the word TONK below it. The description of the shirt explained: "Tonk! Yeah you know the sound . . . no need to explain it. You either know it or you don't!"[15]

Tonk is only one of many racist terms that remain common in the Border Patrol. Agents still frequently use *wetback* and other variations including *wets, mojados* (Spanish for wets), and *POW,* short for *Plain Old Wet*.[16] Agents also use the term *floaters* to refer to people who die when crossing the Rio Grande. When agents apprehend people alive, they will often refer to them as *bodies* rather than people. As in, "I've got three bodies. Send a van to pick them up."[17]

In 2019, a secret Border Patrol Facebook group called "I'm 10-15," which is the code for having people in custody, was revealed by journalists. It had almost 10,000 members, including Carla Provost, the national head of the Border Patrol at the time. Provost was not a passive member of the group; she had even posted in it.[18] Rodney Scott, the Border Patrol chief from 2019 to 2021, was also a member, as was Agent O'Neill who detained Ana and Mimi at the convenience store. "I'm 10-15" was rife with racist and sexist jokes as well as violent imagery that dehumanized migrants. One posting included an image of Elmo saying "Oh, well. If he dies, he dies" in response to the death of a sixteen-year-old Guatemalan boy at a Border Patrol station in Weslaco, Texas. Another included a faked image of Donald Trump forcing Representative Alexandria Ocasio-Cortez to engage in a sex act. A third post included the picture of the face-down bodies of Óscar Alberto Martínez Ramírez and his two-year-old daughter Valeria, who died attempting to cross the Rio Grande in June 2019. The agent who posted the photo expressed no sympathy for the deaths. Instead, he surmised that it was a fake photo because he had never seen "floaters" whose bodies were so clean. After the group was revealed, the Border Patrol investigated 136 people, suspended three dozen, and fired four agents. A 2021 congressional report criticized the agency for the light punishments most agents received.[19]

Attempts to Ban Racial Profiling

There is a broad public consensus in the United States that law enforcement officials should not use racial profiling in their work. A 2020 Monmouth study found that 76 percent of Americans thought that racial discrimination was a big problem in the country, and a 2014 Reason-Rupe survey found that 70 percent of Americans disapprove of police using race as a factor in making traffic stops. A 2020 Kaiser

Family Foundation survey found that 41 percent of Black Americans, 8 percent of Latino/a Americans, and only 3 percent of white Americans reported having been treated unfairly by police due to their race.[20]

Most Americans probably assume that racial profiling is already against the law and that the question revolves around whether police or Border Patrol agents should informally use race in making decisions. Unfortunately, that assumption is wrong. Since the 1990s, a series of lawmakers have attempted, and failed, to pass legislation banning racial profiling by police. Consequently, racial profiling is not officially sanctioned for local and state police officers, but it is not banned either.

The effort to ban racial profiling was led by Democrats in Congress, including late Michigan representative John Conyers and former Wisconsin senator Russ Feingold. Feingold first proposed the law in the Senate in June 2001 along with his cosponsors, Hillary Rodham Clinton (D-NY) and Jon Corzine (D-NJ). The bill never passed, but Feingold submitted it for consideration in every successive term of Congress until he lost his seat in 2011. Senator Ben Cardin of Maryland took up the mantle and has continued to work toward the legislation in the years since.

As the congressional effort to ban racial profiling stalled, in 2014 Attorney General Eric Holder, the first Black man to serve as the top law enforcement official in the United States, directed the Department of Justice to review federal guidelines for the use of race, ethnicity, gender, national origin, religion, sexual orientation, or gender identity in policing. The review resulted in new guidance that "reaffirms the Federal government's deep commitment to ensuring its law enforcement agencies conduct their activities in an unbiased manner." Holder said at the time that racial profiling was "simply not good law enforcement."[21]

The 2014 guidelines ban racial profiling as a general law enforcement technique but allow the consideration of race in a particular case. There is a difference between a police officer being told that a six-foot white man with a red hat stole a motorcycle, and generally operating under the assumption that all white men are suspicious and are more likely to steal motorcycles. In the first instance, the appearance of the individual is important for identifying the specific person who is being sought. In the second, millions of people who have not committed a crime will be stopped, inconvenienced, and potentially found with some other violation when they should have the right to privacy.

The new guidance ensured that most federal officers could not engage in racial profiling, but the guidelines do not affect local or state police officers. Additionally, the ban on racial profiling does not apply to the Border Patrol.[22] The Obama administration's guidelines said, buried in a footnote, "In addition, this guidance does not apply to interdiction activities in the vicinity of the border, or to protective, inspection, or screening activities." Consequently, the Border Patrol is still free to use racial profiling in order to decide whom to stop and interrogate in the border zone. At the time, a DHS official told *The New York Times*, "We can't do our job without taking ethnicity into account. We are very dependent on that."[23]

Status Quo

There is little doubt that Ana and Mimi, the two women who were detained in Montana for speaking Spanish, were subjected to the type of racial profiling that Justice William Brennan warned about in his dissent in the 1976 *Martinez-Fuerte* case. Brennan had concluded that "today's decision would clearly permit detentions to be based solely on Mexican ancestry." In both the *Brignoni-Ponce* and *Martinez-Fuerte* decisions, the Supreme Court allowed the Border Patrol to use racial characteristics when deciding whom to stop and ask questions about their citizenship status. In 1975, *Brignoni-Ponce* listed a series of factors agents could consider when making a roving patrol stop, including "the characteristics of the area in which they encounter a vehicle." It goes on to say, "The Government also points out that trained officers can recognize the characteristic appearance of persons who live in Mexico, relying on such factors as the mode of dress and haircut." In 1976, *Martinez-Fuerte* confirmed that agents could also use the race of individuals at interior checkpoints in the border zone. Justice Lewis Powell's opinion stated, "We further believe it is constitutional to refer motorists selectively to the secondary inspection area at the San Clemente Checkpoint on the basis of criteria that would not sustain a roving-patrol stop. Thus, even if it be assumed that such referrals are made largely on the basis of apparent Mexican ancestry, we perceive no constitutional violation."

The Supreme Court's opinions in *Brignoni-Ponce* and *Martinez-Fuerte* were written over forty years ago, in a different era. The court has twice reconsidered the stop authority of the Border Patrol that it created under *Brignoni-Ponce* that relies on the totality of the circumstances and specific articulable facts from the agents on why they made the stop. In both cases, *United States v. Cortez* (1981) and *United States v. Arvizu* (2002), the justices reaffirmed the 1975 *Brignoni-Ponce* decision. However, neither of those cases considered the racial profiling aspect specifically. In 2000, the Ninth Circuit Court of Appeals did make a decision in *United States v. Montero-Camargo* that carefully considered the impact of racial profiling on border policing. The decision is critical of the practice, but in a legal sense comes to a similar conclusion as the Supreme Court in *Brignoni-Ponce*. The court has never revisited its checkpoint decision in *Martinez-Fuerte*, but it did rule in 2000 that general law enforcement checkpoints were not allowed in *City of Indianapolis v. Edmond*.

In the end, this means that the rules are the same for Border Patrol agents today as they were in in the 1970s. Despite the widespread criticism of unequal racial impacts of policing in the United States, the

Border Patrol continues to be able to use racial profiling in every inter-action they have in the border zone. That profiling is not hypothetical or implied, but explicitly approved by the United States Supreme Court and in the Department of Justice's 2014 guidance that exempts the Border Patrol and other immigration officials from the ban on such profiling. On a roving patrol, agents cannot use the race of the individ-ual as the only factor to justify a stop, but they can consider race along with at least one other factor. Consequently, the detention of Ana and Mimi did not meet that standard. The Department of Homeland Security settled their case in November 2020 and paid them undis-closed damages. Alex Rate, the women's lawyer, concluded, "I would be shocked if what we found here in our case was not present in every Border Patrol sector in the country."[24] If the agent had used additional factors, it could have been a legal stop. At the interior checkpoints, the agents can continue to use race as the only factor when deciding to send someone to secondary inspection for brief questioning, as the check-point monitoring in Arivaca demonstrated was the norm.

Despite the violent actions of agents, the unauthorized use of in-terior checkpoints for general policing, and the use of racial profiling in interactions with the public, the United States Congress has not at-tempted to reform the Border Patrol. Instead, their budget continues to increase. Customs and Border Protection is the largest law enforcement agency in the United States, with access to many new and sophisticated surveillance technologies. As a result, CBP and the Border Patrol have been called upon in an ever-growing series of situations that take the agents further and further away from their original mandate. Rather than a small immigration police force operating in the remote border zone, the leadership of the Border Patrol envisions the agency as a na-tional police force.

18.

The Everywhere Border

THE AIRCRAFT WITH CALL NUMBER CBP 104 STARTED DOWN the runway of Grand Forks Air Force Base in North Dakota at 9:10 a.m. CDT on Friday, May 29, 2020. It was 55°F, an unseasonably cool morning for late May, with cloudy skies and a fifteen-mile-per-hour wind blowing in from Canada to the north. The aircraft was painted gray, with a blue vertical band in the middle. The thin, sleek design, and the unusual feature of a single propeller at the rear, made it look almost like a submarine as it took off. The Predator drone, one of ten operated by Customs and Border Protection, ascended to 20,000 feet, but then it headed southeast, away from the Canadian border where it typically carried out its surveillance.

Rebranded as a front line against terrorist infiltration after 9/11, the Border Patrol reaped the reward in billions of dollars of appropriations. In addition to more than doubling the number of Border Patrol agents, CBP also invested in a wide range of surveillance equipment that would have previously been off-limits due to cost and the sense that sophisticated military equipment was unnecessary for immigration enforcement.

CBP framed every data point in a way that would lead to more funding. For example, in 2019, their Northern Border Threat Analysis Report noted that the vast majority of travel across the Canadian border was normal and legal. However, the routine normalcy itself was described as a threat because the volume of traffic meant that bad actors could blend in and allow "individuals who may pose a national security risk to enter the United States undetected."[1]

Among the flood of new equipment, Air and Marine Operations (AMO) acquired the largest fleet of drones that operates inside the United States, along with a wide range of other aircraft and ships. These included single-engine Cessnas as well as huge Lockheed Martin P-3 Orion long-range tracker planes, which have a crew of eight and are used to search for smuggling submarines in the Gulf of Mexico and off the Florida coast. AMO purchased ten Predator drones, but two have crashed, in 2006 and in 2020. Five of the remaining drones are configured to monitor land environments, and three are maritime variants for missions over oceans. The drones fly out of several different bases, including Sierra Vista, Arizona; Corpus Christi, Texas; San Angelo, Texas; Jacksonville, Florida; and Grand Forks, North Dakota.

Most of the flight plans send the drones straight to the border, where they fly grids above the immediate area. Occasionally, they will deviate to a specific location near the border and fly in a circular pattern, providing eyes in the sky for agents on the ground. The Predator drones have regular and infrared cameras that allow full motion videos, as well as different sensors that allow for measurements of terrain and tracking moving vehicles at night. The Predator drones do not have cameras sensitive enough to use facial recognition software, but CBP also has many smaller tactical drones that do.

In 2014, the inspector general of the Department of Homeland Security found that CBP's Predator drones were expensive to operate, costing $12,255 per flight hour, and had a relatively small impact on apprehensions or drug seizures.[2] Drones cannot make apprehensions on their own, so the data is based on apprehensions in which the drone provided assistance. Even with that broad definition, in 2016 Predator drones played only a part in the apprehension of 1,729 people, or 0.4 percent of all apprehensions that year.[3]

On that Friday morning in May 2020, the Predator drone headed in the opposite direction of the Canadian border. Within a few minutes, it crossed over the Red River, which marked the North Dakota state line with Minnesota. It proceeded southeast over the thousand lakes that dot western Minnesota, then over Saint Cloud, before reaching the urban center of Minneapolis–Saint Paul at 10:47 a.m. It then began a hexagonal-shaped holding pattern over the city at an altitude of 20,000 feet. Minneapolis is outside the one-hundred-mile zone where the Border Patrol normally operates, but the AMO authorization does not have geographical limits.[4]

As the Predator drone circled above, the city of Minneapolis was dealing with the aftermath of the killing of George Floyd. Four days earlier, on May 25, Floyd was accused of trying to pass a counterfeit twenty-dollar bill at a convenience store. When the police arrived, they detained him and pinned him on the ground for over nine minutes with Minneapolis police officer Derek Chauvin's knee pressed on his neck. Floyd died, and the video of the killing set off protests around the city. On May 26, the four officers involved were fired. On Friday, May 29, as the CBP drone circled overhead, Chauvin was arrested on charges of third-degree murder and second-degree manslaughter. Neither charge accused Chauvin of intentionally killing Floyd, which further inflamed protests in Minneapolis, across the United States, and around the world.

The CBP drone, ostensibly purchased to monitor the border for immigration violations, was in the skies over Minneapolis to monitor American citizens protesting the killing of George Floyd. The Predator circled the city for an hour and a half before heading back to Grand Forks at 12:15 p.m. After a reporter noticed the flight pattern and tweeted about it, several news organizations reported on the mission. CBP acknowledged that CBP 104 was their drone: "Earlier today a U.S. Customs and Border Protection, Air and Marine Operations unmanned aircraft system was preparing to provide live video to aid in situational awareness at the request of our federal law enforcement partners in Minneapolis." The CBP spokesperson continued, "AMO carries out its mission nationwide, not just at the border, consistent with federal laws and policies."[5]

The CBP drone deployment to Minneapolis was not a one-off incident. In the first three weeks of the nationwide protests about police killings of Black men and women, there were deployments of CBP helicopters, drones, and airplanes in fifteen cities across the United States from Dayton, Ohio, to New York City. The video surveillance data they produced was not just used in real time; it is also stored in a digital network that can be used later.

In 2019, CBP's Air and Marine Operations did 92,800 hours of flights, including all their aircraft from helicopters to drones, of which 8.6 percent (8,000 hours) were for other agencies.[6] A 2017 assessment of the CBP drone program found that 20 percent of drone flight hours were for operations outside the border and coastal areas where it had FAA preapproval to operate.[7] Many of these flights were in support of Immigration and Customs Enforcement actions inside the United States, but 2 percent were for local law enforcement. These other deployments have included providing surveillance during active shooter incidents or when local police have carried out a large raid. Over the years, CBP drones have been used by the FBI, the U.S. Marshals, the Coast Guard, the Minnesota Bureau of Criminal Investigation, the North Dakota Bureau of Criminal Investigation, the North Dakota National Guard, and the Texas Department of Public Safety.[8]

CBP drones based in Great Falls, North Dakota, have been deployed multiple times to monitor Indigenous environmental activists attempting to prevent the construction of oil pipelines. The CBP monitoring began with the Standing Rock Sioux protests against the Dakota Access Pipeline in 2016 at their reservation that straddles the North and South Dakota border. CBP contributed to the police presence when the local sheriff's office requested and received the use of a drone for surveillance of the protests.

In 2020, journalists at Gizmodo conducted a deeper investigation into CBP flights from the North Dakota base. Using publicly available flight paths, they found that CBP flew missions in February 2020 that tracked the planned route of another pipeline by Canadian energy company Enbridge Inc. The drones also surveilled the homes of anti-pipeline activists, including, on February 21, 2020, an hour spent circling over the remote rural home of Indigenous Environmental Network executive director Tom Goldtooth. The journalists identified five CBP drone flights between February and June 2020 that monitored the homes of Indigenous pipeline opponents.[9]

National Police Force

The expansion of Customs and Border Protection into the largest federal law enforcement agency has allowed the agents to be used for policing well away from the border itself. In the past few years, the Border Patrol has been deployed in an ever-widening range of circumstances that often have little or nothing to do with preventing unauthorized immigration. The most troubling part of the Border Patrol's growth in both size and technical abilities is that it has occurred at the same time that apprehensions have declined substantially from their peak of 1.6 million in 2000. From 2010 to 2020, the Border Patrol averaged only a quarter that number, 435,000 apprehensions per year.[10] The result is a lot of money and a lot agents, and not as much immigration work to do. As Jenn Budd, the former senior agent and now critic of the Border Patrol, explained, "I don't know what they do. They have 20,000 agents and they have a quarter the number [of apprehensions] we used to get with 5,000 agents. So they are not on the border, let me tell you that."[11]

Traditionally, the federal government has not done policing inside the United States, but does maintain law enforcement agencies that conduct investigations or protect government buildings. The Tenth Amendment of the Constitution reserves anything that is not consti-tutionally designated for the federal government as the domain of the states. The Constitution does not authorize a national police force, so policing has been left to local and state governments. Additionally, the Posse Comitatus Act of 1878 prohibits the deployment of the military inside the United States, except under very specific circumstances. The National Guard is also a separate category, because they are always under the command of the governor of the state in which they are deployed.

Despite these restrictions that prevent a national police force, there are dozens of federal law enforcement agencies. However, each of these agencies has a limited purpose that usually revolves around protecting government buildings and officials, investigating federal crimes after they were committed, or locating people who were charged with a crime. On the protective side, the most well-known federal officers are the Secret Service, who are tasked with protecting the president and other high-level government officials. On the investigative side, the FBI is by far the most recognizable, but most agencies, from the Trea-sury Department to the Postal Service, have their own federal agents who conduct investigations.

The FBI and the other investigative agencies are not like beat cops who patrol the streets. Instead, they are only called to investigate after a crime has been committed. The FBI does do counterterrorism investigations that resemble regular police work, but only in that relatively narrow field. Immigration and Customs Enforcement (ICE), which is part of the Department of Homeland Security but separate from Customs and Border Protection, is tasked with locating and arresting people in the interior of the United States. ICE does not patrol neighborhoods for criminal activity. Instead, the agency is given a list of people who have violated immigration laws and then they find them, arrest them, and deport them.

The ability of the Border Patrol to police inside the one-hundred-mile zone, and of AMO to operate anywhere in the United States for surveillance purposes, sets Customs and Border Protection apart from other federal law enforcement agencies. The mandate for the Border Patrol to monitor public spaces allows the agency to take on roles that traditionally were reserved for local or state police. Jenn Budd, the former agent and critic, explained, "They don't want anything to do with immigration anymore. That is why they have the BORTAC units [Border Patrol Tactical Units]. They intend to be a national police force. That's why you are seeing them do actual police work in the joint task forces. They are trying to show 'see, we can do this too.'"[12]

Rodney Scott, the chief of the Border Patrol from 2019 to 2021, was an advocate of the broader role for the agency. As Budd explained, Scott "is one of the ones that really pushed the Border Patrol to go all around the world when he was working in Washington D.C. from 2005 to 2007. He was telling people, if a car bomb goes off, I should know about it. So there is a creep, whether it is a creep into regular policing, or it's a creep into intelligence. The management of the agency is just gung-ho to get their fingers into everything."[13]

In President Donald Trump, the Border Patrol found a strong ally in their efforts to expand their authority. The Border Patrol Union, which represents over 18,000 of the agents, was one of the first major organizations to endorse Trump as a presidential candidate on March 30, 2016. It was the first time the union had ever made a presidential endorsement, and it continued to promote his policies until his election loss in 2020.[14] While he was in office, Trump expanded the authority of the Border Patrol and directed its use in the interior of the United States. In February 2020, Trump authorized using BORTAC units on missions to support ICE operations to "flood the streets" with agents in sanctuary cities.[15] As protests grew after the killing of George Floyd, BORTAC units were deployed to cities around the United States to protect federal buildings and monuments.

The first Border Patrol Tactical Unit was created in 1984, well before the expansion of the agency in the 1990s and the terrorism focus in the twenty-first century. The original purpose was to have a rapid action force that could be deployed quickly to put down riots in immigration detention facilities. BORTAC has since become a multiuse force that operates inside the United States and in other countries for missions and training.[16] Over the years, BORTAC training began to mirror that of other elite special forces such as the Army Rangers and the Navy SEALs. The agents selected for BORTAC go through grueling tests like a six-mile march with a weighted pack and water training, including drowning situations. They are tested in high-stress environments with sleep deprivation.[17] What they are not trained for are de-escalation strategies or civilian interactions, as DHS memos warned prior to the summer 2020 deployments to U.S. cities to deal with crowd control.[18]

Those deployments were not the first time aggressive tactics by BORTAC units had made the national news in the United States. Twenty years earlier, in 2000, a dispute arose over a six-year-old Cuban boy named Elián González. In November 1999, González was on a boat with his mother and twelve others as they attempted the crossing from Cuba to Florida. They set out at 4:00 a.m., but quickly encountered bad weather. The engine of the small boat failed. Waves crashed over the boat, sinking it. The boy's mother and ten others died, but Elián was rescued by an American fishing vessel. The U.S. Coast Guard brought Elián to shore and he was released to his paternal great-uncle, who lived in South Florida.

In Cuba, Elián González's father did not know his wife was taking the boy on the journey. After he found out from relatives in Florida that Elián was alive, he asked the U.S. government to return the boy to him in Cuba. The Florida relatives, however, thought it best for Elián to stay in Florida with them. They contested the repatriation in the courts but lost. Attorney General Janet Reno set a deadline of April 13 for the family to turn over Elián so he could be flown back to Cuba. They refused. On April 22, Reno authorized a BORTAC unit to raid their home and retrieve the boy, which they did.

An Associated Press photographer snapped a picture of the moment a BORTAC agent located the six-year-old Elián in a bedroom. The agent is dressed head-to-toe in green military gear and has an assault rifle held up, with his finger on the trigger, pointed toward the boy and his uncle who is holding him. Elián's face is the epitome of terror as he clings to his uncle for safety. The photo won the 2001 Pulitzer Prize for Breaking News Photography.[19]

Kidnapping People

In the summer of 2020, amid multiple protests over police violence and the killing of George Floyd, President Trump authorized the deployment of Border Patrol agents in several cities around the United States, where they clashed with American citizens and grabbed people off the streets in unmarked vehicles. These deployments were not based on the sections of the U.S. code that traditionally govern the Border Patrol, but rather on little-known and previously unused sections of the U.S. code that give law enforcement authority to the secretary of the Department of Homeland Security. Section 40 USC § 1315 was a post–September 11 provision that allowed the secretary to protect government property. The provisions were written extremely broadly and, with an expansive interpretation, could be seen as authorizing a national police force. The designated agents can make arrests without a warrant for "any felony cognizable under the laws of the United States" and can "conduct investigations, on and off the property in question."[20]

Mitra Ebadolahi, a senior staff attorney at the ACLU, explained, "Because many of these newly established authorities were not immediately invoked, people fell asleep about them. A lot of people do not even know there are these other statutes. These other statutes have a lot of very permissive language, allowing DHS entities like CBP to act like a federal police force."[21]

After President Trump issued an executive order in June 2020, DHS also expanded its guidelines for intelligence gathering to include these new internal policing efforts, including "Protecting American Monuments, Memorials, Statues, and Combatting Recent Criminal Violence."[22] The Border Patrol had a new mandate to conduct policing on America's streets, far from the border itself.

The late-night detention in Portland, Oregon, described in this book's introduction, when heavily armed agents forced a person into a waiting minivan, was carried out by a BORTAC unit operating under this new authorization. The person detained by the Border Patrol on that July 2020 night was Evelyn Bassi, a thirty-year-old Portland resident.

A security camera captured the events leading up to Bassi's detention. Bassi and a friend were standing on the street corner in front of a Starbucks with no one else around. The dark gray Dodge Caravan minivan pulled up beside them, with the sliding door already open and with the heavily armed BORTAC agents sitting inside.

Bassi and the friend put their hands up and said, "We're leaving, we're leaving, we're not causing any trouble." Then, they turned to run. The minivan chased them and Bassi's friend sprinted away. Bassi decided to double back toward the Starbucks, and the minivan did a U-turn to pursue Bassi. At that point, the other pedestrians arrived and used their phones to video the detention.[23]

After Bassi was forced inside the van, it sped away from the scene. The Border Patrol agents drove seven blocks away and then stopped again. Bassi refused to provide a name but asked if it was a detention. The agents responded, "Yes." Bassi asked for what crime, and the Border Patrol agents said someone matching Bassi's description had shined a laser pointer in an officer's eyes. They compared a photo they had with Bassi and decided it was a different person. After ten minutes, they released Bassi, who stood alone in the street and watched the van speed away. Bassi was one of at least four people in Portland who were similarly detained by BORTAC units in July 2020. In each instance, the armed agents swooped in with a minivan, grabbed the individual off the street, and then sped away. None were charged with any crimes.

The abduction of Evelyn Bassi off the streets of Portland appears to be a clear violation of Bassi's First Amendment rights to freedom of speech and peaceable assembly and Fourth Amendment right to be free of unreasonable searches and seizures. Congress took a small step toward regulating the use of federal agents for local and state policing purposes through the National Defense Authorization Act that became law in January 2021. A provision in the law requires federal law enforcement agents deployed to a "civil disturbance" to display a visible identification that includes their name and the government agency that employs them.[24] After the late-night detentions in Portland, Ellen Rosenblum, the Oregon attorney general, filed a complaint that would have required agents to have probable cause or a warrant to detain someone, but a judge ruled the state of Oregon lacked standing in the matter. Several federal lawsuits, questioning the use of the Border Patrol for non-immigration purposes under section 1315, are ongoing.[25] The courts have yet to consider whether the Border Patrol's lower standards of evidence for a stop and interrogation, which were meant to be limited to immigration questions, can be used when the Border Patrol is engaged in other law enforcement purposes.

=

George Floyd was buried in Pearland, Texas, on June 9, 2020. Temperatures pushed past 90°F as thousands of mourners lined the streets for a procession from the Fountain of Praise Church to the Houston Memorial Garden where he was to be laid to rest. Floyd's body was in a golden casket carried by a white carriage with flowers on top, pulled by two white horses. The Houston police chief, Art Acevedo, walked the route beside the carriage, occasionally raising his fist in solidarity with the people gathered along the way.

As Floyd's family mourned his death and television viewers around the country and the world looked on, the Border Patrol was mobilizing nearby. A CBP Predator drone circled overhead as sixty-six BORTAC agents and six snipers monitored the services in Texas. The deployment anticipated protests at the funeral and agents were specifically authorized to use tear gas and deadly force if violence escalated beyond simply throwing objects like water bottles.[26] Nothing of the sort happened and the agents did not use deadly force that day. Nevertheless, they could have.

The increased use of the Border Patrol for missions that lack any immigration enforcement purpose illustrates how the agency has moved closer to becoming a national police force. The Border Patrol was established to conduct immigration checks at the border itself and within a reasonable distance of the border. As that zone expanded to be one hundred miles from the border and coastlines, the agents began to work deep inside the United States. More recently, they have taken on new policing tasks outside their historical focus on immigration. The first new assignment of drug interdiction was border related, but more recent areas of emphasis—from terrorism prevention to protecting federal buildings and monuments—have little or nothing to do with the border. Today, the size of the force, combined with the advanced military technologies at their disposal and their Supreme Court–approved ability to make warrantless stops in large sections of the country, makes the Border Patrol the most dangerous police force in the United States.

Conclusion

It was nearing lunchtime when I paid two dollars to park in the large private lot beside the port of entry between Progreso, Texas, and Nuevo Progreso, Tamaulipas, in November 2018. The other border crossers, gathering their belongings and locking their cars, were a mix of younger women in jeans and plaid shirts with kids in tow and older white retirees headed to Mexico for cheap drinks. I had heard that the best tacos were at Taqueria Victor, a hole-in-the-wall place on the Mexican side, and I was going to cross the border to find out. First, though, I decided to take a walk along the border wall on the U.S. side. It was a sunny and clear day, with a beautiful blue sky. Even in late November, the Rio Grande Valley was still warm and pleasant, so it seemed like a good time to stretch my legs.

The border is often perceived as a dangerous and restricted place, but pedestrians are free to walk along it for as long as they like in most locations. I headed to the west of the port of entry, past Customs and Border Protection office buildings and sheds. All that stood between me and the languid, brown Rio Grande was a ten-foot-high chain-link fence. It had been cut every few feet, and the Border Patrol had opted to mend the damaged sections with concertina wire. After a few hundred feet, the maroon bollard-style barrier began and stretched out in front of me until it curved south, following the path of the river. Except for the wall, the area resembled countless other lonely roads in rural farming communities. To my right was a drainage ditch beside a fallow field with a few withered cornstalks strewn about. There was no one around.

I walked past the bend in the wall and saw a green and white Border Patrol truck parked ahead on the gravel road, facing west. As I came up behind it, I could see that there was one agent seated inside. On a few occasions when I have stumbled upon Border Patrol trucks in isolated locations where the agents were not expecting to see anyone, they were asleep and never even knew I was there. This time the young, white, male agent had his head down, looking at his phone in his lap. He glanced up as I passed, giving me a single nod. Then he went back to whatever he was doing on his phone. I went a little farther down the road before my stomach told me it was time to return to the port of entry and head over to Nuevo Progreso for those tacos. They were delicious.

It might seem odd to conclude a book about the out-of-control Border Patrol with a story in which literally nothing happens, but that is the point. Despite lurid headlines about continuous crises and race-baiting politicians who blame immigrants for every problem in society, the border itself is generally a quiet place. The brief nod from the Border Patrol agent looking at his phone captures all the paradoxes of the United States–Mexico border. On the one hand, the ubiquitous presence of agents gives the border zone the feeling of an occupation. Border Patrol trucks are everywhere, and the dozens of permanent checkpoints and hundreds of temporary locations create the perception that the border is a war zone where constant threats require a massive, militarized response. The occupation seems to justify the violations of the Fourth Amendment that come with it, from vehicle stops based only on a few facts that raise an agent's suspicion to interior checkpoints on interstate highways that stop every single vehicle for questioning and a quick pass by a drug-sniffing dog. The presence of thousands of agents, with expansive powers to stop and interrogate anyone inside the United States, has led to the violent excesses described in this book.

On the other hand, the daily work of the Border Patrol agents is boring. From 2011 to 2020, the average agent made fewer than two apprehensions per month, or one apprehension for every eleven shifts on duty. That means two full weeks of work to find one person in the United States without documents. What that looks like in reality is hours sitting in a truck staring at the border wall. Day. After day. After day. It means hours surfing the internet on a phone, while occasionally looking up as a farmer, or a professor, passes by. It means working shift after shift at an interior checkpoint on an American highway, asking every driver about their citizenship. Even then, as People Helping People's monitoring of the Arizona checkpoint found, days can go by without a single apprehension or drug seizure.

My leisurely walk at Progreso also illustrates how privilege works at the border. As a white American male, I can think it reasonable to cross an international border for lunch. Afterward, I can stroll back into the United States after a few cursory questions from a customs official, even as the family of four standing beside me is aggressively interrogated. They are all short with curly black hair and brown skin and are asked to account for every aspect of their lives while surrounded by three agents, with grim looks on their faces and hands on their hips. I can decide to "stretch my legs" with a walk along the border wall. I can sneak up on and startle a Border Patrol agent without any real concerns. I can be confident that the agent will not even bat an eye when he sees me, mere feet from his truck. I can expect that he would not roll down the window to ask what I was doing or why I was there. I can assume that just by looking at me, he will know that I belong. My white skin is a passport that gives me access to that place.

The Supreme Court gave Border Patrol agents the right to use racial profiling in their work. That profiling happens every day. When racial profiling is discussed, the focus is on what happens to people with brown skin who are asked to explain why they are speaking Spanish in a convenience store in Montana or who are twenty-six times more likely to be asked to show their ID at an interior checkpoint in Arizona. What is often overlooked is that white people are profiled every day. The white people who live in the border zone but have never been pulled over by the Border Patrol were racially profiled. The white people who were waved through an interior checkpoint before they even came to a complete stop were racially profiled. The white people who found the Border Patrol agents they encountered friendly and respectful, just as they expected federal officers to be, were racially profiled.

=

The Supreme Court heard the last major Border Patrol case in 1976, when it allowed interior checkpoints in *Martinez-Fuerte*. In the forty-five years since, the number of Border Patrol agents has increased more than tenfold, even as the number of people apprehended by the Border Patrol has declined. As Mitra Ebadolahi of the ACLU told me, when the Supreme Court ruled on the Border Patrol's procedures, "There were no drugs, there were no sensors, there was no surveillance technology, there were no digital databases. It was a completely different world. We didn't have any border walls. All of the reasoning in *Martinez-Fuerte* is predicated on those facts. None of which exist today, nor have existed for thirty-five years."[1]

Over that same period, the southern border has been transformed in the public's perception. It went from being a sleepy backwater that rarely filtered into the national news to a militarized zone at the center of the national political conversation. In the 2016 presidential campaign, Donald Trump used the border wall as a symbol for his racialized vision for America, where all immigrants were invaders who brought crime and disease, who depressed American wages and destroyed traditional American culture. None of these claims were true. They are racially driven arguments to create fear that immigrants are replacing white Americans.[2]

Over the summer of 2021, a parade of Republican lawmakers made pilgrimages to the border for photo ops about what they called a border crisis. Most kept up the charade that a crisis was happening by wearing bulletproof vests as they toured the Rio Grande on gunboats, even while they passed people swimming at beaches or enjoying the sunny weather on party boats. A few let slip that there was not actually a crisis at the border. In August 2021, Representative Cliff Bentz, a Republican from Oregon, said, "I'm surprised to see . . . the lack of sustained impact. I'm glad to see there's not the impact I was expecting."[3] Even though there is not really a crisis at the border, the relentless framing of it as such has poisoned the discourse to the extent that even politicians who might normally be sympathetic to a more humane border policy are hesitant to say so out of fear of being attacked as anti-American.

Despite the transformation of the border in the public imagination, the people arriving there are largely the same as they always were. The majority are still migrant farm and factory workers from Mexico. In the past few years, they have been joined by entire families fleeing violence in Central America. These families with small children, who turn themselves in to the Border Patrol as soon as they step foot in the United States in order to apply for asylum, pose no threat and deserve humane treatment. However, that is not what they have received. As journalist Garrett Graff memorably put it, "CBP went out and recruited Rambo, when it turned out the agency needed Mother Teresa."[4]

The border needs to be reimagined as a place of connection and movement, not of threat and security. Migration is a normal practice that humans have engaged in for millennia.[5] The ancestors of every single person in the United States migrated there at some point, even those of Native Americans who have been there longer than most. Militarized borders to prevent the movement of civilians are a new phenomenon that emerged in the United States only as non-white immigrants began to arrive in the second half of the nineteenth century. The 1924 Immigration Act established national origins quotas that were meant to ensure that, in the words of the bill's author, Senator David Reed, "the racial composition of America at the present time thus is made permanent."[6] The Border Patrol was created that same year to enforce racial rules about who could enter the United States. Even after the explicitly racial quotas were removed in 1965, the border has continued to be a place shaped by racial exclusion through the present day.

Jenn Budd, the former senior Border Patrol agent, explained to me, "How do you expect this agency not to be racist? Aren't the laws they are enforcing racist?" She continued, "At the heart of this circle is the ugly, beating, racist, white supremacist heart. That has always been in the Border Patrol; that was what the Border Patrol was founded on. It was grown from those seeds, and it is still there."[7]

The decisions of the Supreme Court in the 1970s played a significant role in allowing violence and racial exclusion at the border to continue into the contemporary era. This book seeks to add two of those rulings, *United States v. Brignoni-Ponce* (1975) and *United States v. Martinez-Fuerte* (1976) to the list of the most infamous Supreme Court decisions of the past, such as *Dred Scott v. Sandford*, *Plessy v. Ferguson*, and *Korematsu v. United States*. However, among those now mothballed reminders of America's racist past, *Brignoni-Ponce* and *Martinez-Fuerte* are the only ones still put into practice every day. *Brignoni-Ponce* allowed Border Patrol agents to use race along with at least one other factor to stop a vehicle during a roving patrol on American highways. *Martinez-Fuerte* authorized agents at interior checkpoints to use race as the *only* factor in deciding to send a vehicle to secondary inspection for additional questioning.

These Supreme Court decisions allowed the Border Patrol to become what it is today. As Justice William Brennan wrote in his dissent to *Martinez-Fuerte*, the Supreme Court's Border Patrol decisions amounted to an "evisceration" of the reasonableness requirement in the Fourth Amendment, allowing agents "to stop any or all motorists without explanation or excuse" and "target motorists of Mexican appearance." The Border Patrol's actions in the years since have borne out Brennan's dire predictions. The vast size of the one-hundred-mile border zone, combined with the ability to manufacture suspicion to justify any vehicle stop, results in severe limitations on constitutional protections in a zone that stretches deep into the interior of the United States.

One of the most vexing things about the weakening of Fourth Amendment protections for the Border Patrol is the completely arbitrary size of the border zone. The one-hundred-mile zone was not legislated by Congress. Instead, it was formalized in 1947 through an administrative order without any public comment or oversight. While in the 1930s officials were outraged that the Border Patrol was operating as far as twenty miles inside the United States, after 1947, the one-hundred-mile border zone has remained unchanged and largely unquestioned for almost seventy years.

The enormous border zone is the result of a simple administrative decision that could be reversed immediately by the secretary of the Department of Homeland Security. Similarly, the secretary could immediately end the use of interior checkpoints that inconvenience millions of Americans living in the border zone and kill hundreds of people per year by forcing migrants to trek dozens of miles through the deserts of the U.S. Southwest.

Some of the other problems identified in this book require legislative solutions. Congress has the power to reduce the Border Patrol's enormous budget, cap the number of agents, and restrict Air and Marine Operations' ability to use drones and airplanes for surveillance across the entire United States. Congress could also change the wording of the Border Patrol's authorization to remove the ability to make vehicle stops without a warrant in order to bring the agency into compliance with the *Carroll* doctrine and the Fourth Amendment rules that govern all other police. Finally, Congress should revisit the 9/11-era legislation that gives the Secretary of the Department of Homeland Security broad authority to reassign federal agents for general policing inside the United States.

There are already some positive steps in these directions. In August 2021, the Border Patrol decided to outfit some agents with body cameras, which begins to address the problem of abuse of immigrants in remote locations beyond the view of the public. In addition to Senator Patrick Leahy's efforts to rein in interior checkpoints and shrink the one-hundred-mile zone, a new group of Democratic politicians have questioned the Border Patrol's practices. In August 2021, Representatives Rashida Tlaib of Michigan and Jamie Raskin of Maryland asked the secretary of DHS for an explanation of why the Border Patrol considers Lake Michigan part of the border zone and how it justifies the racially discriminatory outcomes the ACLU identified in its arrest records in Michigan. Tlaib, along with Representatives Alexandria Ocasio-Cortez (New York), Ilhan Omar (Minnesota), and Ayanna Pressley (Massachusetts) also called for substantial reductions to border security funding: "CBP and ICE are rogue agencies that act to inflict harm on our communities and have a pattern of behavior of abuse and mismanagement of funds. This year, the House must hold CBP accountable for their egregious violation of the law by withholding any further funding and imposing additional accountability measures with real consequences."[8]

===

In the end, despite all the changes in American society in the almost one hundred years since the Border Patrol was established, there has been continuity in the actions of the agents themselves. The Border Patrol was founded to enforce racial rules for entry to the United States, the Supreme Court confirmed the legality of their racial profiling, and they continue to conduct racialized policing today. In 2014, the Department of Justice banned racial profiling for other federal law enforcement officers but included an exception for the Border Patrol and other agents involved in immigration enforcement. The very first Border Patrol agent was named after the president of the Confederacy. In 1954, the U.S. government officially termed its effort to crack down on migrant workers "Operation Wetback." Today, Border Patrol agents regularly use racist terms like *tonk*, *wetback*, and *beaner* to describe the people they interact with at the border.

The earliest Border Patrol agents were drawn from frontier law enforcement and had a loose interpretation of the rules. In the 1970s, the Supreme Court ruled that the Fourth Amendment protections against unreasonable searches and seizures did not fully apply in interactions with the Border Patrol. Today, agents engage in illegal activity at a rate far higher than other police officers and are regularly accused of violence in interactions with people they detain. Nevertheless, there is little consequence to their violent actions. No action is taken by the agency in the majority of complaints lodged against agents and no agent has ever been convicted for an on-duty killing, even when there is clear video evidence that the victim posed no threat to the agents involved.

Although the border may feel distant from many people's daily lives, it is much closer than it seems. Warrantless stops, interior checkpoints, and racial profiling are authorized within a vast area that includes the homes of two-thirds of the United States population. Security and surveillance practices tested at the border have a tendency to seep into the society as a whole.[9] This is evident in the use of CBP aircraft for a wide range of surveillance activities inside the United States that have no connection to the border, such as monitoring the homes of Indigenous environmental activists. It is also visible in the deployment of BORTAC units to do internal policing in situations without any immigration purpose, such as standing guard with shoot-to-kill orders at the funeral of George Floyd. The stories of musicians like Snoop Dogg, who was detained by the Border Patrol at an interior checkpoint for marijuana possession while driving from Los Angeles to San Antonio to attend his son's football game, and Evelyn Bassi, who was kidnapped by the Border Patrol while standing in front of a Starbucks in downtown Portland, demonstrate the startling reality: everywhere is becoming a border zone.

Even though the Border Patrol has not yet started to deploy their expansive authority to stop vehicles, use racial profiling, and set up checkpoints on a widespread basis in major American cities, legally they could. It is time to reconsider that authority before they do. Until then, as Thurgood Marshall foresaw almost fifty years ago, "nobody is protected."

Acknowledgments

THERE ARE MANY PEOPLE TO THANK FOR HELPING MAKE this book a reality. First, I want to give thanks to my family for always supporting my work. My children, Rasmey and Kiran, as well as my partner, Sivylay, have traveled with me to many of these research sites. Sivylay also read and commented on the complete draft of the book. Thanks to my parents, Wally and Celia, for their continuous support, and to my brother, Brent, who edits early drafts of my books, before I am ready to show them to anyone else.

Thanks to Todd Miller, Geoff Boyce, and Gabriel Schivone for advice about research on the Border Patrol and Freedom of Information Act requests. Todd and Geoff also read the entire book and provided feedback. Corey Johnson and Md. Azmeary Ferdoush commented on the complete book and Thomas Belfield read sections of it.

Thanks to everyone who agreed to speak with me about the Border Patrol and the Supreme Court. These include Bill Addington, Gilles Bissonnette, Terry Bressi, Jenn Budd, Penny Clark, Mitra Ebadolahi,

Max Granger, Alex Rate, Chris Rickerd, Chuck Sevilla, Sophie Smith, and Christina Whitman. John Jeffries Jr. also provided helpful information on Lewis Powell's time on the court. Thanks to those who spoke with me but preferred not to be named.

I am particularly thankful to the Lewis F. Powell Jr. Archives at Washington and Lee University for digitizing the documents from his Supreme Court years and making those freely available online. This is an important public service and is deeply appreciated. I wish more archives would follow their lead. I also drew on Supreme Court documents from the National Archives in Washington, D.C. Thanks to Cory Lenz at the William S. Richardson School of Law Library who found the documents that confirmed that the one-hundred-mile border zone was established in 1947.

There were several books that proved particularly useful as I delved into the history of Border Patrol. Kelly Lytle Hernández's *Migra!* and Deborah Kang's *The INS on the Line* were critical for understanding the formative years of the Border Patrol. John Jeffries's biography of Lewis Powell provides a nuanced and complete picture of the man. Todd Miller has written several books about the expansion of the Border Patrol after September 11. *Border Patrol Nation* and *Empire of Borders* were particularly useful for this book. I first learned about the *Brignoni-Ponce* case from Mat Coleman, who mentioned it to me in passing in a conversation at a conference, over a decade ago. Thanks for planting one of the seeds that grew into this book.

In March 2019, I gave a talk at the School of Environment and Development at the University of Arizona in Tucson, organized by Orhan Myadar and Stefano Bloch. On the following day, Stefano and Daniel Martínez organized a trip to Ambos Nogales, where we walked the border wall along Calle International where José Antonio Elena Rodríguez was killed. In October 2018, I gave a talk at the University of Texas, Rio Grande Valley, organized by Caroline Miles and

Dennis Hart. It was my first visit to the South Texas borderlands and the trip gave me the opportunity to visit many sections of the border wall. Thanks also to Scott Nicol for showing me around the border in McAllen and Mission, Texas.

Thanks to the John Simon Guggenheim Foundation for financial support for this project through the fellowship program, and to the Social Science Research Institute at the University of Hawaiʻi at Mānoa for a Research Support Award in 2018–19 that funded the early research for this project. I owe particular gratitude to my research assistant Md. Azmeary Ferdoush who located many old congressional records, manuscripts, and reports about the various people and organizations that feature in this book. Thanks also to Kevin Morris for research assistance on old case files in the law library.

My agent, Julia Eagleton of Janklow & Nesbit, provided excellent guidance and assistance for the book proposal. Thanks to everyone at Counterpoint Press for bringing the book to publication, including Dan Smetanka and Dan López on the editorial side, Laura Berry in production, and Lena Moses-Schmitt, Megan Fishmann, Rachel Fershleiser, and Mandy Medley in marketing. Thanks to Katherine Kiger for careful copyedits. Finally, mahalo nui loa to my colleagues who make the Department of Geography and Environment at the University of Hawaiʻi at Mānoa such a great place to live and work.

Notes

Introduction: Out of Control

1. Agent Terrance J. Brady's testimony in the original trial states that the stop was in the early evening. However, later rulings by the Appeals Court and Supreme Court put it in the early morning. Records and Briefs of the United States Supreme Court, 1973 term.

2. Latin surnames, like Brignoni-Ponce, can be complicated to use in English because they typically include both the father's (Brignoni) and the mother's (Ponce) last names. The most accurate way to describe Felix Brignoni-Ponce would be Mr. Brignoni. However, in all the cases, the courts opted to hyphenate the two surnames. Consequently, for clarity, throughout this book the hyphenated surnames will be used. There is a debate about whether to use the terms *Hispanic*, *Latino/a*, or *Latinx*, which lacks consensus at the time of publication. *Latino/a* is used in this book. McCarthy, Justin, and Whitney Dupreé, "No Preferred Racial Term Among Most Black,

Hispanic Adults," Gallup, August 4, 2021, https://news.gallup.com /poll/353000/no-preferred-racial-term-among-black-hispanic -adults.aspx.

3. The terms *alien* and *illegal alien* are used in this book when they appear in the historical record. In 2021, the US government decided to retire the term and instead use *noncitizen*. In this book, *undocumented* will be used as well.

4. "Criminal Justice Memorial for Howard Turrentine," San Diego County Bar Association, https://www.sdcba.org/index.cfm?pg= CriminalJusticeMemorial#Turrentine.

5. "Video Shows Federal Agents Detaining People in Portland Based on Inaccurate, Insufficient Information," *The Washington Post*, September 10, 2020.

6. Bree Newsome Bass, Twitter, July 18, 2020. https://twitter.com /BreeNewsome/status/1284613358600302592.

7. I briefly recounted this story in my first book. Reece Jones, *Border Walls: Security and the War on Terror in the United States, India, and Israel* (London: Zed Books, 2012).

8. Justin Rohrlich and Zoë Schlanger, "Border officers are arrested 5 times more often than other US law enforcement," *Quartz*, July 16, 2019; Human Rights Watch, "'They Treat You Like You Are Worthless': Internal DHS Reports of Abuses by US Border Officials," October 21, 2021; Jeremy Slack, Daniel Martinez, Scott Whiteford, and Emily Peiffer, *In the Shadow of the Wall: Family Separation, Immigration Enforcement and Security* (Tuscon: The Center for Latin American Studies, University of Arizona, 2013); Guillermo Cantor and Walter Ewing, "Still No Action Taken: Complaints against Border Patrol Agents Continue to Go Unanswered," American Immigration Council (2017).

9. Southern Border Communities Coalition, *Deaths by Border Patrol* report (2021); Carrie Johnson, "Former Border Protection

Insider Alleges Corruption, Distortion in Agency," *NPR*, August 28, 2014. The story of Border Patrol agent Lonnie Swartz killing José Antonio Elena Rodríguez on October 10, 2012 is described in chapter 12; ACLU *Rodriquez v. Swartz*, summary; Mark Binelli, "10 Shots Across the Border," *The New York Times Magazine*, March 3, 2016.

10. Jacob Soboroff, *Separated: Inside an American Tragedy* (New York: HarperCollins, 2020).

11. Chapin, Angela. "57 Migrant Women Say They Were Victims of ICE Gynecologist," The Cut, October 28, 2020. https://www.thecut.com/2020/10/migrant-women-detail-medical-abuse-forced-hysterectomies.html.

12. Congressional and Administrative News, 2117-8.

13. 40 USC § 1315.

14. There are many important books on the border and the Border Patrol. Miguel Díaz-Barriga and Margaret Dorsey, *Fencing in Democracy: Border Walls, Necrocitizenship, and the Security State* (Durham: Duke University Press, 2020); Kevin Johnson, "How Racial Profiling Became the 'Law of the Land': *United States v. Brignoni-Ponce* and *Whren v. United States* and the Need for Rebellious Lawyering," UC Davis Legal Studies Research Papers Series (2009), 174; Deborah S. Kang, *The INS on the Line: Making Immigration Law on the US–Mexico Border, 1917–1954* (Oxford: Oxford University Press, 2017); Kelly Lytle Hernández, *Migra! A History of the U.S. Border Patrol* (Oakland: University of California Press, 2010); Todd Miller, *Border Patrol Nation: Dispatches from the Frontlines of Homeland Security* (San Francisco: City Lights Books, 2014); Todd Miller, *Empire of Borders: The Expansion of the US Border around the World* (New York: Verso, 2019); John Washington, *The Dispossessed: A Story of Asylum and the US–Mexican Border and Beyond* (New York: Verso, 2020).

15. From 2010 to 2020, the Border Patrol averaged 439,000 apprehensions per year. During that era, there were an average of 20,400 agents on duty.

16. American Immigration Council, "Rising Border Encounters in 2021: An Overview and Analysis," August 2, 2021.

Chapter 1: Send Two Coffins

1. Dale Cox, *The History of Jackson County, Florida: The Civil War Years*, Amazon Digital (2010).

2. "Suicide of Gov. Milton, of Florida," *The New York Times*, May 1, 1865.

3. Doug Swanson, *Cult of Glory: The Bold and Brutal History of the Texas Rangers* (Viking, 2020), 10.

4. James Gillett, *Six Years with the Texas Rangers, 1875–1881* (New Haven: Yale University Press, 1925), xxvii.

5. Details on Milton's life are from Clement Hellyer, *The U.S. Border Patrol* (New York: Landmark Books, 1963), 21–22; Thomas Correa, *The American Cowboy Chronicles: Old West Myths & Legends, the Honest Truth, Book 1* (New York: Page Publishing, 2019); Thomas Correa, "Jeff Milton & George Scarborough – Cowboys, Lawmen, Gunfighters," The American Cowboy Chronicles website, October 10, 2014, http://www.americancowboychronicles.com/2014/10/jeff-milton-george-scarborough-cowboys.html.

6. Correa, *American Cowboy Chronicles*, 46.

7. Correa, "Jeff Milton & George Scarborough."

8. James Ely, Bradley Bond, and Charles Wilson, *The New Encyclopedia of Southern Culture, Volume 10, Law and Politics* (Chapel Hill: University of North Carolina Press, 2008), 129.

9. Gary Potter, *The History of Policing in the United States* (Richmond, KY: Eastern Kentucky University, 2013), 3.

10. Garrett Epps, "The Second Amendment Does Not Transcend All Others," *The Atlantic*, March 8, 2018.

11. Sally Hadden, *Slave Patrols: Law and Violence in Virginia and the Carolinas* (Chapel Hill: University of North Carolina Press, 2001).

12. Hidetaka Hirota, *Expelling the Poor: Atlantic Seaboard States and the Nineteenth Century Origins of American Immigration Policy* (Oxford: Oxford University Press, 2017); Anna Law, "The Historical Amnesia of Contemporary Immigration Federalism Debates," *Polity* 47, 2015, 302–319; Anna Law, "Lunatics, idiots, paupers, and Negro Seamen." *Studies in American Political Development* 28, 2014, 107–128.

13. US Congressional Records, 1882, p. 1546.

14. US Congressional Records, 1890. The Executive Documents of the Senate of the United States, 97, part 5. Washington, D.C.: Government Printing Office.

15. Hellyer, *The U.S. Border Patrol*, 1963, 21–2.

16. Hellyer, *The U.S. Border Patrol*, 1963, 29.

Chapter 2: The Texas Rangers

1. Julia Cauble Smith, "Brite Ranch Raid," Handbook of Texas Online, last modified August 14, 2015, https://tshaonline.org/handbook/online/articles/qyb02.

2. Robert Keil, *Bosque Bonito: Violent Times along the Borderland during the Mexican Revolution,* ed. Elizabeth McBride, (Alpine, TX: Center for Big Bend Studies, 2002).

3. Keil, *Bosque Bonito.*

4. Glenn Justice, "Porvenir Massacre Archaeology Most Revealing," Glenn's Texas History Blog, Rimrock Press, December 16, 2015, http://www.rimrockpress.com/blog/index.php?entry=entry151216-162435.

5. Swanson, *Cult of Glory*, 10.

6. Swanson, *Cult of Glory*, 56.

7. Swanson, *Cult of Glory*, 56.

8. Swanson, *Cult of Glory*, 66.

9. Swanson, *Cult of Glory*, 116.
10. Swanson, *Cult of Glory*, 118–9.
11. "John Coffee 'Jack' Hays." Texas Rangers Hall of Fame and Museum website, last updated January 17, 2021, https://www.texasranger.org/texas-ranger-museum/hall-of-fame/john-coffee-jack-hays/.
12. Greg Grandin, *The End of the Myth: From the Frontier to the Border Wall in the Mind of America* (New York: Metropolitan Books, 2019).
13. Treaty of Guadalupe Hidalgo, signed on February 2, 1848.
14. Michael Dear, *Why Walls Won't Work* (Oxford: Oxford University Press, 2013).
15. Gillett, *Six Years with the Texas Rangers*.
16. Lytle Hernández, *Migra!*, 36.
17. Keil, *Bosque Bonito*.
18. The account of cavalry member Bob Keil, written decades later, absolves the cavalry of any blame in the incident, saying they went and found the bodies and were appalled. This does not match other accounts of the event.
19. Swanson, *Cult of Glory*, 265.
20. Charles Harris and Louis Sadler, *The Texas Rangers and the Mexican Revolution: The Bloodiest Decade, 1910–1920* (Albuquerque: University of New Mexico Press, 2007).

Chapter 3: Closing the Back Gate

1. David Reed, "America of the Melting Pot Comes to an End," *New York Times*, April 27, 1924.
2. Immigration Act of 1924.
3. Kelly Lytle Hernandez, "How Crossing the US-Mexico Border Became a Crime," *The Conversation*, April 30, 2017.
4. U.S. Congressional Record, House of Representatives, 1924, 6476.
5. U.S. Congressional Record, House of Representatives, 1924, 6477.

6. Mae M. Ngai, *Impossible Subjects: Illegal Aliens and the Making of Modern America* (Princeton: Princeton University Press, 2004).

7. Mary Kidder Rak, *Border Patrol* (Boston: Houghton Mifflin Company, 1938).

8. Kang, *The INS on the Line.*

9. Lytle Hernández, *Migra!*, 34, 38.

10. "Border Patrol History," U.S. Customs and Border Protection website, last updated July 21, 2020, https://www.cbp.gov/border-security/along-us-borders/history.

11. Lytle Hernández, *Migra!*, 34.

12. 43 Sta. 1049–105; 8 U.S.C. 110.

13. Registry of Aliens Act and Act of March 4, 1929 create penalties for entry.

14. Lytle Hernández, *Migra!*, 48.

15. Clifford Perkins, *Border Patrol: With the U.S. Immigration Service on the Mexican Boundary 1910–1954* (El Paso: Texas Western Press, 1978) 116–7.

16. Lytle Hernández, *Migra!*, 58.

17. Lytle Hernández, *Migra!*, 62.

Chapter 4: They Have No Right to Go into the Interior

1. "Ogden Mills Dies Suddenly at 53," *The New York Times*, October 12, 1937.

2. William MacDonald, "Ogden Mills Speaks in Behalf of 'The 17 Million,'" *The New York Times*, August 29, 1937.

3. The Committee on Interstate and Foreign Commerce, House of Representatives. 1930. Hearing on H.R. "A Bill to Regulate the Entry of Persons into the United States, to Establish a Border Patrol in the Coast Guard, and for Other Purposes." April 24–25.

4. Lytle Hernández, *Migra!*, 47–8, 52.

5. Lytle Hernández, *Migra!*, 52.

6. Kang, *The INS on the Line*, 51; David Reed, 68 Cong. Rec., part 3, 3202 (February 9, 1925).

7. Kang, *The INS on the Line*, 60; *Lew Moy v. United States* (1916), 237 Fed. 50. Cited in 1944 training manual.

8. Kang, *The INS on the Line*, 61.

9. Committee on Interstate and Foreign Commerce transcript 1930, 11.

10. Kang, *The INS on the Line*, 59; June 9, 1930, 71st Cong 2nd session, 1828, pp. 6–7.

11. Kang, *The INS on the Line*, 77.

12. Kang, *The INS on the Line*, 79.

13. "Daniel W. MacCormack," U.S. Citizenship and Immigration Services website, last updated April 6, 2020, https://www.uscis.gov/history-and-genealogy/our-history/commissioners-and-directors/daniel-w-maccormack.

14. Hellyer, *The U.S. Border Patrol*, 97.

Chapter 5: Unreasonable Searches and Seizures

1. *Carroll v. United States*, 267 U.S. 132 (1925).

2. Edwin Harwood, "Arrests Without Warrant: The Legal and Organizational Environment of Immigration Law Enforcement," *Davis Law Review*, 17, no. 2 (1984): 505–48; Tracy Maclin, *The Supreme Court and the Fourth Amendment's Exclusionary Rule* (Oxford: Oxford University Press, 2012); Thomas McInnis, *The Evolution of the Fourth Amendment* (Lanham, MD: Lexington Books, 2009).

3. *Terry v. Ohio*, (1968) 392 U.S. 1, 14–15.

4. *Terry v. Ohio*, (1968) 392 U.S. 38.

Chapter 6: A Reasonable Distance

1. "For the Prosecution Herbert Brownell Jr," *The New York Times*, June 28, 1957.

2. "The Cabinet: Cleanup Man," *Time Magazine*, February 16, 1953.

3. Gladwin Hill, "Tide of 'Wetbacks' Reaches Crest; 1,500,000 in Southwest in 1952," *The New York Times*, January 12, 1953.

4. President's Commission (1951), 76; K. Calavita, *Inside the State: The Bracero Program, Immigration and the I.N.S.* (New York: Routledge, 1992).

5. John Crewdson, *The Tarnished Door: The New Immigrants and the Transformation of America* (New York: Times Books, 1983).

6. Calavita, *Inside the State*.

7. Kang, *The INS on the Line*, 107.

8. Act of August 7, 1946. 60 STAT 865; U. S. C. 110.

9. *Federal Register* 12, no. 149 (July 31, 1947): 5047.

10. Public law (S 1851).

11. 98 Cong. Rec., part 1, 1355 (February 25, 1952).

12. Willard Kelley, "The Wetback Issue," *The I & N Reporter*, January 1954, 39.

13. President's Commission (1951), 69.

14. Calavita, *Inside the State*, 48.

15. Louis Hyman and Natasha Iskander, "What the Mass Deportation of Immigrants Might Look Like," *Slate*, November 16, 2016.

16. "Brownell Tours 'Wetback' Border," *The New York Times*, August 16, 1953.

17. "Mexico Cites Difficulties," *The New York Times*, August 18, 1953.

18. Joan Cook, "J. M Swing, Wartime Airborne Commander," *The New York Times*, December 12, 1984.

19. "Guard of the Borders, Joseph May Swing," *The New York Times*, April 24, 1958.

20. Gladwin Hill, "Plan Gains to End Use of 'Wetbacks,'" *The New York Times*, June 27, 1954.

21. Lytle Hernández, *Migra!*.

22. Gladwin Hill, "700 on Coast Open 'Wetback' Drive," *The New York Times*, June 18, 1954.
23. Gladwin Hill, "'Wetback' Stream Stemmed in Part," *The New York Times*, June 20, 1954.
24. Some reports say they were all stuck in a locked truck, but I could not find confirmation of that. Hearings before the Subcommittee on Equipment, Supplies, and Manpower of the Committee on Agriculture, House of Representatives (March 16, 17, 21, 22, 1955): 214.
25. Lytle Hernández, *Migra!*
26. Calavita, *Inside the State*, 55.
27. Customs and Border Protection, "U.S. Border Patrol Total Apprehensions (FY 1925–FY 2020)," n.d., https://www.cbp.gov/newsroom/media-resources/stats.
28. *Federal Register* 22, no. 236 (Friday, December 6, 1957): 9808, https://tile.loc.gov/storage-services/service/ll/fedreg/fr022/fr022236/fr022236.pdf.
29. Calavita, *Inside the State*.
30. "Ban on Braceros," *The New York Times*, June 3, 1964.
31. "New Door for Braceros?" *The New York Times*, December 9, 1964.
32. Kang, *The INS on the Line*, 87.

Chapter 7: Law and Order
1. Charles Lamb and Stephen Halpern, eds., *The Burger Court: Political and Judicial Profiles* (Champaign: University of Illinois Press, 1991), 132.
2. Evan Thomas, *First: Sandra Day O'Connor* (New York: Penguin, 2018).
3. Lamb and Halpern, *The Burger Court*, 316–9.
4. The Burger Court reinstated capital punishment in 1976 in *Gregg v. Georgia*.

5. John Jeffries, *Justice Lewis F. Powell: A Biography* (New York: C. Scribner's Sons, 1994), 142.

6. Jeffries, *Justice Lewis F. Powell: A Biography*, 214; Lewis Powell, "Address," *Nebraska Law Review* 44 (1965): 358; Lewis Powell, "Civil Disobedience: Prelude to Revolution?" *New York State Bar Journal* 40 (1968): 172.

7. Lewis Powell, "An Urgent Need for More Criminal Justice," *American Bar Association Journal* 51 (1965): 437–44, 438–9.

Chapter 8: Terrorists in Suits

1. Chanoux passed away eight years later, in 1981, at the still-young age of forty-eight while vacationing in Texas. "Obituary for James A. Chanoux," *Chula Vista Star-News*, February 26, 1981.

2. The details on John Cleary's life were gathered through interviews with Chuck Sevilla and his academic profiles. Unfortunately, Cleary passed away on January 31, 2020, before I was able to interview him.

3. Rate My Professors site, rating of "John Cleary," August 15, 2005, https://www.ratemyprofessors.com/ShowRatings.jsp?tid=50617.

4. Oral arguments, *United States v. Martinez-Fuerte.*

5. The oral arguments for all Supreme Court cases since 1955 were recorded and are publicly available. They are held at the National Archives and are posted on websites such as www.oyez.org.

6. *Alexander v. United States*, 1966; *United States v. Ramsey*, 431 U.S. 606, 616 (1977).

7. Interview, Chuck Sevilla, January 31, 2020.

Chapter 9: Change of Heart

1. J. Harvie Wilkinson III, *Serving Justice: A Supreme Court Clerk's View* (New York: Charterhouse, 1974).

2. Jeffries, *Justice Lewis F. Powell: A Biography*, 431.

3. Interview, Christina Whitman, January 21, 2021.

4. I suspect but could not confirm that the identity of the clerk is J. Harvie Wilkinson. Wilkinson had a close relationship with Powell and recounts a similar story, without specifying the exact case, in his book *Serving Justice*, 33, 63, and 116.

5. Bob Woodward and Scott Armstrong, *The Brethren: Inside the Supreme Court* (New York: Simon & Schuster, 1979), 259-60.

6. Jeffries, *Justice Lewis F. Powell: A Biography*, 265.

7. Powell Papers, *Almeida-Sanchez*, 178.

8. *Almeida-Sanchez v. United States*, 413 U.S. 266, 275.

Chapter 10: Rank Racism

1. Ninth Circuit Court of Appeals, *Brignoni-Ponce*. 499 f.2d 1109 (1974).

2. Section 287 of the U.S. Code.

3. *United States v. Brignoni-Ponce*. Supreme Court Case Files Collection. Box 25. Powell Papers. Lewis F. Powell Jr. Archives, Washington & Lee University School of Law, Virginia (p. 3 74-114 document).

4. Interview, Penny Clark, February 20, 2020.

5. Powell Papers, Brignoni-Ponce 9.

6. Email correspondence with Chuck Sevilla, April 25, 2021.

7. Patricia Brennan, "Seven justices, on camera," *Washington Post*, October 6, 1996.

Chapter 11: Mexican Haircuts

1. Quoted in Lamb and Halpern, *The Burger Court*, 188, from William Douglas, *The Court Years: The Autobiography of William O. Douglas* (New York: Random House, 1988), 329–30.

2. Woodward and Armstrong, *The Brethren*.

3. *U.S. v. Ortiz*. Supreme Court Case Files Collection. Box 24.

Powell Papers. Lewis F. Powell Jr. Archives, Washington & Lee University School of Law, Virginia. 33–34.

4. Powell Papers, Brignoni-Ponce 23.

5. Powell Papers, Brignoni-Ponce 32.

6. Powell Papers, Brignoni-Ponce 44.

7. Powell Papers, Brignoni-Ponce 45.

8. Powell Papers, Brignoni-Ponce 53.

9. Powell Papers, Brignoni-Ponce 54.

10. Powell Papers, Brignoni-Ponce 65.

11. Powell Papers, Brignoni-Ponce 67.

12. Powell Papers, Brignoni-Ponce 72.

13. Interview, Penny Clark, February 20, 2020.

14. Interview, Penny Clark, February 20, 2020.

15. Interview, Penny Clark, February 20, 2020.

16. Johnson, "How Racial Profiling in America Became the Law of the Land."

Chapter 12: A Sixth Sense

1. David Zimmerle, "Border Check," *The San Clemente Times*, April 8, 2010.

2. *United States v. Martinez-Fuerte*, 9th Circuit Court (1975), 313.

3. *United States v. Baca*, 368 F. Supp. 398 (S.D. Cal. 1973).

4. *United States v. Martinez-Fuerte*, 9th Circuit Court (1975).

5. *United States v. Martinez-Fuerte*, 9th Circuit Court (1975), 314.

6. *United States v. Martinez-Fuerte*, 9th Circuit Court (1975), 315.

7. *United States v. Martinez-Fuerte*, 9th Circuit Court (1975), 318.

8. Interview, Christina Whitman, January 21, 2021.

9. Powell Papers, *Martinez-Fuerte*, 10.

10. Powell Papers, *Martinez-Fuerte*, 14.

11. Oral arguments from the *United States v. Martinez-Fuerte* are cited through the next three pages.

12. Interview, Christina Whitman, January 21, 2021.
13. *Terry v. Ohio*, 392 U.S. (1968).

Chapter 13: Free to Stop Any and All Motorists
1. Interview, Christina Whitman, January 21, 2021.
2. *United States v. Martinez-Fuerte*, 428 U.S. 543 (1976).
3. Woodward and Armstrong, *The Brethren*, 443.
4. *United States v. Martinez-Fuerte*, 428 U.S. 543 (1976).

Chapter 14: America's Frontline
1. *ACLU Rodriquez v. Swartz*, summary. Mark Binelli, "10 Shots Across the Border," *The New York Times Magazine*, March 3, 2016.
2. Joseph Nevins, *Operation Gatekeeper and Beyond: The War on "Illegals" and the Remaking of the U.S.-Mexico Boundary* (Oxfordshire, UK: Routledge, 2010).
3. Katy Murdza and Walter Ewing, "The Legacy of Racism within the U.S. Border Patrol," The American Immigration Council, January 2021.
4. Robert Reinhold, "A Welcome for Immigrants Turns to Resentment," *The New York Times*, August 25, 1993.
5. Border Patrol, "Border Patrol Strategic Plan 1994 and Beyond: National Strategy."
6. Timothy Dunn, *Blockading the Border and Human Rights: The El Paso Operation that Remade Immigration Enforcement* (Austin: University of Texas Press, 2009); Nevins, *Operation Gatekeeper*.
7. Todd Miller, *Border Patrol Nation: Dispatches from the Front Lines of Homeland Security* (San Francisco: City Lights, 2014).
8. 6 USC § 211(f)(3)(C).
9. "About CBP," U.S. Customs and Border Protection website, last updated December 18, 2020, https://www.cbp.gov/about.

10. Reece Jones, "Border Wars: Narratives and Images of the US-Mexican Border on TV," *ACME* 13, no. 3 (2014): 530–50.

11. *Family Members of Anastasio Hernández-Rojas v. United States,* complaint, Inter-American Commission on Human Rights, March 2016, 30.

12. Debbie Nathan, "How the Border Patrol Faked Statistics Showing a 73 Percent Rise in Assaults Against Agents," *The Intercept,* April 23, 2018.

13. Ted Hesson, "U.S. to outfit Border Patrol agents with body cameras in major oversight move," Reuters, August 4, 2021, https://www.reuters.com/world/us/us-outfit-border-agents-with-body-cameras-major-oversight-move-2021-08-04/.

14. Jeremey Slack, Daniel Martinez, Scott Whiteford, and Emily Peiffer, *In the Shadow of the Wall: Family Separation, Immigration Enforcement and Security,* (Tucson: The Center for Latin American Studies, University of Arizona, 2013); Guillermo Cantor and Walter Ewing, "Still No Action Taken: Complaints against Border Patrol Agents Continue to Go Unanswered," American Immigration Council, 2017.

15. Binelli, "10 Shots."

16. The Police Executive Research Forum, "U.S. Customs and Border Protection Use of Force Review: Cases and Policies," 2013.

17. "Perez, C. Y. v. United States," Hold CBP Accountable website, last modified June, 24, 2021, https://holdcbpaccountable.org/2016/04/12/perez-c-y-v-united-states/.

18. Perla Trevizo, "Not guilty: Jury acquits Border Patrol agent Lonnie Swartz of involuntary manslaughter," *Arizona Daily Star,* November 22, 2018.

19. *Hernandez v. Mesa,* 589 U.S (2020).

20. Southern Border Communities Coalition, *Deaths by Border Patrol.*

Chapter 15: Hostile Terrain

1. Amy Wang, "Border Patrol agents were filmed dumping water left for migrants. Then came a 'suspicious' arrest," *The Washington Post*, January 24, 2018, https://www.washingtonpost.com/news /post-nation/wp/2018/01/23/border-patrol-accused-of-targeting -aid-group-that-filmed-agents-dumping-water-left-for-migrants/.

2. Interview, Max Granger, March 18, 2021.

3. Fernanda Santos, "Border Patrol Raids Humanitarian Aid Group Camp in Arizona," *The New York Times*, June 16, 2017, https:// www.nytimes.com/2017/06/16/us/border-patrol-immigration-no -more-deaths.html.

4. Complaint, "Dr. Scott Warren Motion to Dismiss Due to Selective Enforcement," 14. https://www.scribd.com/document/40202 0760/Dr-Scott-Warren-Motion-to-Dismiss-due-to-Selective -Enforcement.

5. Complaint, "Dr. Scott Warren," 15.

6. Adrian Skabelund, "The graveyard in Arizona's borderlands," *The Lumberjack*, March 2, 2017.

7. Jason De León, *The Land of Open Graves: Living and Dying on the Migrant Trail* (Berkeley: University of California Press, 2015).

8. Border Patrol, "Border Patrol National Strategic Plan 1994 and Beyond," July 1994.

9. Geoffrey Boyce, Samuel Chambers, and Sarah Launius, "Bodily Inertia and the Weaponization of the Sonoran desert in US Boundary Enforcement: A GIS modeling of Migration Routes through Arizona's Altar Valley," *Journal on Migration and Human Security*, 7, no. 1 (2019): 23–3; Samuel Chambers, Geoffrey Boyce, Sarah Launius, and Alicia Dinsmore, "Mortality, Surveillance and the Tertiary 'Funnel Effect' on the US-Mexico Border: A Geospatial Modeling of the Geography of Deterrence," *Journal of Borderlands Studies*, 36, no. 3 (2021): 443–468.

10. No More Deaths, "Left to Die: Border Patrol, Search and Rescue, and the Crisis of Disappearance," February 3, 2021, https://no moredeaths.org/new-report-left-to-die-border-patrol-search-rescue -and-the-crisis-of-disappearance/.

11. Rob O'Dell, Daniel Gózález, and Jill Castellano, "'Mass disaster' grows at the U.S.-Mexico border, but Washington doesn't seem to care," *USA Today*, n.d., https://www.usatoday.com/border-wall /story/mass-disaster-grows-u-s-mexico-border/1009752001/.

12. No More Deaths, "Left to Die," 74.

13. Border Patrol, "Border Patrol Agents Rescue Man Missing for Eight Days," March 16, 2021, https://www.cbp.gov /newsroom/local-media-release/border-patrol-agents-rescue -man-missing-eight-days.

14. No More Deaths, "Left to Die," 10.

15. No More Deaths, "Left to Die," 11.

16. No More Deaths, "Left to Die," 12.

17. No More Deaths, "Left to Die."

18. Interview, Max Granger, March 18, 2021.

19. 90-191, *United States of America v. Scott Daniel Warren*, No. 17-00341MJ-001-TUC-RCC (US District Court, D. Arizona 2019).

20. "Drop all charges against No More Deaths volunteer Scott Warren," petition, MoveOn.org, https://sign.moveon.org/petitions/drop-all -charges-against-7.

21. Scott Warren, "I gave water to migrants crossing the Arizona desert. They charged me with a felony," *The Washington Post*, May 28, 2018.

22. Isaac Stanley-Becker, "An activist faced 20 years in prison for helping migrants. But jurors wouldn't convict him," *The Washington Post*, June 12, 2019.

23. Ryan Devereaux, "Humanitarian Volunteer Scott Warren Reflects

on the Borderlands and Two Years of Persecution," *The Intercept*, November 23, 2019, https://theintercept.com/2019/11/23 /scott-warren-verdict-immigration-border/.

24. No More Deaths, "No More Deaths Volunteers Win #cabeza9 Appeal: Convictions Reversed," February 4, 2020.

25. No More Deaths, "Second Military Style Raid in Two Months: Border Patrol Detains 12 people Receiving Humanitarian Aid," October 7, 2020, https://nomoredeaths.org/second-military-style -raid-in-two-months-border-patrol-detains-12-people-receiving -care-at-humanitarian-aid-station/.

26. Geneva Sands, "Border Patrol Tallies Record 557 Migrant Deaths on US-Mexico Border in 2021 Fiscal Year," CNN, October 29, 2021.

Chapter 16: Checkpoint Nation

1. Interview, Terry Bressi, February 11, 2021.

2. 8 U.S.C. § 1357(a)(3).

3. Tim Gaynor, "Ex-Arizona governor, 96, detained at checkpoint in sweltering heat," Reuters, July 5, 2012.

4. *United States v. Martinez-Fuerte*, 428 U.S. 543 (1976).

5. *United States v. Martinez-Fuerte*, 428 U.S. 543 (1976).

6. Alex Nowrasteh, "Border Patrol Checkpoints Do Not Work—End Them," The Cato Institute, November 20, 2017.

7. ACLU, "Record of Abuse: Lawlessness and Impunity in Border Patrol's Interior Enforcement Operations" (2015).

8. General Accountability Office, *Border Patrol: Issues Related to Agent Deployment Strategy and Fixed Checkpoints* (Washington, D.C.: Government Printing Office, 2017), 39.

9. General Accountability Office, *Border Patrol*, 52.

10. Al Reinart, "The best little checkpoint in Texas," *Texas Monthly*, August 2013.

11. John Burnett, "At 'checkpoint of the stars,' Texas sheriff takes a pass on pot cases," *Morning Edition*, National Public Radio, October 1, 2015.
12. *Drewniak v. U.S.* complaint (2020), 13.
13. *Drewniak v. U.S.* complaint (2020), 13.
14. Interview, Gilles Bissonnette, February 03, 2021.
15. *State of New Hampshire v. Daniel McCarthy* (2018) Docket #469-2017-CR-01888.
16. Interview, Jenn Budd, February 01, 2021.
17. The videos of over 300 of Terry Bressi's checkpoint encounters are available at https://vimeo.com/user66259598.
18. Federal Emergency Management Agency, "Operation Stonegarden (OPSG) Program," solicitation, 2019.
19. Office of Inspector General, "FEMA and CBP oversight of Operation Stonegarden program needs improvement," Department of Homeland Security, November 9, 2017.
20. Jasmine Demers, "Pima County supervisors reject Operation Stonegarden grant funding 3-2," *Arizona Daily Star*, February 4, 2020.
21. Patrick Leahy, "Leahy, Murray and Welch Reintroduce Legislation to Curtail Warrantless Vehicle Checkpoint Stops and Property Searches Away from the Border," press release, 2019.

Chapter 17: Somebody Speaking Spanish
1. Details of the interactions between Suda, Hernandez, and O'Neill are described in the complaint. Additional details from an interview with their lawyer, Alex Rate, March 19, 2021.
2. Census data, 2019 estimates.
3. Matt Volz, "Backlash over Border Agency lawsuit forces Montana Women to leave town," Associated Press, September 20, 2019.
4. ACLU, "Customs and Border Protection Settles Federal Lawsuit

with American Citizens Racially Profiled and Unlawfully Detained for Speaking Spanish," press release, November 24, 2020.

5. Border Patrol, "M-69 The Law of Arrest, Search, and Seizure for Immigration Officers," INS 1981 Investigator's Handbook.

6. Customs and Border Protection, "CBP Enforcement Law Course, 510-1" (2012). This document was obtained by Max Rivlin-Nadler of *The Intercept* through a Freedom of Information Act Request; Max Rivlin-Nadler, "Newly Released FOIA Documents Shed Light on Border Patrol's Seemingly Limitless Authority," *The Intercept*, January 7, 2019.

7. ACLU, "Fact Sheet: Implementing Law Enforcement Best Practices for our Nation's Biggest Police Force (CBP)" (2015).

8. ACLU Michigan, *The Border's Long Shadow: How Border Patrol Uses Racial Profiling and Local and State Police to Target and Instill Fear in Michigan's Immigrant Communities* (2021), 4; Mat Coleman and Austin Kocher, "Rethinking the 'Gold Standard' of Racial Profiling: §287(g), Secure Communities and Racially Discrepant Police Power," *American Behavioral Scientist* 63, no. 9 (2019): 1185–1220; Geoff Boyce and Todd Miller, "An anti-Latin@ policing machine: Enforcing the US/Mexico border along the Great Lakes and the 49th Parallel," *Handbook on Human Security, Borders and Migration*, eds. Natalia Ribas-Mateos and Tim Dunn (London: Edward Elgar, 2021).

9. ACLU Michigan, *The Border's Long Shadow*, 5.

10. *United States v. Martinez-Fuerte*, 428 U.S. 543 (1976).

11. Interview, Sophie Smith, March 23, 2021.

12. *Jacobson et al. v. DHS et al.*, Nos. 14-02485.

13. Yoohyun Jung and Perla Trevizo, "Group finds racial profiling at Amado border checkpoint," *Arizona Daily Star*, October 19, 2014.

14. ACLU, "CBP tapes show systemic racism," November 24, 2020.

15. Interview, Jenn Budd, February 1, 2021; Fernanda Echavarri,

"Border Patrol's Toxic Culture Goes Way Beyond Facebook Groups. It's Actually for Sale on a T-Shirt," *Mother Jones*, July 19, 2019.

16. Francisco Cantú, *The Line Becomes a River: Dispatches from the Border* (New York: Penguin Random House, 2019), 101.

17. The term is used frequently in the TV series *Border Wars*.

18. A. C. Thompson, "Inside the Secret Border Patrol Facebook Group where Agents Joke about Migrant Deaths and Post Sexist Memes," ProPublica, July 1, 2019.

19. A. C. Thompson, "House Committee to Subpoena Records on Discipline Related to Secret Border Patrol Facebook Group," *Government Executive*, November 3, 2020; Maria Sacchetti and Nick Miroff, "Border agents who made violent, lewd Facebook posts faced flawed disciplinary process at CBP, House investigation finds," *The Washington Post*, October 25, 2021.

20. Monmouth University Polling Institute, "Protestors' Anger Justified Even if Actions May Not Be," June 2, 2020; Reason-Rupe Poll, "Poll: 70% of Americans Oppose Racial Profiling by the Police," October 9, 2014; Kaiser Family Foundation, "Poll: 7 in 10 Black Americans Say They Have Experienced Incidents of Discrimination or Police Mistreatment in Their Lifetime, Including Nearly Half Who Felt Their Lives Were in Danger," June 18, 2020.

21. U.S. Department of Justice, "Guidance for Federal Law Enforcement Agencies Regarding the Use of Race, Ethnicity, Gender, National Origin, Religion, Sexual Orientation, or Gender Identity" (2014).

22. Chris Rickerd, "A Dangerous Precedent: Why Allow Racial Profiling at or Near the Border?" ACLU, December 8, 2014.

23. Matt Apuzzo and Michael Schmidt, "U.S. to Continue Racial, Ethnic Profiling in Border Policy," *The New York Times*, December 5, 2014.

24. Interview, Alex Rate, March 19, 2021.

Chapter 18: The Everywhere Border

1. General Accountability Office, "Northern Border Security," GAO-19-470 (2019).
2. Office of the Inspector General, "U.S. Customs and Border Protection's Unmanned Aircraft System Program Does Not Achieve Intended Results or Recognize All Costs of Operations, Department of Homeland Security" (December 24, 2014): 1.
3. General Accountability Office, "Border Security: Additional Actions Needed to Strengthen Collection of Unmanned Aerial Systems and Aerostats Data" (February 27, 2017).
4. Tom McKay and Dhruv Mehrotra, "Customs and Border Protection flew a Predator Surveillance drone over Minneapolis Protests Today," *Gizmodo*, May 29, 2020.
5. Jason Koebler, Joseph Cox, Jordan Pearson, "Customs and Border Protection is Flying a Drone over Minneapolis," *Vice Motherboard*, May 29, 2020.
6. Zolan Kanno-Youngs, "U.S. Watched George Floyd Protests in 15 Cities Using Aerial Surveillance," *The New York Times*, June 19, 2020.
7. General Accountability Office, "Northern Border Security," 9.
8. Jennifer Lynch, "Customs & Border Protection Logged Eight-Fold Increase in Drone Surveillance for Other Agencies," Electronic Frontier Foundation, July 3, 2013.
9. Yessenia Funes and Dhruv Mehrotra, "CBP Drones Conducted Flyovers Near Homes of Indigenous Pipeline Activists, Flight Records Show," *Gizmodo*, September 18, 2020.
10. Customs and Border Protection, "U.S. Border Patrol Total Apprehensions (FY 1925–FY 2020)."
11. Interview, Jenn Budd, February 1, 2021.
12. Interview, Jenn Budd, February 1, 2021.
13. Interview, Jenn Budd, February 1, 2021.

14. Ryan Devereaux, "An Unchecked Union," *Intercept*, December 27, 2020.

15. Caitlin Dickerson, Zolan Kanno-Youngs, Annie Correal, "'Flood the Streets': ICE Targets Sanctuary Cities with Increased Surveillance," *The New York Times*, March 5, 2020.

16. Miller, *Empire of Borders*.

17. Customs and Border Protection, "Border Patrol Tactical Unit," n.d., https://www.cbp.gov/sites/default/files/documents/Border%20Patrol%20Tactical%20Unit.pdf.

18. Sergio Olmos, Mike Baker, and Zolan Kanno-Youngs, "Federal Officers Deployed in Portland Didn't Have Proper Training, D.H.S. Memo Said," *The New York Times*, July 18, 2020.

19. Elián González is in his twenties now, and is an industrial engineer at a state company in Cuba.

20. 40 USC § 1315, (b) (2) (C) and (E). Interview with Mitra Ebadolahi, August 3, 2021.

21. Interview with Mitra Ebadolahi, August 3, 2021.

22. Steve Vladeck and Benjamin Wittes, "DHS Authorizes Domestic Surveillance to Protect Statues and Monuments," *Lawfare*, July 20, 2020.

23. "Video Shows Federal Agents Detaining People in Portland Based on Inaccurate, Insufficient Information," *The Washington Post*, September 10, 2020.

24. Kate Oh, "New Law Requires Federal Agents to Identify Themselves to Protesters," ACLU, January 4, 2021.

25. *Don't Shoot Portland v. Wolf*, 1:20-cv-02040 (D.D.C.) https://clearinghouse.net/detail.php?id=17742; *Pettibone v. Trump*, 3:20-cv-01464 (D. Or.)

26. ACLU, "Documents Obtained by ACLU Reveal Border Patrol Agents Were Authorized to Use Deadly Force at George Floyd's Burial," October 1, 2020.

Conclusion

1. Interview, Mitra Ebadolahi, August 3, 2021.
2. This is the argument of my previous book. Reece Jones, *White Borders: The History of Race and Immigration from Chinese Exclusion to the Border Wall* (Boston: Beacon Press, 2021).
3. Emma Dumain, "'Trash Public Lands?' Republicans take a Fraught Border Hike," E&E News, August 5, 2021, https://www.eenews.net/articles/trash-public-lands-republicans-take-fraught-border-hike/.
4. Garrett Graff, "The Border Patrol Hits Its Breaking Point," *Politico*, July 15, 2019.
5. Sonia Shah, *The Next Great Migration: The Beauty and Terror of Life on the Move* (New York: Bloomsbury, 2020).
6. Reed, "America of the Melting Pot."
7. Interview, Jenn Budd, February 1, 2021.
8. Jamie Raskin, "Subcommittee Requests Briefing from DHS after Allegations of Discrimination by Border Patrol Agents in Michigan," press release, August 5, 2021, https://raskin.house.gov/press-releases?ID=0160EA15-BF08-4B54-B33D-346237E6DE33; Alexandria Ocasio-Cortez, "'The Squad' Calls for Reductions to U.S. Customs and Border Patrol Budget," press release, July 16, 2020, https://ocasio-cortez.house.gov/media/press-releases/squad-calls-reductions-us-customs-and-border-patrol-budget.
9. Jack Herrera, "The Government Is Testing Mass Surveillance on the Border before Turning It on Americans," *Medium*, October 16, 2019.

© Sivylay Jones

REECE JONES is a Guggenheim Fellow. He is a professor and the chair of the Department of Geography and Environment at the University of Hawai'i. He is the author of three books, the award-winning Border Walls and Violent Borders, as well as White Borders. He is the editor in chief of the journal Geopolitics and he lives in Honolulu with his family.